D1327301

Civil Commitment and
Social Control

Civil Commitment and Social Control

Martin L. Forst
University of California

Lexington Books
D.C. Heath and Company
Lexington, Massachusetts
Toronto

Library of Congress Cataloging in Publication Data

Forst, Martin Lyle.
   Civil commitment and social control.

   Includes index.
   1. Sentences (Criminal procedure)—California. 2. Insane—Commitment
and detention—California. 3. Sex crimes—California. I. Title.
KFC1172.F66   345'.794'077   77-14626
ISBN 0-669-01988-7

Published simultaneously in Canada.

Printed in the United States of America.

International Standard Book Number: 0-669-01988-7

Library of Congress Catalog Card Number: 77-14626

To Marvis

Contents

List of Figure and Tables

Preface

At the turn of the century the traditional criminal sanction—imprisonment or fine—was employed to handle most forms of deviant behavior. For a variety of reasons, this method of social control came to be viewed as ineffective or inhumane for certain individuals. To deal with these particular classes of deviants, there developed what was then considered the "enlightened" alternative to the criminal sanction—the civil commitment. From its limited application a century ago, the civil commitment in all its statutory variations has become a major form of social control through law in American society.

The greater part of this work represents an empirical investigation into the operation and functioning of one such civil commitment statute and its relationship to the criminal justice system. The particular law under study is California's "Mentally Disordered Sex Offender" (MDSO) statute, which provides for a civil commitment of one day to life in a maximum security mental institution for convicted sex offenders. The MDSO law is California's version of what are known in most states as "Sexual Psychopath" laws. Since this study deals with the relationship between the civil and the criminal commitment, the imposition of criminal sentences for sex offenders was also studied in detail. A central assumption of this book is that it is impossible to completely understand the imposition of one form of sanction without knowing as well the criteria used in imposing the other, given the close relationship of the two sanctioning systems.

This study evolved from a concern for the uses and abuses of civil commitments, particularly involving persons who would have formerly received a criminal sanction. A fear has been voiced that civil commitments can be imposed without the same strict procedural safeguards accorded persons under the criminal sanction, threatening the values of individual liberty in a free society. Furthermore, it has been claimed that the duration of the civil commitment is often disproportionate to the behavior exhibited by the person against whom the civil proceedings are initiated. A good example would be a possible life commitment in a mental institution for exhibitionism.

Although this book is essentially a detailed comparative analysis of the functioning of one particular civil commitment law, it is hoped that insights into the theoretical and policy issues surrounding the use of any civil commitments will carry over. In theory, there are a variety of important issues distinguishing the civil and the criminal commitments and, more generally, the civil and criminal law—issues that address the question of the nature of law and social control in modern society. These theoretical issues are important, for they serve as the bases for statutes and policies that legally control deviant behavior. This study should aid lawmakers and judges, as well as sociologists, since it will provide them with a realistic understanding of the actual operation of a civil commitment law within the context of the criminal justice system.

Because civil commitment statutes were originally hailed for their humanitarian emphases on care and treatment, there was little concern over either the procedural or the substantive aspects of those statutes. As long as the state was perceived as acting in a benevolent manner, the lack of procedural safeguards and excessive restraints was overlooked by the courts and the legislatures. As abuses in the operation of the civil commitment laws mounted, however, a great deal of criticism erupted. Consequently, the courts are becoming more aware of the real and potential dangers of elastic civil commitment statutes and, as a result, are taking steps to prevent further abuses. Through this process, there has, in effect, been a "criminalization of the civil commitment" over the last decade; both procedurally and substantively, the civil commitment is assuming the characteristics of the traditional criminal sanction. It is further suggested that this trend is desirable, that it is occurring throughout the country (although at different rates), and that it will most likely continue until the functional differences between the civil and the criminal commitment are negligible.

Acknowledgments

On completing this book, I would like to express my gratitude to those persons and agencies that lent intellectual, moral, or financial support. Phillip E. Johnson assisted me by greatly enhancing my understanding of the legal aspects of the disposition of sex offenders at the trial court level. Bernard L. Diamond helped me understand the role of the psychiatrist in the courtroom as well as the ethical consequences of modifying the current sex offender laws. Jerome H. Skolnick contributed his ideas about the theoretical distinctions between the civil and criminal commitments and offered suggestions on how to organize the study and make it interesting to others. A special thanks to Sheldon L. Messinger, who lent his support on this project from its inception through to its completion. With his assistance, the book developed a theme and a theoretical orientation.

The completion of this project would have been very difficult without the financial support I received from the National Institute of Mental Health (NIMH). At the University of California, Berkeley, I was awarded an NIMH Traineeship, administered through the Center for the Study of Law and Society, and an NIMH Predoctoral Fellowship through the School of Criminology.

My thanks must also be extended to the criminal justice personnel whose cooperation made this study possible. In each of the counties I worked, the court personnel were very courteous, helpful, and patient in responding to my inquiries and requests. I appreciated this all the more as I became aware of the demands made on them by their daily work.

And finally, a special expression of gratitude to my wife, Marvis, who assisted me at every stage of this project.

1

Introduction

Distinctions between the Civil and the Criminal Sanction

When one thinks of social control through law, various images of criminal sanctions come to mind—an offender may be incarcerated in prison, he may be fined, or he may be put under some type of state surveillance. To come under a criminal sanction, a person must commit an act that society proscribes and seeks to discourage with the threat of punishment. Once in the criminal justice system, he must be found guilty in a court of law after receiving all the benefits of a broad range of specified procedural safeguards. Yet there is another form of social control through law that operates extensively in American society—the civil commitment. Despite deep roots in the history of law, this legal mechanism, with its current statutory variations, represents a new and unique form of state coercion. Theoretically, a civil commitment may be characterized as a noncriminal process, which commits gravely disabled or otherwise dependent persons—without their consent—to an institution for care, treatment, or custody rather than punishment. Because the emphasis is placed on cure in a clinical setting, the rationale for instituting civil commitment proceedings is considered to be very appealing. In addition to the espoused benefits for the individual, society feels both more protected from whatever dangers such a person might pose if left at liberty and less threatened by a recurrence on the rehabilitated person's release.

Traditional civil commitment, well-established in law and principle, permits the state to quarantine persons with contagious diseases and to protect and to care for mental incompetents. The authority for this type of civil commitment derives from two legal principles, the state's right and responsibility to assume guardianship over persons suffering some disability (*parens patriae*) and the police power to take whatever steps necessary, within constitutional limitations, to protect society. Historically, civil commitment proceedings were rarely initiated against persons who had violated criminal laws; instead the state used civil commitment to protect the individual's or its own best interests.

Jurisprudential scholars have written extensively about the basic differences between situations calling for the use of the civil or the criminal sanctions and, more generally, the differences between the civil and the criminal law. Before the turn of the century, there was no significant disagreement concerning the distinctions between the traditional civil commitment and the criminal sanction. In this century, however, another type of civil commitment exists, which is frequently identified as a quasi-criminal commitment. Given this label because it frequently deals with persons who could be or have been proceeded against criminally, quasi-criminal commitment includes sex offenders, heroin addicts, defective delinquents, juvenile delinquents, and the like. The current trend toward using this type of civil commitment against persons for whom the traditional criminal sanctions are deemed inappropriate is often justified as a useful and humane means of diverting selected types of deviants from the criminal justice system into the mental health system. By labeling the sanction civil rather than criminal, the person is subjected to legal proceedings with fewer procedural protections, but as a consequence he avoids the formal penal sanction. As this procedure becomes more common, the features that distinguish the two types of legal sanctions have blurred, and the relationship between the criminal justice and mental health systems has become more complicated. As a result, substantial confusion has arisen for the courts and legislatures, both of which try to formulate sound policy for the legal control of deviant behavior.

The difficulties in understanding the theoretical distinctions between criminal and quasi-criminal commitments are clearly revealed when one reviews the appellate courts' attempts to distinguish between them. The appellate courts have used a variety of means—often not very sophisticated—to decide whether a statute is civil or criminal in nature. One method is to determine in which Code the law is found. If it is in the Criminal Code, it is deemed criminal in nature; if written in the Civil Code, it is civil. This method, however, has not proved sufficient for other courts, which have decided that location in a particular code should not be decisive in determining if the law is considered criminal or civil in nature. An alternative approach favored by some courts is to examine the title of the statute; if it deals with punishment, it is held to be criminal in nature; if the statute's title pertains to treatment, it is considered civil. Other courts tend toward a deeper and more thoughtful analysis by trying to interpret the legislative intent of the statute, without regard to its title or location in the codes.

While these judicial interpretations are generally not considered sufficient by serious legal academicians, two schools of thought—the "procedural" and the "substantive"—have developed, which outline the theoretical distinctions between the civil and the criminal sanction. For the procedural school, the distinction between the civil and the criminal law lies in the rules and methods involved in imposing sanctions. For instance, the criminal law, as set forth in the United States and the state constitutions, is characterized by a certain set of procedural rules and regulations, which act as safeguards for persons subject to that sanction. A defendant in a criminal action has the right to a trial by jury, to confront witnesses against him, to avoid testifying against himself, and so on. One asks the question, "What is criminal law?" The answer is, quite simply, law that uses criminal procedures. Civil law encompasses all remaining law: It is a different type of law with a different set of procedural rules.[1]

The claim that the mere presence of rigid procedural safeguards controls the civil or criminal designation has frequently been criticized. Certainly, if the law were originally civil in substance, the addition of procedural safeguards that ordinarily pertain to criminal proceedings would not convert the proceedings from a civil one to a criminal one.[2] Asserting that procedural distinctions are insufficient, the adherents of the substantive school believe that the nature of the behavior or status to which the sanction is applied, as well as the substantive effect of the sanction, are the crucial determinants in employing the criminal or the civil law label. For example, if a person behaves in a manner that would subject him to the moral condemnation of the community, the criminal law comes into play. As Henry Hart states, "What distinguishes a criminal from a civil sanction and all that distinguishes it, it is ventured, is the judgment of community condemnation which accompanies and justifies its imposition."[3] Moral condemnation is imposed only when dealing with intentional behavior, which requires a state of mind capable of deciding to act in an unlawful manner.

In contrast, the civil sanction is imposed when the formal moral condemnation of the community is not at issue. This situation may arise if the behavior is intentional but not morally blameworthy, as in a civil suit for damages, or if the behavior would have been morally blameworthy, but because of mental impairment, criminal culpability is either mitigated or negated. In the latter instance, the civil issue is not the person's *behavior* but his *status*. If an unfortunate status has befallen someone (e.g., the state of being a drug addict or a mental defective), he is not to be held morally responsible for that condition. This person is seen to deserve treatment, not punishment, even if the treatment requires deprivation of liberty in a mental institution. This attitude is exemplified in a recent observation by Justice Fortas: "Our morality does not permit us to punish for illness. We do not impose punishment for involuntary conduct, whether the lack of volition results from 'insanity,' addiction to narcotics, or from other illnesses."[4] In one leading case, the U.S. Supreme Court held that it is unconstitutional, on the grounds of cruel and unusual punishment, to imprison someone for a status that can be recognized medically.[5] If a person is to be punished, it is to be done under the auspices of the criminal law; it is the punitive character of a law that determines whether it is criminal in nature.[6] If treatment is deemed appropriate, the civil law is invoked. It is asserted that what distinguishes the criminal from the civil sanction is the substantive effect of the law, not its procedural aspects.

As the debate between the two schools continues, there have been attempts to synthesize the various approaches and make a more functional classification of the criminal and civil sanctions. Dession, for one, points out that the general assumption that the two sanctions differ substantially is not supported by the evidence. Both sanctions may result in severe restrictions on personal liberty. He concludes: "A more functional classification of sanctions involving deprivations might distinguish between those utilizing deprivations as an instrument, and those to which deprivation was incidental."[7]

Although the interpretations of theoretical differences between the civil and criminal sanction have a bearing and are important in understanding the underlying ideology of the criminal justice and mental health systems, the practical significance of this issue is reflected in the fact that pragmatic decisions must be made by legal personnel whenever a person becomes entwined in the court apparatus. At such a time, he must be classified into either the criminal or civil law categories—for which different sanctions are applicable and from which different dispositions follow. The nature of the commitment decision may thus have profound implications for the social control of deviant behavior.

The Increased Utilization of the Quasi-Criminal Commitment and Its Consequences

As mentioned above, civil commitments are employed with increasing frequency in the control of deviant behavior.[8] Mentally defective individuals (although not criminally insane) previously subject to criminal sanctions for their behavior are now coming under the aegis of the civil sanction. As Kittrie states:

In its quest for social order, criminal law has functioned primarily as a system for assessing individual blame, and for meting out criminal penalties that fit the severity of the offense and the degree of guilt. In recent years, however, America has seen a departure from criminal sanctions and a concomitant utilization of a different system or model of social controls, described as "civil," "therapeutic," or "*parens patriae.* . . ."[9]

Where legislatures have passed statutes mandating the development of treatment programs, many programs are similar in effect to the old penal measures: "Many of the statutes reflect that interesting exercise of word-magic which results in labeling procedures 'civil' rather than 'criminal.' "[10]

A brief examination of the statistics involving the multiple forms of civil commitment will strikingly reveal the extent to which they are used as a form of social control through law. Because it is well known that official statistics are sometimes inaccurate, usually incomplete, and almost always difficult to interpret, the reader should be forewarned that the following data are no exception. The figures are not presented to account for the precise number and types of current civil commitments, but to offer the reader a general impression of the relative numbers of persons who are legally controlled by means of the civil, as compared to the criminal, commitment.

In 1960 there were approximately 1,887,000 residents of the United States classified as inmates of various institutions. Of these, 346,000 were housed in correctional institutions, while 630,000 resided in mental hospitals.[11] Over the last decade and a half, however, there has been a decline in the number of residents at state mental institutions as indicated by more recent data. By 1970, there were 2,126,719 people classified as residents of various institutions; of those, 328,020 were incarcerated in correctional institutions, while 433,890 stayed in mental institutions.[12] Revealing a further decline in the mental hospital population in the last few years, Alan Stone cites the most recent data. As of June 30, 1973, there were 248,562 patients in state and county mental facilities;[13] this figure is nevertheless larger than the 204,349 inmates in state correctional institutions for that same year.[14]

Of course the standard civil commitment for mental illness and incompetency is only one of the many types of civil commitments used to control deviant behavior. Quasi-criminal commitments represent another sizable portion of persons under state control through the use of the civil sanction, the commitment of juvenile delinquents being the largest single population within this quasi-criminal grouping. In 1960 there were 45,695 juvenile delinquents in custody in juvenile training schools and another 10,821 in some form of detention home.[15] By 1971, the Department of Health, Education, and Welfare estimated that roughly 1,125,000 delinquency cases (excluding traffic offenses) were handled by all juvenile courts in the country.[16] By the end of that year, there were approximately 77,000 juvenile delinquents incarcerated in a training school or a detention home.[17] This number compares with the 198,061 adults imprisoned at year's end in 1971.[18]

While the amount of other types of quasi-criminal commitments do not represent the same high volume as juvenile commitments, the potential for controlling a significant number of individuals does exist. A case in point is the rise in civil commitments for chronic alcoholics. In volume, drunkenness represents one of the major social problems in the United States; approximately two million people (33 percent of all arrests) are arrested for that offense each year. If alcohol-related offenses (such as driving under the influence of alcohol, vagrancy, and disorderly conduct) are added to this category, drunkenness accounts for 40 to 49 percent of all arrests. The traditional criminal law approach has not worked well with this type of offender. Accordingly, alternatives have been developed not only to attempt to rehabilitate the offender, but also to save time and money for the criminal justice system. The current trend, as recommended by the President's Task Force, is to establish "civil detoxification centers" for chronic alcoholics.[19] If this trend continues, a substantial percentage of the arrestees in this country will be subject to some form of civil control.

Although it is difficult to determine accurately the extent of heroin addiction in the United States, because of the vast amount of "hidden" drug abuse, estimates range from 50,000 to 250,000 addicts.[20] Traditionally, the criminal sanction was used to control heroin addicts, for addiction itself was considered a criminal offense. This situation changed substantially, however, when the U.S. Supreme Court held in *Robinson* v *California*[21] (1962) that drug addiction per se could not be a crime and that it would constitute cruel and unusual punishment to incarcerate a drug addict in a penal institution for no reason other than his addiction. However, the Court stated *in dicta* that it would be constitutionally permissible to *civilly* commit drug addicts for care and treatment to mental health facilities. At just that time, California had enacted a civil commitment law for addicts, and shortly after the *Robinson* decision, New York State and the federal government passed similar laws. Since 1962, there have been about 30,000 persons committed to the three principal civil addict programs (California, New York, and the federal program), and it is likely that the number of civil commitments for heroin addicts will remain substantial for the next several years.

Finally, there exists a curious amalgam of persons subject to various other quasi-criminal commitments. This group contains persons who may be proceeded against civilly for being sex offenders (variously known as Sexual Psychopath, Sexually Dangerous Person, or Mentally Disordered Sex Offender), defective delinquents, defendants too insane to stand trial, and persons not criminally guilty by reason of insanity. At this time there are no accurate and comprehensive data to indicate the exact number of persons civilly confined according to any of those statutory categories. Knowledgeable sources do, however, attempt estimates. Rubin, for one, believes that the number of persons subject to these quasi-criminal commitments ranges from 20,000 to 30,000.[22] While that figure does not represent a significant percentage of this country's population, great concern should be expressed for these individuals, because they are often confined for the longest periods of time with the least judicial review and fewest procedural protections.

Another related development in the field of criminal justice is the process of diversion. It is a legal process through which persons charged with relatively minor crimes are taken out of, that is diverted from, the formal systems of criminal or juvenile justice before the issue of guilt is determined. The medical model is frequently used to justify the diversion process, since persons are often diverted into treatment and rehabilitative groups, psychiatric counseling, inpatient or outpatient drug programs, or other facilities in the mental health system. The ramifications for both juveniles and adults are significant, in part because of the possible infringement of constitutional rights of those involved. The diversion process often takes place in the least visible segments of the criminal justice system, i.e., with the police or the prosecutor with only a limited amount of formal supervision by a court of law and little or no legal representation available. Furthermore, the use of this process could result in a substantial increase in persons under some form of state control.

Although the data presented here are admittedly rather sketchy, a major point can be made: The various types of civil commitments (including quasi-criminal commitments) constitute one of the primary forms of social control through law in American society. In fact this form of social control is more extensive in volume of cases than the social control exercised by the traditional criminal commitment. Moreover, the trend toward the increased utilization of the civil commitment is not abating. To be sure, for some forms of civil commitment, more restrictive criteria for commitment are required that decrease the number of persons subject to them; the standard civil commitment for mental illness or incompetency is an example. However, the statutory variations of civil commitments, particularly those closely associated with the criminal justice process, are multiplying, and it appears that the extended use of these sanctioning alternatives will continue.

The increased utilization of the quasi-criminal commitment to socially control deviant behavior has affected more than official statistics. It has had a substantial impact on the relationship between the criminal justice and mental health systems and on the nature of social control through law. Previously, the criminal justice and mental health systems handled separate and distinct clienteles. With the rise of the quasi-criminal commitment, however, these two dominant systems of social control in American society have developed a strong reciprocal relationship to the extent of handling largely overlapping, if not identical, groups of persons.[23] Although there has been a decrease in the population of some categories of offenders in the criminal justice system (because of the decriminalization of certain offenses and the process of diversion), the conclusion cannot be made that there has been a similar reduction in the *level* of social control over these persons. Whereas the labels and procedures may have changed in the legal nomenclature, the substantive degree of social control has remained essentially the same. The locus and definition of that control has merely shifted from the criminal sanction to the civil commitment into the mental health system. As a result, some individuals considered deviant are still controlled by the state, through what has been called the "civil-criminal labeling game."[24]

The close relationship between these two social control systems allows the clients to move from one to the other with relative ease. This situation is described by a practicing psychiatrist discussing his experiences with the two systems. After disclosing society's intolerance of mentally disordered behavior, he states: "If the entry of persons exhibiting mentally disordered behavior into the mental health system of *social control* is impeded, community pressure will force them into the criminal justice system of *social control.*"[25] There has thus developed such a close working relationship between the criminal justice and mental health systems that they reciprocate to control deviant behavior in modern society, regardless of the mental characteristics of the persons involved.

The shift in the nature of social control through law and the close reciprocal relationship between the criminal justice and mental health systems have their roots in the rethinking that has taken place in legal theory over the past century. With the increasing stress that legal sanctions against deviant behavior should fit the "criminal" and not the "crime," there has been a concomitant decrease in emphasis on the principle of moral guilt or blameworthiness, as well as on the concept of *mens rea* (criminal intent) in defining crime.[26] Rather than a continued concern over the person's guilt or innocence,[27] his perceived deviance or social malevolence has become the important issue. A corollary to this development is that the previous system of criminal penalties has been deemed inappropriate, and the indeterminate sentence employed extensively with both the criminal and civil commitments. Therefore, it is possible for someone to receive a civil commitment for treatment in a mental institution ranging from one day to life because of a relatively minor form of deviant behavior, such as exhibitionism.

Reasons for Quasi-Criminal Commitments

Different names have been suggested to describe the increased use of the civil law in cases that were previously considered the domain of the criminal law. Allen claims that this reflects the "rehabilitative ideal,"[28] with its emphasis on treatment and cure, rather than on punishment and revenge. This new area usurped by the civil law is called the "borderland of criminal justice."[29] Kittrie asserts that the incursion of the civil law has resulted in a "divestment of the criminal law"[30] and that new types of treatment programs are leading to the emergence of a "therapeutic state."[31] Although they may differ in their terminology, both writers agree that a very significant trend is developing with important implications for individual liberty. Allen and Kittrie's primary concern (and other authorities')[32] is that the civil sanction, with its emphasis on treatment rather than punishment, is being used to control persons perceived as deviant without according them the constitutional procedural safeguards granted criminal defendants. As Dershowitz states: "By attaching this label [civil], the state has successfully denied defendants almost every important safeguard required in criminal trials."[33] Furthermore, there are substantive, as well as procedural, objections to the use of civil commitments. In the name of treatment, individuals can be subjected to extremely long periods of incarceration, which do not fairly reflect what they have actually *done* but simply bear on what they are perceived *to be*. The implication of this trend is clearly stated by Allen: "This reference to the tendency of the rehabilitative ideal to encourage increasingly long periods of incarceration brings me to my final proposition. . . . [T]he rise of the rehabilitative ideal has often been accompanied by attitudes and measures that conflict, sometimes seriously, with the values of individual liberty and volition."[34]

The explanations for the increased use of civil commitment are diverse. There are those (the positive criminologists) who view the increase as a beneficial shift from the traditional emphasis on punishing people to rehabilitating them. Their confidence that such rehabilitation was possible was based largely on an awareness of the modern scientific advances made by psychiatry and the social sciences. Not only did they believe that rehabilitation could reduce the crime rate,[35] but also that certain offenders by reason of their youth or mental state deserved special consideration and less punishment than the average criminal.[36] These suggestions of the positive criminologists were opposed by members of the classical school of criminology with their "moral concerns" that people who commit crimes should be caught, tried, and punished for their misdeeds.

Those who supported the emphasis on treatment and rehabilitation contended that advanced diagnostic techniques and expert psychiatric testimony could easily screen persons in need of such treatment out of the criminal courts and place them in proper hospitals or clinics. This view is based, however, on certain dubious assumptions. As Allen makes the argument:

First, they assume a body of knowledge and technique that enables its practitioners to identify with reasonable accuracy those persons likely to commit dangerous . . . acts in the future and exclude with reasonable certainty those posing no such danger. If this assumption is false, if there is no such knowledge or technique, these laws, when applied, present the grave threat of depriving persons who constitute no serious threat to the community of their liberty. Second, these laws assume that there is therapy adequate to treat and cure [such an individual], once he has been committed to an institution. If this assumption is false, these statutes are not rehabilitative measures, whatever verbalisms may be employed to describe them. Third, these statutes assume, not only that such knowledge and technique exist, but that, as a practical matter, they are available to the state in the administration of these laws. I shall content myself by saying that many competent observers doubt that any of these assumptions are able to bear the weight of fair and impartial investigation.[37]

Another explanation for the increased use of civil commitments (the divestment of the criminal law) is that the civil commitment serves as a substitute for, or a supplement to, the criminal law in order to socially control undesirable forms of behavior. Claims are made that there exists a conspiracy on the part of the power elite to circumvent the constitutional safeguards accorded criminal defendants. Those who subscribe to this view are products of such diverse disciplines as psychiatry, sociology, and law.[38] Szasz, for instance, believes that mental illness is a "myth" and that the concept merely functions to "disguise and thus render more palatable the bitter pill of moral conflicts in human relations."[39] Platt attempts to show that the development of the juvenile court was based not on the benign motivation of humanitarians, but on punitive, romantic, and intrusive efforts to control the lives of lower-class, urban adolescents and thus maintain their dependent status.[40] No one, however, has summarized the theory as well as Kittrie.

The therapeutic state's recent history reveals, however, that the divestment of criminal justice and the concurrent therapeutic expansion have not always arisen, as they did in the case of insane and youthful offenders, from religious and humanitarian considerations or from a sense of wardship toward the disadvantaged. With regard to psychopaths, drug addicts, and the diverse candidates for sterilization, shock therapy, and lobotomy, divestment has not served primarily as a means of the removal of criminal stigmas from offenders who are not fully responsible for their actions. Instead, the *parens patriae* model has become a pragmatic tool for accomplishing under therapeutic auspices what could not be done at all in the criminal realm. Divestment has thus increasingly served as the vehicle for bringing into the American scene the social defense formulas advanced by the late nineteenth-century positive criminologists; the substitution of the indeterminate commitment that "fits the criminal" for the inadequate determinate sentence that merely "fits the crime"; orienting the process of sanctions toward the offender's total personal deficiency rather than toward the manifestations of the particular offense; placing greater emphasis on who the deviate *is* and what his propensities are than upon his *overt* antisocial past *act*; granting greater discretion to the treatment and correctional arms of the state, often represented by social and behavioral scientists, in formulating programs that might more effectively curb and modify deviant behavior.[41]

Although the preceding explanations for the increased use of civil commitment may contain elements of truth, they are not sufficient. This book contends that the inadequacies of the previous theories stem from their limited focus and restricted units of analysis. Even as the traditional explanation emphasizes the personality of the individual, thereby using him as the unit of analysis, and the newer theory relies on a macroanalysis of the larger trends in civil commitments along with a sinister notion of social control by the power elite, the complete structure and the function of the actual organization making the classifications and commitment decisions are largely ignored. This book will provide new and important information, supported by empirical data, about the role of such a formal organization in the decisionmaking process.

Purpose and Organization of the Book

The different situations calling for the use of the civil or the criminal sanction have infrequently been studied empirically. The principal purpose of this book, therefore, is to determine the extent to which the theoretical arguments discussed above are valid within the organization imposing the legal sanctions. It explores the criteria used by the trial courts in making the decision to impose one or the other class of sanctions. An explanation is offered that will show how certain patterns of social phenomena, in this instance the classification of individuals into different legal categories, can be understood by the social and legal organizations with which they are associated.

Another purpose of this study is to generate empirical data that address some of the important policy issues concerning the use and abuse of civil commitment as a form of social control through law. Criticism of civil commitments for criminal offenders is constantly growing. Some critics advocate the revision or abolition of all civil commitment laws, because, they argue, the constitutional rights of the persons subject to them are violated, and the procedural safeguards associated with them are not as stringent as in the criminal justice system. Others oppose civil commitment because it allows people to avoid the degree of punishment they deserve. Although they may differ in their underlying philosophies, the various criticisms of civil commitment laws have one thing in common—they are generally devoid of compelling empirical data to support their case. To make policy decisions on weak or nonexistent empirical data may not only be bad policy, it may also be morally reprehensible. Allen believes that mere ignorance of the facts is bad enough, "But when, in our eagerness to find 'better ways' of handling old problems, we rush to measures affecting human liberty and human personality, on the assumption that we have knowledge which, in fact, we do not possess, then the problem of ignorance takes on a more sinister hue."[42] Since the future development of laws regulating civil commitments ultimately rests in the hands of the lawmakers (the judiciary and the legislatures), it is important to provide a strong empirical grounding for their policy decisions.

To accomplish this goal, an empirical study was made of one process of reclassifying persons subject to the criminal sanction and their resulting diversion into the mental health system. This example was the imposition of sanctions on convicted sex offenders, specifically under the "Mentally Disordered Sex Offender" statute in California, which is that state's version of the Sexual Psychopath Laws existing in about two-thirds of the states.

At the time of sentencing a sex offender, California Superior Courts have, at their discretion, the authority to impose either a criminal or a civil sanction. The criminal sanction involves the same processes and procedures employed in traditional sentencing, e.g., probation, fine, county jail, or a commitment to state prison. The alternative sanction, technically labeled "civil," consists of designating the offender a "Mentally Disordered Sex Offender" (MDSO), thereby suspending the standard criminal procedures and placing the offender in a maximum-security mental institution under the authority of the Department of Mental Hygiene. Since this commitment is deemed civil in nature, its duration is truly indeterminate—from one day to life. After the offender, or the "patient" as he is now called, is returned to the committing criminal court, that court may then impose a criminal penalty for the offense, since the involuntary incarceration in the mental institution was civil or "therapeutic" in nature.

By analyzing the decisionmaking process at the Superior Court level, this author determined the extent to which the classification and disposition of offenders was the result of the unique policies (both formal and informal) of the decisionmakers within the court organization, rather than a reflection of the mental characteristics of those persons classified. It is the hypothesis of this author that one cannot gain a complete understanding of the function and implementation of the MDSO civil commitment without a close examination of the organization that makes that decision.

This perspective was adopted because it was the most appropriate orientation for explaining court commitment rates and the decisionmaking process. Practical decisionmaking within the organization was stressed. The courts, in this instance, faced the practical problem of what to do with defendants after a conviction had been secured. In dealing with this problem, the courts considered many factors concerning internal organizational pressures as well as the uncertainty presented when the defendant was changed from one environment to another, e.g., to state prison or to a mental institution. Any study of this complex organization had to discern both the rationality of the internal decisionmaking process and how well the organization adapted to and minimized uncertainty within its environment. The decision involved in designating an individual an MDSO and sending him to a maximum-security mental institution was the same type of decision as any of the other criminal dispositional alternatives, and therefore it had to be viewed within the context of all the possible alternatives at the court's disposal. Only in this way could sense be made of the criteria used for making the civil commitment decision.

To examine the Superior Court's formal decision to designate a defendant an MDSO and to commit him to a mental institution, strategic decisions about research design had to be made. A comparative study was required to illuminate most effectively the organizational aspects of the Court's decisionmaking process. From data gleaned from the California Bureau of Criminal Statistics, it was revealed that the commitment rates of MDSOs varied significantly among jurisdictions in California. To explain how this variation might result from differing organizational policies, the jurisdictions with the greatest variation in commitment rates were selected for examination. Orange County had the highest, San Francisco County had the lowest, and Contra Costa County had an average commitment rate of MDSOs in the state. A sample of sex offender cases processed in each county over a given period of time was studied. Analysis of these cases, supplemented by extensive interviews with the Superior Court decisionmakers, furnished a reasonable explanation for the variation in commitment rates and the reasons for the use of the civil commitment within each jurisdiction.

Admittedly, the findings of a study of the classification and commitment of sex offenders in California may be of limited application. Applying the specific empirical findings to other situations throughout the country will depend, of course, on the degree of similarity between those civil commitment statutes and the "Mentally Disordered Sex Offender" law. Nevertheless, the general conclusions drawn address important legal, social, and ethical issues facing all types of civil commitments everywhere. It is suggested that (1) the current trends for MDSOs in California are, to a greater or lesser degree, also occurring with other types of civil commitments in most areas of the United States and (2) the trends are likely to continue. It is hoped that this book will furnish information concerning the nature and functioning of civil commitment laws as a means of social control in our society.

It might be helpful, before proceeding further, to present a brief outline of the chapters to come. Chapter 2 describes the statutory provisions of the MDSO Act with an historical review of statutory and case law. Chapter 3 presents a general description of the MDSO law in everyday practice at the criminal court, stressing the similarities within the three counties. A comparison of the three jurisdictions, focusing on the decisionmakers—judges, district attorneys, and defense attorneys—will be found in Chapter 4. The analysis in Chapter 5 will shift to the assistants to the court—the probation officers and the psychiatrists. Chapter 6 dissects the administration of justice in the three counties, considering such issues as capricious and arbitrary sentencing policy, discretion in sentencing, and the relations between the Superior Court and the hospital to which the MDSOs are committed. The concluding chapter illustrates the fusion of the two types of sanction—civil and criminal—and the extension of this book to analogous civil commitment proceedings. Finally, the methods used in this study, theoretical considerations, and actual operations will be presented in the Appendix. For those interested in the empirical aspects of this research, it is suggested that the methodology section be read before proceeding to the substantive chapters.

Notes

1. For an example of this orientation, see Glanville Williams, "The Definition of Crime," *Current Legal Problems* 8 (1955):107-130. The biggest problem in the definition of civil law, according to Williams, is that ". . . [T]here are no common features of civil proceedings, in respect either of procedure or of the relief sought. . . ." (p. 124).

2. See People v Levy, 151 Cal. App.2d 460, 465, 311 P.2d 897, 900 (1957).

3. Henry M. Hart, "The Aims of the Criminal Law," *Law and Contemporary Problems* 23 (1958):404. Also see George H. Dession, "Justice after Conviction," *Connecticut Bar Journal* 25 (1951):217.

4. Budd v. California, 385 U.S. 909, 912-913 (1966) (dissenting opinion).

5. Robinson v. California, 370 U.S. 660 (1962).

6. See Kennedy v. Mendoza-Martinez, 372 U.S. 144 (1963).

7. George H. Dession, *Criminal Law Administration and the Public Order,* Charlottesville, Virgo: Michie Casebook Corporation, 1948, p. 198. Also see Walter Gellhorn, *Administrative Law Cases and Comments,* Chicago: The Foundation Press, 1940, pp. 427-430; Morris R. Cohen, "On Absolutisms in Legal Thought," *University of Pennsylvania Law Review* 84 (1936):686.

8. Nicholas N. Kittrie, *The Right to Be Different,* Baltimore and London: The Johns Hopkins Press, 1971, pp. 4-8.

9. Ibid., p. 3.

10. Francis A. Allen, *The Borderland of Criminal Justice,* Chicago: The University of Chicago Press, 1964, p. 14.

11. U.S. Bureau of the Census, *Statistical Abstracts of the United States, 1971,* Table 52, p. 41. The reason the residents of the correctional and mental institutions do not equal the total of all residents in institutions is that several categories of institutions were not calculated. These other institutions include those for the aged and dependent, the mentally handicap-

ped, the physically handicapped, dependent or neglected children, and persons suffering from TB or other contagious diseases. According to Alan Stone's estimates, approximately 55 percent of the mental hospital residents were admitted voluntarily. Alan Stone, *Mental Health and Law: A System in Transition,* Rockville, Mary.: National Institute of Mental Health, 1975, p. 44.

12. U.S. Bureau of the Census, *Statistical Abstracts of the United States, 1975,* Table 62, p. 45.

13. Stone, *Mental Health and Law,* p. 44.

14. U.S. Bureau of the Census, *Statistical Abstracts of the United States, 1975,* Table 293, p. 169.

15. Ibid., Table 287, p. 167.

16. Department of Health, Education, and Welfare, *Juvenile Court Statistics,* DHEW pub. no. SRS 73-03452 (1971).

17. U.S. Bureau of the Census, *Statistical Abstracts, 1975,* p. 167.

18. Ibid., p. 169.

19. The President's Commission on Law Enforcement and Administration of Justice, *Task Force Report: Drunkenness,* Washington, D.C.: U.S. Government Printing Office, 1967, p. 5.

20. The President's Commission on Law Enforcement and Administration of Justice, *Task Force Report: Narcotics and Drug Abuse,* Washington, D.C.: U.S. Government Printing Office, 1967, p. 2.

21. 370 U.S. 660 (1962).

22. Bernard Rubin, "Prediction of Dangerousness in Mentlly Ill Criminals," *Archives of General Psychiatry* 27 (September 1972): 397.

23. Other studies agree with this assessment. See David Biles and Glenn Mulligan, "Bad or Mad—The Enduring Dilemma," *British Journal of Criminology* 13 (1973):275-279.

24. Stone, *Mental Health and Law,* p. 6.

25. Marc F. Abramson, "The Criminalization of Mentally Disordered Behavior," *Hospital and Community Psychiatry* 23, no. 4 (1972):103.

26. Anthony A. Cuomo, "Mens Rea and Status Criminality," *Southern California Review* 40 (1967):463-526.

27. Sanford H. Kadish, "The Decline of Innocence," *Cambridge Law Journal* 26 (1968):273-290. Kadish has used the phrase "loss of innocence" to reflect this development.

28. Francis A. Allen, "Criminal Justice, Legal Values, and the Rehabilitative Ideal," *Journal of Criminal Law and Criminology* 50 (1959):226-232.

29. Allen, *Borderland of Criminal Justice.*

30. By "divestment of the criminal law," Kittrie refers to a "relinquishing of its jurisdiction over many of its traditional subjects and areas."Kittrie, *Right to Be Different*, p. 4.

16

31. Ibid., pp. 39-49.

32. For example, see "Liberty and Required Mental Health Treatment," *University of Pennsylvania Law Review* 114 (1965):1067-1080; Alan M. Dershowitz, "Psychiatry in the Legal Process: A Knife That Cuts Both Ways," *Judicature* 51 no. 10 (1968):370-377; H.A. Ross, "Commitment of the Mentally Ill: Problems of Law and Policy," *Michigan Law Review* 57 (1959):945-1018; Leonard V. Kaplan, "Civil Commitment 'As You Like It,' " *Boston Law Review* 49 (1969):14-45.

33. Alan M. Dershowitz, "Preventive Confinement: A Suggested Framework for Constitutional Analysis," *Texas Law Review* 51 (1973):1296.

34. Allen, *Borderland of Criminal Justice,* p. 35.

35. For examples of this point of view, see Marcel Frym, "What Psychiatry Can Do for Criminology," *Bulletin of the Menninger Clinic* 25, no. 4 (1961):196-205; Manfred Guttmacher, "The Psychiatric Approach to Crime and Correction," *Law and Contemporary Problems* 23 (1958):633-649; Karl Menninger, "Medico-Legal Proposals of the American Psychiatric Association," *Journal of Criminal Law and Criminology* 19 (1928):367-377; Karl Menninger and J. Satten, "The Development of Psychiatric Criminology," *Bulletin of the Menninger Clinic* 25 (1961):164-172; more recently, see Karl Menninger, *The Crime of Punishment,* New York: The Viking Press, 1966.

36. For a review of the literature in this area, see Tony Platt, *The Child Savers,* Chicago: The University of Chicago Press, 1969, Chapter 1; Kittrie, *Right to Be Different,* Chapter 1; Allen, *Borderland of Criminal Justice,* the chapter on Garofalo's Criminology; Seymour Halleck, "American Psychiatry and the Criminal: A Historical Review," *American Journal of Psychiatry* 121, Supplement (1965):I-XXI.

37. Allen, *Borderland of Criminal Justice,* pp. 14-15.

38. For examples of this orientation, see Platt, *The Child Savers;* Thomas Szasz, *Law, Liberty and Psychiatry,* New York: Collier Books, 1963; Kittrie, *Right to Be Different.*

39. Thomas Szasz, "The Myth of Mental Illness," in *Ideology and Insanity,* Garden City, N.Y.: Anchor Books, 1970, p. 24.

40. Platt, *The Child Savers.*

41. Kittrie, *Right to Be Different,* p. 344.

42. Francis A. Allen, "The Borderland of the Criminal Law: Problem of 'Socializing' Criminal Justice," *Social Service Review* 32 (1958):114.

2

Historical Development and Current Status of the Mentally Disordered Sex Offender Statute

Description of the Mentally Disordered Sex Offender Law

California's Mentally Disordered Sex Offender (MDSO) Law is found in the Welfare and Institutions Code, beginning at Section 6300.

As used in this article "mentally disordered sex offender" means any person who by reason of mental defect, disease, or disorder, is predisposed to the commission of sexual offenses to such a degree that he is dangerous to the health and safety of others. Wherever the term "sexual psychopath" is used in any code, such term shall be construed to refer to and mean a "mentally disorderd sex offender."

The MDSO proceedings are initiated in two general ways: (1) at the discretion of the court or (2) because of the nature of the crime. The court has the discretion to start MDSO proceedings after a person has been convicted of a criminal offense—whether or not it is a sexual offense—if the court finds that there is probable cause for believing the offender is an MDSO.

Under two conditions it is mandatory that the court initiate MDSO proceedings: (1) if a person is convicted of a felony sex offense involving a child under the age of fourteen, or (2) if a person is convicted of a misdemeanor sex offense involving a child under the age of fourteen, and the offender has been previously convicted of a sex offense in California or any other state.

If the court in which the criminal charge was adjudicated decides to initiate MDSO proceedings, the criminal proceedings are suspended and held in abeyance while the new civil proceedings are conducted. With the criminal proceedings suspended, this same court must certify the offender to the Superior Court of that jurisdiction, stating that the person has been "alleged to be an MDSO" and that the Superior Court must hold a hearing for a determination of the defendant's status. If the person is charged with a felony that is adjudicated at the Superior Court level, the proceedings are not transferred; if the crime is a misdemeanor, the offender is transferred from the Municipal Court to the Superior Court. When the alleged MDSO is before the Superior Court, the judge informs him of his right "to make a reply and to produce witnesses in relation thereto" (the allegation).

The court then refers the matter to a probation officer, who in-

17

vestigates the circumstances surrounding the offense and the legal and social history of the person. When the probation report is completed, the probation officer submits the report to the psychiatrists appointed by the court. The court appoints at least two, but not more than three, psychiatrists (one of whom is to be on the staff of a state hospital or county psychiatric facility). The psychiatrists examine the alleged MDSO and determine whether he is, within the meaning of the law, an MDSO. Each psychiatrist submits his findings to the court—that is, his opinion as to whether or not the person is an MDSO as well as his judgment as to whether he is likely to respond to care and treatment in a state hospital.

After the psychiatric reports have been submitted, a hearing is ordered (unless it is waived by the alleged MDSO) at which all relevant witnesses appear, and evidence is heard. If the offender has no attorney nor the funds to retain one, the court appoints a public defender to represent the offender at this hearing.

If, at the Superior Court hearing, the alleged MDSO is judged not to be an MDSO, he is returned to the court in which the criminal charge originated. The civil proceedings are terminated; the criminal proceedings are reinstated; and the court is to give "such disposition as the court may deem necessary and proper." If the court finds that the person is an MDSO, but would not benefit from care and treatment in a state hospital, there are two options. First, the court may return the offender for action on the criminal charge. Second, the court may submit an order committing the person for an indefinite period of time to the Department of Mental Hygiene—which will place him in a state mental institution.

The other possible outcome of the hearing is that the individual may be found to be an MDSO who would benefit from care and treatment in a state mental institution. In this case, once again, the court has two options. First, the court may return the offender to the court in which the criminal charge originated for final disposition of the criminal charge, or the court may make an order committing the person to the Department of Mental Hygiene for placement in a state mental institution for an indefinite period of time. For approximately 95 percent of the offenders judged to be MDSOs, this means a civil commitment to Atascadero State Hospital, a maximum security mental institution.

If the offender, or anyone on his behalf, is dissatisfied with the order of the committing judge, he may demand, within ten days after the order has been made, that the question of his being an MDSO be tried by a jury in the Superior Court. If this demand is made, the court must set the case for hearing at a date not less than five nor more than ten days from the date of the demand. The trial is to be conducted as provided by law for the trial of criminal cases, even though the criminal proceedings are suspended.[1]

After the person has been incarcerated in a state mental institution for an indefinite period of time, the superintendent of the institution can make one of two recommendations. An "A" recommendation signifies that the person has been treated to such an extent that he will not benefit from further treatment and that he is no longer a danger to the health and safety of others. A "B" rcommendation means that the person would no longer benefit from care and treatment, but that he is still a danger to others.

If the person receives an "A" recommendation, he may be returned to the committing court for further action on the criminal conviction. The court then terminates the civil proceedings, reinstates the criminal proceedings, and may either sentence the offender or put him on probation for not less than five years.[2] If a sentence is imposed, the time spent on an indefinite commitment as an MDSO is credited in fixing the term of sentence.

With the "B" recommendation, several alternatives are available to the court. The committing court can return the person to the original court, where a sentence can be imposed or probation granted for not less than five years.[3] The original court may also return the offender to the Superior Court, which may then recommit the person to the Department of Mental Hygiene for an indefinite period of time.

If the hospital does not make a recommendation after the person has been confined for a period of not less than six months, the committing court, on the motion of a person acting on behalf of the offender, may order the superintendent to make such a recommendation. After it has been received and the appropriate action taken, the court, or the person acting on behalf of the offender, must wait at least six months before making a similar motion. Motions can be made every six months thereafter.

Historical Context: 1900-1939

To make the current MDSO statute more comprehensible, an examination of the social and historical context from which it developed and of the social climate surrounding the passage of the original Sexual Psychopath Law is essential. It is not sufficient to study the national mood or the general social conditions of a given time; one must also look at the interest groups involved, which often had the power and ability to formulate specific social policy. The major interest groups that supported the enactment of the Sexual Psychopath Law (psychiatric reformers, a segment of the concerned public, and conservative law and order organizations) will be discussed.

Opinions differ regarding the extent to which psychiatrists were involved in the legal and penal reform movements before 1900. Some estimate that the psychiatrists' role was limited and place emphasis on social and political forces instrumental in reform. Others contend that medical personnel performed a greater role than was previously believed.[4] Whatever the role of the psychiatrist before the turn of the century, his role in the reform of the law and corrections was undoubtedly more prominent after 1900. At that point more articles about the psychiatric approach to crime and corrections began to appear in professional journals, and there was an urging on the part of the psychiatrists for increased cooperation between law and psychiatry.

The fact that the psychiatric and scientific approaches were considered closely related contributes to an explanation of the increased involvement of psychiatry in the field of crime and corrections. The faith in the ability of scientists to solve problems was prevalent, and this was extended to the psychiatrists, whose expertise was thought to enable them to make judgments about and suggest cures for different types of offenders.[5]

The medical specialty of psychiatry was not only rapidly expanding in its own right, but during the 1920s there was an increasing liaison between law and psychiatry. In 1927 the American Psychiatric Association (APA) formed an official committee, which was charged with the task of informing the legal profession about recent scientific developments in the field of psychiatry. The committee was to recommend the best ways to deal with offenders. In the first report of this committee, Karl Menninger discussed the psychiatric concept of justice and the role psychiatry would play in the protection of society and the treatment of the individual offender.

. . . [S]cientists [psychiatrists] frankly avow the aim of protecting society rather than achieving justice. It is often claimed that the psychiatrist is more interested in the individuals than in society; this is only true in private practice, and not always then. The psychiatrist has to consider both sides of the problem, but from the standpoint of assisting society and in reducing the menace of crime, psychiatrists aim only at the ideal of protecting society from individuals incapable of living safely within it. The fact that the psychiatrist is not the least interested in justice, and perhaps even doubts its existence, might lead us to much philosophical and metaphysical discussion. The fact is that doctors never talk about the justice of a medical case; the hospital is never concerned with whether or not the treatment of a case is just treatment, but only if it is beneficial or expedient. Similarly, scientists engaged in advising with respect to criminals would be not at all concerned with whether or not what they advised was just.[6]

Therefore, the APA recommended: "The permanent legal detention of the incurably inadequate, incompetent, and anti-social offenders irrespective of the particular offense committed. . . ."[7]

Sheldon Glueck, a lawyer and one of the principal spokesmen for the participation of psychiatry in the law, provided a further example of this type of thinking in 1927, under the heading "Basic Criterion of a Penal System." Using Ferri's basic commitment criteria, Glueck maintained:

The legal and institutional provisions for the protection of society must be based not so much upon the gravity of the particular act for which an offender happens to be tried, as upon his personality, that is, upon his dangerousness, his personal assets, and his responsiveness to peno-correctional treatment.[8]

Glueck urged the establishment of "scientific" treatment boards, which would be able to judge more accurately than laymen what type of individualized treatment would be best for each inmate and an appropriate release date for an individual serving time under an indeterminate sentence.

Among some psychiatrists there was concern for the individual liberties of the offender, although such feelings did not dominate. To many psychiatrists, individual liberties and constitutional guarantees were only barriers to the psychiatric reforms they sought. After discussing a penal system based on the individualization of justice, William White claimed:

I know the alleged constitutional barriers that stand in the way but I have faith that if we are right we can find ways to overcome such obstacles, else our plastic Constitution that can adjust to growing demands has no meaning and will sooner or later become an obstacle to progress.[9]

There is no doubt that the psychiatric reformers of the day sought to increase their influence in criminal justice. As the proposals indicate, the interest of the psychiatrists was not limited to one type of offender, but it extended to all offenders who seemed psychiatrically abnormal. To many psychiatrists, this meant *all* offenders.

Progress toward these goals was slow. When the opportunity arose to pass new laws relating to sexual psychopaths, there were mixed reactions from the psychiatric reformers. Some felt that the law should encompass other categories of individuals and that there was no logical or psychiatric reason for the law to pertain only to sex offenders. Eventually, the sexual psychopath legislation won general acceptance, although it was viewed as a compromise. Two prominent authorities reached the following conclusion:

Perhaps the only valid justification for separate legislation for sexual psychopaths is a pragmatic one. Such legislation permits experimenting with new procedures in a limited area, procedures which would be considered too radical for general acceptance. If they prove themselves, they can be extended in scope later.[10]

The passage of this and similar laws increased the influence of psychiatry in the criminal justice system.

The rise of psychiatry and psychiatric pressure groups was not the only force at work for the enactment of the sexual psychopath laws. Public opinion and outcry over what was thought to be an increase in sex crimes, especially against children, was another important factor. Several authors feel that the role of public pressure may have been underestimated.[11]

During the time period directly preceding the passage of these laws (1935-1940), there was a perceived increase in the number of sex crimes throughout the country, although there was actually no substantive increase. This perception can be explained by several factors: (1) the normal increase in crimes as a result of the general population increase; (2) several sensational sex crimes in California; and (3) heightened interest in sex crimes on the part of journalists and the expanding coverage of such crimes in newspapers and popular magazines.[12] This type of journalism, reflecting the public outcry, undoubtedly had an effect on influential groups concerned with establishing control over sex deviates (state legislators, law-and-order interest groups, police, and district attorneys).

The motives of the proponents of the Sexual Psychopath Act were varied. It may well have been that some people who favored the law did so with benevolent and humanitarian motives. However, a contradictory explanation is also tenable. The district attorneys and police groups realized that the passage of the Act would increase their ability to incarcerate dangerous individuals with a minimum of procedural safeguards. There would be few safeguards to hamper the courtroom proceedings, and a defendant would not have to be convicted of a crime. Once incarcerated, there would be no limit to the time that he could be confined and kept off the streets.[13]

The passage of the Sexual Psychopath Act reflected the formation of a curious coalition of interest groups—the psychiatric reformers and the law-and-order advocates. The psychiatric reformers were able to expand their sphere of influence in the field of criminal justice, and the conservative law-and-order groups gained greater control over the deviants—for the purpose of the new law was to incarcerate dangerous offenders in a secure institution for an extended period of time. The Act provided for more punishment and more treatment at the same time; there was to be more protection of society and more treatment for persons thought to be suffering from mental disorders. It is therefore obvious that the new law satisfied two concerned groups—the treatment-minded and the punishment-minded.

Similar formations of this opportune coalition were witnessed in many states during this period. Sexual Psychopath Acts were passed in Illinois in 1937, in Michigan in 1938, and in California in 1939. Numerous other states followed the example, so that by 1950, twelve states and the District of Columbia had some form of sexual psychopath act.[14] By 1960 twenty-six states and the District had such laws.[15] Although these laws have been variously titled (Sexual Psychopath Act, Sexually Dangerous Persons Act, Mentally Disordered Sex Offender Act), they are essentially the same. They provide for civil commitment including care and treatment, and they either bypass the standard criminal procedures or are used in conjunction with them.[16]

History of the Sexual Psychopath Law in California

The first law in California to contain the term *sexual psychopath* was passed in 1939 and stated:

As used in this chapter "sexual psychopath" means any person who is affected, in a form predisposing to the commission of sexual offenses against children, and in a degree constituting him a menace to the health or safety of others, with any of the following conditions:

a) Mental disease or disorder
b) Psychopathic personality
c) Marked departures from normal mentality

The opening paragraph and other sections of this new law caused a great deal of concern and debate. The section that aroused immediate controversy stated that the civil commitment could be instituted and the defendant involuntarily incarcerated without having been convicted of a crime. This section of the statute clearly raised questions of due process of law: according to the California and U.S. Constitutions no person could be incarcerated on a criminal charge unless certain minimal safeguards had been met. This objection was met by the courts when they held that the standard criminal safeguards were not applicable to the Sexual Psychopath Act, since the statute was civil, not criminal, in nature. Although the courts held fast to this logic, there was continued criticism on constitutional grounds, and some actual abuses of the law were exposed. In response to such criticism and abuses, the law was amended in 1950 to state that a person had to be convicted of a criminal offense before the civil proceedings could be initiated.

A further criticism focused on the phrase "menace to the health or safety of others"; the question was raised as to what constituted a "menace"—a vague and nebulous word. It was frequently asked how one discerned the thin line between offensiveness or obnoxiousness and menace or danger. The courts initially resisted this criticism, however, and claimed that this word was no more difficult to interpret than words in any other law. The court further decided that mental or emotional trauma, such as in reaction to a man exhibiting himself to a child, is as much an injury to the victim as a bone fracture and that this type of psychological trauma constituted a menace.[17] Criticism of this interpretation eventually proved effective, however, for in 1963 the wording of the law was changed to its present form—"*dangerous* to the health and safety of others."

The portion of the law that drew the most criticism was the term "sexual psychopath." The criticism was based on the notion that "sexual psychopathy" was not a valid psychiatric entity and that it was very difficult, if not impossible, to diagnose.[18] Bowman and Rose believed that there were no specific criteria for determining whether or not an individual had a psychopathic personality. The main indication for diagnosing psychopathic personality, they noted, was simply a long record of recidivism.[19] But how long is a long record, and how many repetitions must there be to constitute a pattern of recidivism? Bowman and Rose conclude:

Experience has proved the sexual psychopath laws to be as difficult to apply as traditional sex legislation. Their failure is due primarily to the fact that they assume psychiatric knowledge and terminology in the field of sexual abnormality to be a great deal more exact than they in fact are.[20]

Confronted with this type of evidence, the court considered the arguments and held that the term "sexual psychopath" was not vague to the degree that it should be held unconstitutional. Although the court's rationale was based on logic and analogy, the argument was essentially pragmatic. In one leading case the following opinion was given:

The Legislature does not have detailed knowledge of psychiatry. In this field the best that it can do is to adopt general broad definitions and leave it to the common sense and fairness of the courts to see that individual rights are not illegally affected. There are many similar statutes that are as "vague" as the one under consideration. . . . While the definition of "sexual psychopath" contained in the statute is somewhat general, considering our present knowledge in the field of mental sciences, any specific definition would unduly fetter expansion and experimentation in the field. Certainly we know that all psychiatrists do not agree as to the nature of the type of mental illness here involved, so that, by necessity, any legal definition must be a broad one.[21]

Although the courts did not change this opinion, the constant criticism in academic journals must have influenced the legislature, for in 1963 the statute was amended, and the term "sexual psychopath" was replaced with the present phrase, "mentally disordered sex offender."

Another consistent criticism of the Sexual Psychopath Act (which has more recently been made of the MDSO Law) is that the statute permits double jeopardy.[22] Civil libertarians have generally felt that incarcerating an individual two separate times in two different types of institutions for the same crime constitutes double jeopardy. The courts reply that since the MDSO commitment is essentially civil in nature, the individual safeguards that apply in criminal cases are not necessarily accorded to the MDSO. In one leading case, the court found:

It is obvious therefore that the primary purpose of the Legislature was to protect society against the activities of sexual psychopaths, and that it was not intended to make sexual psychopathy a mitigating circumstance. On the contrary, the sexual psychopath may be removed from society under the Sexual Psychopath Law until he is cured or until he is no longer considered a menace to the health and safety of others. The court may thereafter resume the criminal proceedings and impose the punishment allowed by law since the confinement as a sexual psychopath is not a substitute for punishment, the entire statutory procedure being civil in nature rather than penal.[23]

The basis for the state's authority to enact a sexual psychopath statute is said to rest in the "police power" of the state and the doctrine of *parens patriae*. The police power is the power of the state to pass laws for the protection of the public health, safety, morals and welfare of the community.

The only limitation set on this power is that the laws passed cannot be "unreasonable or arbitrary." The court's role in making judgments about laws passed in the name of the police power is to reconcile the public advantage derived from the legislation with the possible violation of civil liberties. This is the "balancing" function of the courts.

It seems futile to attempt to argue on a philosophical level whether or not the sexual psychopath laws are "unreasonable and arbitrary." What can be done is to state the view of the courts in this matter. The courts have held that the state has a right, based on the police power, to protect its citizens and that the law is not unreasonable or arbitrary. In the court's words: "The main purpose of the Act is to protect society against the activities of the sexual psychopath. The secondary purpose is to rehabilitate the sexual psychopath."[24] This secondary purpose of the Act—to rehabilitate the sex psychopath—is based on the doctrine of *parens patriae*.[25] The courts have acknowledged this doctrine with the reaffirmation that the statute is civil in nature. Therefore, the courts have held that incarceration under the authority of the Department of Mental Hygiene is to be viewed as treatment.

The Sexual Psychopath Act, as has been shown, has gone through many changes. The inferences to be drawn from these changes are many and, to a great extent, contradictory; two major trends can be identified in the nature and the administration of the law. On the one hand, increased emphasis has been placed on the civil liberties of the individual. That is, many of the Constitutional safeguards accorded regular criminal defendants are granted to those civilly committed. In the current form of the law, the person must be convicted of an offense, not merely charged; he has the right to a jury trial governed primarily by the rules of criminal procedure; he has the right to legal representation in all phases of the proceedings; and he has the right to confront witnesses, challenge expert testimony, and file for release every six months. In general, the proceedings have taken on a very criminal flavor—with the distinction between these and criminal proceedings becoming increasingly vague.

On the other hand, there has been an expansion of the scope of the law; the domain of the law has spread to include a wider variety of cases. The original law was concerned primarily with child molesters; at that time the terms *sexual psychopath* and *child molester* were almost synonymous in the eyes of the legislators. Also, sexual psychopathy was viewed as a single clinical entity. With the numerous revisions of the law, including a change in phrases, from the term "sexual psychopath" to "mentally disordered sex offender," sanctions against any person who seemed mentally disordered and who was involved in illegal sexual activity might be imposed by the court. The law granted greater protection to the individuals who were processed, but it expanded the range of behaviors subject to the law.

Notes

1. People v. Burnick, 14 Cal. 3d 306 (1975).
2. According to the data published by the Bureau of Criminal Statistics, the chances of getting mandatory probation after receiving an "A" recommendation are about 95 percent. Ronald H. Beattie and Virginia Vanich, *The Mentally Disordered Sex Offender in California,* Sacramento, Calif.: Bureau of Criminal Statistics, 1972, p. 39.
3. Ibid. The probability of receiving probation with a "B" recommendation is about 30 percent.
4. Tony Platt, *The Child Savers,* Chicago and London: The University of Chicago Press, 1969. "The self-image of penal reformers as doctors rather than guards and the domination of criminological research in the United States by physicians, helped to encourage the acceptance of 'therapeutic' strategies in prisons and reformatories. As Arthur Fink has observed, 'the role of the physician in this ferment is unmistakable. Indeed, he was a dynamic agent. . . . Not only did he preserve and add to existing knowledge—for his field touched all borders of science—but he helped to maintain and extend the methodology of science.' Perhaps what is more significant is that physicians furnished the official rhetoric of penal reform." (p. 29).
5. For examples, see L.A. Tulin, "The Problem of Mental Disorder in Crime: A Survey," *Columbia Law Review* 32 (1932):958; Louis Cohane, "Psychiatry and the Criminal Law," *The American Journal of Medical Jurisprudence* 1 (1938):153; "Report of the Committee on Psychiatric Jurisprudence," *The American Journal of Medical Jurisprudence* 1 (1938):22.
6. Karl A. Menninger, "Medicolegal Proposals of the American Psychiatric Association," *Journal of Criminal Law and Criminology* 19 (1928):372-376. Reprinted with permission.
7. Ibid., p. 376.
8. Sheldon Glueck, "Principles of a Rational Penal Code," *Harvard Law Review* 41 (1927-1928):469.
9. William A. White, "Need for Cooperation between Lawyers and Psychiatrists in Dealing with Crime," *American Bar Association Journal* 13 (1927):553.
10. Manfred Guttmacher and Henry Weihofen, "Sex Offenses," *Journal of Criminal Law and Criminology* 43 (1952-1953):171-172.
11. Frederick Hacker and Marcel Frym, "The Sexual Psychopath Law in Practice: A Critical Discussion," *California Law Review* 43 (1955):766-780; Alan Swanson, "Sexual Psychopath Statutes: Summary and Analysis," *Journal of Criminal Law and Criminology* 51 (1960):215-227; Gordon Kamman, "Evolution of Sex Psychopath Laws,"

Journal of Forensic Sciences 6 (1961):170-179; William Foley, "California's Sexual Psychopath—Criminal or Patient," *University of San Francisco Law Review* 1 (1967):332-339.

12. For example, see Charles J. Dutton, "Can We End Sex Crimes?" *Christian Century* 54, no. 2 (December 22, 1937):1595.

13. Hacker and Frym, "Sexual Psychopath Law in Practice," p. 777. "There has, in our experience, never been the slightest doubt in the minds of any of the offenders or the law enforcement officers that this type of forced institutionalization is primarily punishment, regardless of its precautionary or therapeutic aspects. . . ."

14. Edwin H. Sutherland, "The Diffusion of Sexual Psychopath Laws," *American Journal of Sociology* 56 (September 1960):142-148.

15. Swanson, "Sexual Psychopath Statutes," p. 215.

16. For a review of the literature of Sexual Psychopath Laws, see R.C. Bensing, "A Comparative Study of American Sex Statutes," *Journal of Criminal Law and Criminology* 42 (May 1951):57-72; Edwin H. Sutherland, "The Sexual Psychopath Laws," *Journal of Criminal Law and Criminology* 40 (1949-1950):543-554; Swanson, "Sexual Psychopath Statues," pp. 215-227; Paul Tappan, "Sex Offender Laws and Their Administration," *Federal Probation* 14 (September 1950):32-37.

17. People v. Stoddard, 227 Cal. App.2d 40 (1964).

18. Thomas Meyers, "Psychiatric Examination of the Sexual Psychopath," *Journal of Criminal Law and Criminology* 56 (1965):27. He states, "The hard fact is that there are no pathognomonic signs of sexual deviation other than the behavioral background."

19. Karl Bowman and Milton Rose, "A Criticism of the Current Usage of the term 'Sexual Psychopath,' " *American Journal of Psychiatry* 109 (1952):177-182.

20. Ibid., p. 179.

21. People v. Levy, 151 Cal. App.2d 460, 467-468 (1957).

22. In 1938, directly after the Michigan Sexual Psychopath Law was passed, the Michigan Supreme Court found it unconstitutional on the grounds of double jeopardy (People v. Frontzack, 286 Mich. 51, 281 N.W. 534, 1938). It was so ruled because the law was located in the criminal code, making the procedures essentially criminal in nature. The California law was part of the civil code (Welfare and Institutions Code), thereby countering the double jeopardy argument.

23. People v. McCracken, 39 Cal.2d 336, 346 (1952).

24. People v. Levy, 151 Cal. App.2d 460, 468 (1957).

25. "The doctrine of *parens patriae* to which we hereafter make reference and application may be defined as the inherent power and authority of a legislature of a state to provide protection of the person and property of persons non sui juris (not his own master), such as minors, insane, and incompetent persons." McIntoch v. Dill, 205 P. 917,925 (1922).

3

General Considerations for the Imposition of Sanctions

Most human decision-making, whether individual or organizational, is concerned with the discovery and selection of satisfactory alternatives; only in exceptional cases is it concerned with the discovery and selection of optimal alternatives.[1]

The primary concern of the Superior Court is what to do with offenders—what sort of sanctions should be imposed. While the court is also concerned with guilt and innocence, that issue is not the major preoccupation, since the vast majority of defendants plead guilty, thereby waiving their Constitutional right to a trial by jury. This is not meant to imply that defense attorneys, particularly public defenders, do not avail themselves of every opportunity to secure acquittals for their clients. Rather, the point is that a considerable amount of the time spent by the court personnel and most of the negotiations conducted involve the making of decisions about the defendant's future *after* the question of guilt has been determined.

Blumberg claims the criminal justice system of any large metropolitan area resembles a "sieve."[2] By this he means that from the time individuals are arrested to the time they are sentenced, there is a tremendous attrition rate. A very small percentage of the cases that are originally admitted into the criminal justice system ultimately emerge at the Superior Court level.

During interviews with prosecuting and defense attorneys in the three counties studied, the administrative concern to settle cases was consistently emphasized. An explanation for this is the pressure on the district attorney of each jurisdiction to maintain a high conviction rate, to foster an efficient organization, and to keep the Criminal Master Calendar as clear as possible. Therefore, all the cases in which it is believed the defendant is not guilty of the charge are eliminated during the screening. The result of this strategy is that only the "good" cases (from a prosecution point of view) are certified to the Superior Court, and consequently the conviction rate is very high.

Every defense attorney seeks to have his client acquitted, and most struggle arduously to achieve this goal. It is commonly noted that most of the court personnel, defense attorneys included, are keenly aware of the fact that the odds favoring acquittal are not great. Since an acquittal for each client is not possible, the defense attorney attempts to secure the "best possible disposition for the client." What constitutes a good disposition? If the client has pleaded guilty, a choice must be made from among a few rather undesirable dispositional alternatives. The alternative is selected to correspond to the court's perceptions of the dangerousness of the defendant and the seriousness of his activities. Selecting among alternatives and deciding what to do with the offender are the primary tasks of the court.

Sentencing in Superior Court is a very practical enterprise. In many cases options are limited, and the court faces its awesome responsibility with pressures impinging from all sides. Decisions must be made that may have profound effects on the defendant, his family, and the community; the decisionmaking participants must consider many factors, some conflicting, and the resulting frustration is enormous.

This chapter will focus on an examination of how the court, in making its determinations about the nature of a particular case, lays the foundation for administering an appropriate sanction. To deal with the large number of cases that flow through the system, general categories must be set up to ensure that similar cases receive similar dispositions.

Categorization of Typical Cases

In one sense, all criminal cases, like people, are different. However, when numerous cases are processed through the courts, certain patterns emerge (at least in the eyes of the court personnel) so that cases can be viewed as falling into one or another category. The process of classification or categorization is not unique to the criminal courts but is common to all organizations. When people work together in an organization, there is a need to maximize efficiency in communications so that the members of the organization do not have to describe in great detail all the information that must be communicated. Therefore, methods must be devised to communicate large amounts of information with relatively few symbols. To do this, organizations develop: (1) a standardized or technical language whose symbols have a definite and common meaning to the members of the organization; and (2) a classification, or categorization, scheme for establishing shared assumptions of meaning.

The technical vocabulary and classification schemes in an organization provide a set of concepts that can be used in analyzing and in communicating about its problems. Anything that is easily described and discussed in terms of these concepts can be communicated readily in an organization; anything that does not fit the system of concepts is communicated only with difficulty. Hence, the world tends to be perceived by the organization members in terms of the particular concepts that are reflected in the organization's vocabulary. The particular categories and schemes of classification it employs are reified, and become, for the members of the organization, attributes of the world rather than mere conventions.[3]

The importance of a classification scheme for an organization becomes very clear when one realizes the tremendous volume of material that must be translated into the organization's conceptual scheme. With a commonly understood classification scheme, organization members can transmit inferences about the raw material rather than the raw material itself.

Classification or categorization schemes can be viewed as facts of organizational life. The important issue, when examining a specific organization, is to look at the criteria on which the classifications are based. In the traditional Weberian model of bureaucracy, classification is based on formal, preconceived, and elaborated criteria. Merton summarizes the Weberian model:

Within the structure of hierarchically arranged authority, the activities of "trained and salaried experts" are governed by general, abstract, clearly defined rules which preclude the necessity for the issuance of specific instructions in each specific case. The generality of the rules requires the constant use of categorization, whereby individual problems and cases are classified on the basis of designated criteria and are treated accordingly.[4]

Since this classical model was proposed, sociologists have come to realize that the classification schemes used in organizations may not be based completely on formal criteria. The task of the researcher of organizations, then, is to ascertain the nature of the "true" classification scheme and the extent to which it is related to the formal one. This task is especially important for a researcher studying an organization that processes people, whether it be a mental hospital, a social welfare agency, or a criminal court. Scheff, for instance, suggests that an important area of social research in such agencies is the "typification of diagnosis."[5]

Such studies of organizations have begun to appear in the areas of criminal and juvenile justice. Sudnow's study of "normal crimes" is a classic example of informal classification in the adult criminal court,[6] while Emerson's study exemplifies research in juvenile court classification.[7] The intent of these studies is the same—to discern the "functional units" employed by the court personnel to carry out the business of the court.[8]

Here, analyzing the categories used by the court personnel to sort out and classify sex offenders meant determining the extent to which the categories used were those formally designated in the California Penal Code or whether they were categories that had evolved through repeated contact with "typical cases" in the court's everyday activities. Both types of categories, formal and informal, are used by the court personnel. For the purposes of this study, however, discussions of cases in terms of the formal numbered categories in the Penal Code proved to be less valuable. These formal numbered categories are very broad, and any number of real situations can fall within each formal category. Therefore, individual cases are discussed in terms of the very specific fact situations; the cases are compared to the abstracted "typical cases" and to similar cases that have been processed through the court previously.

When discussing specific cases before the bench, the court personnel examine all the facts of the case that seem relevant for determining how serious the offense is, how dangerous the offender is, and how severe a sanction should be leveled against the defendant. In weighing the gravity of the case to determine the appropriate disposition, the court decisionmakers compare by analogy that case with similar cases previously processed through the court. The facts of the case, the characteristics of the offender, and the sanctions meted out are considered, so that an equitable sentence can be imposed.

As opposed to Sudnow's findings that attorneys speak entirely in terms of "normal crimes," this study found that the court personnel tend to speak in detailed terms about the specific facts of recent cases in the court. The comparison of a current case with a recent one is a much more common approach than a comparison with "typical cases," although such typical cases are used as general reference points. Since there are some commonalities of cases and some patterns that emerge, it should prove useful to outline briefly and describe these "typical cases" and to point out some of the factors that are at issue as the court decides which case is more serious and which deserves a more severe sanction. These issues will be mentioned only briefly in connection with the typical cases, since a detailed analysis of conceptions of the severity of offenses and sanctions will be presented shortly.

Rape Cases

The details surrounding a classical rape case can vary, but the important elements seem to be that the offender and victim generally do not know each other and that the male seeks out an unsuspecting and unwilling victim for purposes of sexual exploitation and gratification. The male becomes sexually involved with the victim by force or threat of great bodily harm with no indication from the victim that she is willing to participate in the sexual relations. The important issues for comparison in these cases are how much force was used, whether a weapon was wielded, how much harm was perpetrated against the victim, and the offender's mental attitude at the time of the offense.

Rape cases involving females hitchhiking were very common in all three jurisdictions studied and are closely related to the classical rape situation. The primary difference in the eyes of the court personnel is that in the hitchhike situation, the victim places herself in a dangerous position voluntarily. While this does not mean that the court decisionmakers handle the hitchhike rape case nonchalantly, they have a much more difficult time determining to what extent there may have been complicity or agreement to have sexual relations. Operationally, this means that the deputy DA has a more difficult time proving the case in court, and the defense can drive a harder bargain and secure a less severe sanction for his client.

In the crude category of rapes resulting from a dating situation, the individuals involved are a male and a female who have known each other—even if for only a short period of time. A typical case involves a male who approaches a female in a bar and after several hours of conversation invites her to his apartment; she agrees. At some point the male decides that it is time for sexual relations and acts very surprised if the female claims she had no intention of becoming sexually involved. The challenge facing the male is to convince the female to comply with his wishes; he often resorts to different forms of persuasion, including force. The main issue facing the court is to determine how much coercion or force was used.

In California the statutory rape law was repealed in 1971, and was replaced with a new law entitled "Unlawful Sexual Intercourse." The new law resembles the old, but the word rape is not included. The key factor remains the age of the victim, namely whether she is under 18 years of age. Of relevance and interest to the court is the amount of coercion employed and the age differential. For example, if a nineteen-year-old male has had a sexual affair with his seventeen-year-old girlfriend, and the mother of the girl reports the crime to the authorities, this is not viewed as a particularly serious matter. However, a teenager's compliance to a much older man's demands, especially if he is threatening her with bodily harm, is cause for greater concern on the part of the court.

Child Molest Cases

The type of case that Sudnow described as the "Normal Crime of Child Molest" involves an adult male who molests a child, and the victim and the male do not know each other. The child informs his or her parents, who in turn report the offense to the police. We found this type of child molest case to be relatively rare. When it did occur, there was a great deal of concern on the part of the district attorney and the judge. The issues facing the court are what the offender actually did in the molest—from fondling to penetration—and the age of the child. One final consideration is how "dangerous" the offender is perceived to be, for the court fears that the simple child molest case could easily escalate into a kidnapping. If there are indications that the offender is potentially a kidnapper or that he might commit similar, although more serious, offenses in the near future, the court would view this as a very serious situation.

Intrafamily child molest cases are more or less common depending on the actual blood relationship involved. Perhaps the most frequent subtype of child molest case is that of a stepfather molesting his stepdaughter. Most commonly the mother is absent, and the husband becomes increasingly familiar and affectionate toward his stepdaughter(s). Eventually, the mother discovers the situation and reports the case to the police. The issues involved are the age of the victim, the specific nature of the molestation, and the degree of coercion used by the stepfather.

The child molest case perpetrated by a neighbor occurs more frequently than the classical case and generally involves a relatively young child who visits a neighbor's house and is molested. The main issue is the nature of the behavior that took place, for the seriousness factor varies with the assumed repugnance of the act and the resulting trauma.

Miscellaneous Cases

The typical exhibitionism case is usually that of a male in a public place who exposes himself to passers-by. The offender may or may not be masturbating at the time of exposure. One issue for consideration by the court is the number of prior arrests and convictions. The other important concern is the extent to which there was potential for a more serious crime to occur in conjunction with the act of exhibitionism. For example, did the person simply expose himself to the children and then depart, or did he invite them to get into his car and talk? The latter situation is viewed as much more serious, because it could easily develop into a child molest or a kidnapping case.

The homosexual case involving two adult males discovered by the police in a public restroom or a park with one male orally copulating the other can be considered the typical homosexual case. Since this case involves consenting adults, it is viewed as the least serious sex offense in the Superior Court and is frequently eliminated from the criminal justice system at a lower level. There is the possibility, however, of a similar case involving consenting individuals with one of the participants a minor; this is viewed as a much more serious situation. Generally, nothing of significance would happen to the young male, because the court may feel he was led astray; the older partner may receive a more serious sanction, especially if he has similar, prior offenses on his record.

Assessing the Seriousness of the Offense

The complexities involved in the process to determine the appropriate sanction for an offender are obvious. The court personnel must assess the nature of the offense at issue, namely, the type of behavior involved, the extent of force used, and other details of the crime. Beyond that, the relevant characteristics of the defendant, such as the number of prior convictions, his attitude, and potential for further dangerous activities are considered. Both aspects of the offense, the specifics of the act and the information about the individual, contribute to the judgments made about the "case." (From this point the word "case" will refer to consideration of both aspects.)

The formal legal categories in the Penal Code are only one of the many factors considered in assessing the attitudes of the court decisionmakers toward sentencing. There are other issues, which will be discussed later. Since such categories are one of the major factors, they can serve as the starting point in determining conceptions about seriousness of offense.

To obtain a crude indication of the relative severity of the formal offense categories and to compare the perceptions of severity among counties and among agencies within each county, a questionnaire was administered to judges, deputy district attorneys, deputy public defenders, and probation officers in each of the three counties. The respondents were asked to rate the seriousness of a variety of offenses, mostly sex offenses, that seemed to occur the most frequently at the Superior Court level. The respondents were instructed that the least severe rating was 1 and the most severe rating was 100. After the questionnaires had been returned, they were scored— first, by averaging the ratings for each of the agencies in each of the three counties and then by ranking the ratings of each individual respondent and averaging the rankings for each agency in each county. The averaged numerical responses to the questionnaire are given in Tables 3-1 and 3-2. Table 3-1 presents the average ratings of the seriousness of offenses for each agency in each of the three counties. Table 3-2 presents the average rankings of the seriousness of offense for each agency in each of the three counties. Since there were twenty offenses to be ranked, the number 1 indicates the least severe and the number 20 the most severe offense.

From both tables, it can be discerned that, in general, there is substantial agreement about the relative severity of the various offenses. In other words, the perceptions of the key decisionmakers in each agency in each of the three counties are quite uniform, although there is some variance with respect to a few offenses. For example, there is some disagreement about whether robbery or forcible rape is the more serious offense, since each was ranked as the most severe by different agencies. However, there is almost total agreement that both of these offenses are more serious than, say, child molest or rape by threat. Similarly, although child molest and rape by threat have roughly the same ranking, they are both viewed as more serious than exhibitionism or oral copulation. Although the administered questionnaire had some obvious limitations, as explained in the Appendix, there remains substantial uniformity in the court decisionmakers' perceptions of the seriousness of crimes in the formal offense categories.

Table 3-1
Average Ratings of Seriousness of Offense

Penal Code Sections[a]	N	Burglary (459 PC)	Felony Child Molest (288 PC)	Exhibitionism (314.1 PC)	Unlawful Sexual Intercourse (261.5 PC)	Incest (285 PC)	Robbery (211 PC)	Forcible Rape (261.3 PC)	Rape by Threat (261.4 PC)	Lewd Vagrancy (647a PC)	Oral Copulation (288a PC)
CCC[b] Judges	4	62.5	92.5	17.5	23.8	43.8	96.3	87.5	86.4	21.3	32.5
CCC DAs	6	62.5	72.0	22.0	28.7	61.7	90.3	82.5	75.3	24.5	54.8
CCC PDs	5	61.0	75.0	18.8	14.0	51.0	83.0	82.0	68.8	34.4	18.0
CCC POs	10	59.7	86.7	20.8	24.3	51.6	90.7	88.8	82.1	35.9	31.3
SFC[c] Judges	0	–[d]	–	–	–	–	–	–	–	–	–
SFC DAs	7	86.9	89.3	57.9	30.7	62.9	93.6	95.7	91.1	41.4	44.3
SFC PDs	13	65.0	85.3	18.3	35.0	42.9	92.9	91.3	86.3	20.4	21.8
SFC POs	10	81.0	92.8	37.5	40.0	72.3	89.2	92.5	89.4	28.3	42.0
OC[e] Judges	7	67.1	78.6	26.6	25.7	60.1	95.7	94.9	91.4	19.0	32.6
OC DAs	6	81.3	87.3	34.2	34.2	86.7	97.5	95.7	91.7	44.3	54.3
OC PDs	13	62.3	76.7	21.7	12.5	55.5	91.5	88.5	82.3	20.0	20.0
OC POs	14	72.1	86.4	32.9	46.5	73.8	94.6	94.5	92.7	33.7	56.6

(1 = least serious, 100 = most serious)

[a]Based on pre-1970 Penal Code revision except 261.5 (Unlawful Sexual Intercourse), which was formerly "Statutory Rape."

[b]CCC = Contra Costa County

[c]SFC = San Francisco County

[d]San Francisco judges refused to answer the questionnaire.

[e]OC = Orange County

Penal Code Sections	N	Mayhem (203 PC)	Assault with Intent to Commit Rape (220 PC)	Assault with Intent to Commit Violent Injury (240 PC)	Tattooing a Minor (653 PC)	Loitering around Schoolyard (653g PC)	Obscene Conduct (311.7PC)	Resisting Arrest (148 PC)	Bigamy (281 PC)	Sodomy (286 PC)	Failure to Register as a Sex Offender (290 PC)
CCC Judges	4	93.8	82.5	88.8	8.8	15.0	17.5	62.5	10.0	18.8	23.8
CCC DAs	6	75.0	74.5	63.2	10.5	27.2	24.7	44.5	22.7	54.8	23.7
CCC PDs	5	86.4	69.8	80.2	12.2	28.4	5.2	23.7	17.4	32.8	27.6
CCC POs	10	90.8	78.9	83.9	14.6	38.3	26.0	50.2	11.5	34.3	22.1
SFC Judges	0	–	–	–	–	–	–	–	–	–	–
SFC DAs	7	85.0	86.3	62.1	20.0	35.0	25.0	55.7	27.1	57.7	23.6
SFC PDs	13	91.3	81.7	75.8	17.1	22.5	13.0	21.2	11.3	32.7	10.3
SFC POs	10	86.5	87.9	89.3	30.1	38.7	31.1	48.1	28.5	19.1	31.1
OC Judges	7	80.0	84.3	84.3	15.3	19.0	22.3	55.0	18.7	37.3	40.1
OC DAs	6	92.5	89.3	82.0	17.5	36.6	18.8	44.8	15.8	59.2	35.8
OC PDs	13	78.8	65.2	61.9	12.4	18.6	1.5	23.5	8.3	19.8	12.8
OC POs	14	85.7	89.1	86.9	20.4	32.0	34.0	54.8	20.4	50.9	35.0

Table 3-2
Average Ranking of Seriousness of Offense

Penal Code Sections[a]	N	Burglary (459 PC)	Felony Child Molest (288 PC)	Exhibitionism (314.1PC)	Unlawful Sexual Intercourse (261.5 PC)	Incest (285 PC)	Robbery (211 PC)	Forcible Rape (261.3 PC)	Rape by Threat (261.4PC)	Lewd Vagrancy (647a PC)	Oral Copulation (288a PC)
CCC Judges	4	12.1	17.6	5.4	7.5	10.8	18.4	16.5	16.0	6.4	7.4
CCC DAs	6	13.1	15.1	4.3	7.3	13.4	18.8	17.0	16.2	5.3	11.6
CCC PDs	5	13.8	15.3	6.6	6.4	12.4	16.4	17.4	15.5	7.4	6.3
CCC POs	10	10.9	16.7	5.8	5.1	10.0	17.4	17.9	15.8	6.8	7.8
SFC Judges	0	–	–	–	–	–	–	–	–	–	–
SFC DAs	7	15.1	16.0	10.0	4.9	10.8	17.8	18.8	16.9	7.9	7.9
SFC PDs	13	13.8	16.0	6.0	9.4	10.9	17.3	17.3	16.2	6.8	6.8
SFC POs	10	13.6	17.1	7.5	7.3	11.7	15.8	17.5	16.4	4.8	7.3
OC Judges	7	13.1	15.4	6.3	5.3	12.0	18.4	18.2	17.5	5.4	7.6
OC DAs	6	12.1	15.2	7.1	6.5	14.3	19.3	18.6	16.3	7.3	8.8
OC PDs	13	12.4	15.7	8.2	5.5	12.6	19.0	18.7	17.8	7.7	6.8
OC POs	14	11.8	15.3	5.8	8.1	12.9	18.3	18.2	16.8	5.8	9.7
Total	95										

[a]Based on pre-1970 Penal Code revision except 261.5 (Unlawful Sexual Intercourse), which was formerly "Statutory Rape."

Penal Code Sections	N	Mayhem (203 PC)	Assault with Intent to Commit Rape (220 PC)	Assault with Intent to Commit Violent Injury (240 PC)	Tattooing a Minor (653 PC)	Loitering around Schoolyard (653g PC)	Obscene Conduct (311.7 PC)	Resisting Arrest (148 PC)	Bigamy (281 PC)	Sodomy (286 PC)	Failure to Register as a Sex Offender (290 PC)
CCC Judges	4	17.5	14.9	16.0	3.0	4.4	6.3	12.9	2.9	5.9	7.4
CCC DAs	6	15.3	15.8	12.6	1.6	4.9	6.0	9.4	5.6	11.3	4.2
CCC PDs	5	17.6	14.1	15.7	5.4	7.1	2.5	7.7	4.9	9.4	7.1
CCC POs	10	17.4	15.2	16.0	4.6	8.3	6.6	9.4	3.3	7.5	5.3
SFC Judges	0	–	–	–	–	–	–	–	–	–	–
SFC DAs	7	14.0	14.9	11.6	2.6	5.3	4.2	9.5	5.4	9.8	4.9
SFC PDs	13	16.5	14.8	13.8	6.3	7.2	4.5	7.8	4.6	9.0	3.8
SFC PDs	10	14.8	16.0	16.2	5.5	6.8	5.3	9.1	5.3	4.7	4.6
OC Judges	7	14.5	15.5	14.6	4.5	5.3	5.4	11.0	4.1	7.6	7.9
OC DAs	6	16.6	15.3	13.6	3.1	6.7	3.5	7.6	3.0	9.3	6.2
OC PDs	13	16.8	13.6	13.2	5.2	7.0	2.5	7.8	4.6	6.7	5.9
OC POs	14	14.8	16.4	15.9	3.0	5.4	5.7	8.9	2.6	8.7	5.5
Total	95										

Interviews with respondents to the questionnaire revealed a general agreement that the questionnaire had not allowed for an accurate reflection of the seriousness of a particular offense. The respondents stated that although the questionnaires were useful in eliciting a rough idea of relative seriousness, such information could be misleading, since the formal categories were so broad as to include many different fact situations. This problem created the possibility that one offense category normally seen as more serious could in fact be less serious—given the particular circumstances of the offense. How the decisionmakers judge the seriousness of an offense will now be examined.

One factor consistently discussed in the interviews with court personnel was the consideration of how much harm was done to the victim. The more harm, the more serious the offense was considered—without regard to the formal legal category used for the conviction. Although harm can be both physical and psychological, physical harm is viewed as more serious. In a rape or child molest case with severe physical harm perpetrated against the victim, the offender is very likely to be sent to prison. If the psychological damage is so serious as to require extensive psychiatric counseling, the offense would be considered very serious.

Closely related to the concept of harm, although not synonymous, is the amount of force used in the offense. Naturally, the more force employed, the more serious is the offense. To illustrate that the amount of force is not reflected in the formal legal categories, consider the following two cases. In the first, two males are found orally copulating, charged with oral copulation, and a conviction is secured. In the second case, a person is attacked and forced to submit to oral copulation; an arrest and conviction result. In both cases a conviction was secured under the same section of the penal code, yet clearly, the court will consider the latter situation more serious.

The state of mind of the offender at the time of the offense is also an important consideration. This is a vague concept, concerned with such issues as intent, degree of premeditation, and malice. The court tends to look less kindly on an offender if he appears to have planned the offense and acted in a malicious manner. Under some circumstances, the court may view the offender's state of mind as a mitigating circumstance. For instance, if a nondrinking offender were accused of attempted rape while under the influence of alcohol, the court would be likely to view this situation as less serious than that of a man who became drunk for the purpose of committing a rape.

In some cases the age differential between the victim and the offender is considered very important by the court. This concern is most apparent in cases of unlawful sexual intercourse, formerly called statutory rape. If the male and female are very close in age and toward the upper end of the statutory limit (eighteen years), the court is not likely to be overly concerned, assuming the relations are consensual in nature.

And finally, when the court attempts to gauge the seriousness of an offense, it is very concerned with the number of counts lodged against the defendant; did the rape involve assault, burglary, sodomy? The number of separate offenses involved in one incident contributes to the court's estimate of the seriousness of the offense.

Assessing the Seriousness of the Offender

Although the seriousness of the actual offense, including harm done and force used, may be the single most important determinant of the appropriate sanction, the court also considers other factors. Most of these other factors involve an evaluation of the offender himself. While no one of the following factors is of overriding importance, their appearance in different combinations (in conjunction with the appraisal of the seriousness of the offense) contributes to the court's sentencing decision.

Of primary interest to the court decisionmakers is the offender's prior legal history. This includes not only prior criminal activities, but also legal sanctions imposed for such activities. In general, the more prior convictions, especially if similar to the current offense, the more likely the court is to impose a severe sanction. If an offender is convicted for his first offense, the court would probably be lenient in setting his sentence, even if the offense is relatively serious.

Consideration is not limited to formal convictions, for the court is interested, although to a lesser extent, in police and court contacts that did not result in a conviction. Many of the court personnel believe that cases might well have been dismissed because the defendant cannot be proven guilty due to a legal technicality. A few police contacts that resulted in dismissal are of no great consequence, since it is assumed that the police can easily arrest someone by mistake. When there is a record of numerous police contacts, however, the court personnel find it reasonable to assume that the individual was involved in some criminal activity at one time or another.

The last part of the offender's prior legal history of concern to the court is the number and types of sanctions imposed against him in the past. When determining the appropriate sanction in the current case, the court makes an assessment of the effect of various sanctions on the offender. The court employs some version of a sanctioning gradient, and if a lenient sanction has been tried in the past and another offense has been committed, the court tends to select a more severe sanction. For instance, if a man is convicted of exposing himself, a misdemeanor sanction might be applied. With the second conviction, the same offense might become a felony, although the court would be unlikely to impose a severe sanction. However, repeated convictions with no apparent progress toward rehabilitation would result in progressively more severe sanctions—jail, a civil commitment to Atascadero, or prison.

There are many aspects of the offender's social life of interest to the court. The court will look at his marital, work, and military history to assess his stability. It is advantageous for the offender if there is evidence that he has maintained a marriage and/or a family, that he has been a working member of the community, and that he has been able to survive successfully the discipline and demands of military service. The absence of military service is not considered important unless evidence indicates that the individual was considered unacceptable.

The nature of the military discharge—honorable, dishonorable, or medical—may provide the court with further insight. In the case of a dishonorable or medical discharge, the court would seek out evidence of the individual's prior problems. An honorable discharge may work on the defendant's behalf, but it is not considered a conclusive statement of his character.

In sex cases the court is very interested in looking at the offender's psychiatric history for information about the types of treatment or therapy to which he has been exposed. If the offender has had extensive psychiatric help in the past, the court is likely to infer that further hospitalization would be useless, and an alternative in the form of a criminal sanction might be sought.

The offender's current "attitude" is also deemed important by the court. Attitude is a rather vague concept, but it has to do with the degree of remorse the offender feels over his criminal acts and how much he appears motivated to change his behavior. An offender who appears very remorseful will be judged more favorably than someone who does not or than someone who displays contempt for the court. Since the willingness to change is at the very center of the rehabilitative process, those who seem willing to work toward such an end are granted special consideration.

All this information is sought because the court is concerned with what the offender might do in the future. The court reviews the offender's prior criminal record, social history, current attitude, and psychiatric history to determine, as accurately as possible, whether or not the offender is likely to commit a dangerous offense in the near future. If it is believed that the defendant poses a very real danger to others, institutionalization becomes an increasingly appropriate alternative.

No single factor listed under seriousness of offense or seriousness of offender determines any particular sanction; the combinations of mitigating or aggravating circumstances that arise in any particular case must be examined. Being convicted of a serious offense does not necessarily indicate a serious sanction will be meted out if the offender has no prior record, a good social history, a positive attitude, and if there is a strong possibility that he will not commit another offense. The converse also holds; a person convicted of a relatively minor offense might receive a relatively severe sanction if there were numerous prior convictions and if he shows a lack of interest in changing his behavior.

What develops at the Superior Court level, then, is a very elaborate ranking system for examining and weighing the numerous factors judged significant by the court personnel. The issue for the court decisionmakers, after they have established the relative ranking of severity of the offense and the offender is to fit that ranking with a sanction of an appropriate degree of severity.

Assessing the Severity of Sanctions

The process of plea bargaining implies alternatives, which are viewed as more or less attractive to each party. Defense attorneys constantly state that their goal is "the best possible disposition for the client." In a study of sentencing policy the immediate questions are: (1) How do the various actors in the decisionmaking process view the available dispositional alternatives, and (2) given the type of case before the bench, what is the "best possible disposition" from each adversary's point of view? An understanding of these issues must include a firm conception of what the numerous dispositional alternatives represent.

Exposure to the literature on civil commitments, especially civil commitments of criminal defendants, might lead one to assume that civil commitments are used primarily to circumvent constitutional safeguards accorded criminal defendants and to expedite the involuntary incarceration of defendants for a longer period of time than commitment by standard criminal procedures would allow. Given this assumption, it would seem reasonable that defense attorneys would oppose a civil commitment and that prosecuting attorneys would favor it.

Contrary to these expectations, close observations of the Superior Court proceedings revealed that in most cases that involve a possible commitment as an MDSO to Atascadero, the defense attorney was in favor, and the prosecution was opposed. In a small proportion of the cases (perhaps 5 to 10 percent) the defense attorney was opposed to committing an offender to Atascadero as an MDSO, and the prosecution was in favor of it. Upon inquiry, defense and prosecuting attorney alike explained that attitudes toward Atascadero and MDSO commitments varied depending on the type of case before the bench. With very serious cases, the civil commitment as an MDSO was viewed by both attorneys as a relatively lenient sanction; with minor cases, the MDSO commitment was considered severe.

To determine in a systematic manner to what extent these views were uniformly held by the key decisionmakers in each of the three counties, two questionnaires were devised to assess their perceptions of the relative severity of possible sanctions—one for minor sex cases and another for serious sex cases. The questionnaires were administered to judges, deputy district attorneys, deputy public defenders, and probation officers in each of the three counties. Respondents were instructed to rate the severity of the sanctions from least severe to most severe. The questionnaires were scored, and the results are presented in Tables 3-3 and 3-4.

From an examination of Table 3-3, it is clear that there is unanimous agreement among all agencies in all three counties that for minor cases (misdemeanors) a commitment to Atascadero as an MDSO is the most severe sanction possible; a county jail sentence is the next most severe sanction. In contrast, the results of the second questionnaire (Table 3-4) reveal that for serious sex cases an MDSO commitment is not the most severe sanction. No agency in any of the three counties believed that a commitment to Atascadero was more severe than a commitment to state prison. In one agency in one county (the public defenders of San Francisco) these two sanctions were ranked equally as being the most severe. In all other instances, a commitment to state prison was viewed as a more severe sanction.

To explain why the civil commitment was viewed differently, depending on the case, intensive interviews were conducted with many of the key decisionmakers—judges, defense attorneys (private and public), prosecuting attorneys, and probation officers. There was almost unanimous agreement among all the decisionmakers in all counties that the primary consideration in sentencing is the *amount of time to be served*; the secondary consideration is the *quality of the time to be served.* If it were revealed to the defendant and defense attorney that they were faced with the choice of eighteen months of therapy at Atascadero or twelve months of incarceration in the county jail, most would select the county jail sentence.

If the court decides to sentence an offender for a specific amount of time, there is generally only one way for the court to ensure that its pronouncements are carried out—by sentencing the offender to the county jail. When an offender is sentenced to jail, the judge can specify the precise length of incarceration. If, however, the court feels that the offender should be sent out of the community, it cannot specify the time to be served because of the indeterminate sentencing law in California, which is applicable for commitment to both the Department of Corrections (state prison) and the Department of Mental Hygiene (Atascadero State Hospital). If an offender is sentenced to state prison, the judge merely states: "You are hereby sentenced to the Department of Corrections for the term prescribed by law"; it is the responsibility of the California Adult Authority (California's version of the parole board) to set the specific

Table 3-3
Average Ranking for Severity of Misdemeanor Dispositions

	N	Small Fine	Probation (No Supervision)	Atascadero S.H.	Dismissal	Jail (6 mos.)	Probation (Supervision)	Fine & Jail	Suspended Sentence
CCC Judges	4	2.4	3.0	7.5	1.1	6.9	5.3	6.1	3.5
CCC Deputy DAs	6	3.1	2.7	7.9	1.3	6.8	5.0	6.1	3.2
CCC Deputy PDs	5	3.4	3.4	7.8	1.0	6.8	4.8	5.4	3.4
CCC Deputy POs	10	2.9	3.1	7.5	1.1	7.4	4.9	5.9	3.0
SFC Judges	0	–[a]	–	–	–	–	–	–	–
SFC Deputy DAs	7	2.4	3.7	8.0	1.1	7.0	4.9	6.1	2.8
SFC Deputy PDs	13	2.5	3.6	7.8	1.0	6.8	4.9	6.3	3.0
SFC Deputy POs	10	3.1	2.8	8.0	1.2	6.6	5.1	6.2	3.1
OC Judges	7	2.8	3.3	7.6	1.7	6.8	5.4	6.1	2.3
OC Deputy DAs	6	2.5	3.4	7.7	1.1	6.8	5.2	6.3	3.0
OC Deputy PDs	13	2.7	3.6	8.0	1.0	6.8	5.6	5.3	3.0
OC Deputy POs	14	3.3	3.3	7.6	1.3	7.1	5.1	6.0	2.4
Total	95								

(1 = Lowest Ranking and 8 = Highest)

[a]The judges in San Francisco County refused to answer the questionnaire.

Table 3-4
Average Ranking for Severity of Felony Dispositions

	N	Small Fine	Probation (No Supervision)	Atascadero S.H.	Dismissal	State Prison	Jail (6 mos.)	Probation (Supervision)	Fine & Jail	Suspended Sentence
CCC Judges	4	2.1	3.4	8.0	1.3	9.0	6.6	5.6	5.8	3.3
CCC Deputy DAs	6	2.8	2.8	8.1	1.6	8.9	6.4	5.5	5.9	3.1
CCC Deputy PDs	5	3.2	3.0	7.8	1.0	9.0	7.0	5.0	5.4	3.8
CCC Deputy POs	10	2.8	3.4	7.4	1.1	9.0	7.2	5.5	5.8	3.0
SFC Judges	0	–	–	–	–	–	–	–	–	–
SFC Deputy DAs	7	2.3	3.2	8.2	1.2	8.6	6.6	5.2	6.0	3.2
SFC Deputy PDs	13	2.3	3.6	8.5	1.0	8.5	6.5	5.0	6.2	3.3
SFC Deputy POs	10	3.1	3.1	8.1	1.2	8.9	6.6	5.1	6.1	2.9
OC Judges	7	2.6	3.3	8.0	1.6	8.8	6.3	5.8	5.6	2.8
OC Deputy DAs	6	2.7	3.8	7.5	1.2	9.0	6.7	5.6	6.2	2.5
OC Deputy PDs	13	2.6	3.5	7.9	1.0	9.0	6.3	5.8	5.2	3.6
OC Deputy POs	14	2.9	3.1	7.5	1.6	8.9	6.6	5.9	5.8	2.8
Total	95									

(1 = Lowest Ranking; 9 = Highest)

length of the sentence. Likewise, if the judge sends the offender to Atascadero State Hospital, it is primarily up to the staff at Atascadero to determine either that the offender has received sufficient treatment and can be safely returned to the community or that treatment is no longer helpful, and the offender is still a danger to the community.

Although the commitment to state prison or Atascadero is theoretically indeterminate, each institution has established general policies concerning the length of the incarceration for different types of offenders; these policies may fluctuate slightly from time to time. Despite the slight fluctuations, the decisionmakers at the Superior Court have very definite ideas about how long a particular type of offender will be retained in either institution. The feeling is uniform among all court personnel that, generally, an offender will spend less time in Atascadero than in state prison for a roughly comparable offense. The court personnel claim that if an offender is sent to Atascadero on a relatively serious case, such as rape or felony child molest, he is likely to spend eighteen months to two years, depending on the circumstances of the case. The court personnel acknowledge that if the same defendant were sent to state prison, he would probably be there between two and three years. For this reason, Atascadero is viewed as a less severe sanction for serious cases; that is why the defense attorney would favor it and the prosecuting attorney oppose it.

The situation is exactly the opposite for relatively minor offenses for which state prison is not an alternative. If an offender received a civil commitment to Atascadero for a relatively minor offense, the court personnel believe that he would spend approximately eighteen months there. The same offender given a criminal commitment would not spend more than six months to one year in the county jail. Facing these two alternatives, the defense attorney generally opposes the civil commitment, and the prosecuting attorney favors it, since the offender will be incarcerated for a longer period of time.

The second, less important, concern when sentencing is the quality of the time to be served; that is, how much physical and psychological harassment will result from each of the dispositional alternatives? It is believed by the court decisionmakers that most offenders, notably child molesters, receive a greater degree of physical and psychological abuse under a criminal commitment, especially to state prison, than under the civil commitment to Atascadero.

Cases in which a defendant has previously been beaten by inmates in the county jail and is afraid of being sentenced to state prison are not uncommon. Such a defendant has discovered that passive sex offenders in general, and child molesters in particular, are at the lowest level in the inmate subculture's hierarchy. Therefore, as an inmate at a state prison, he can look forward to several years of exploitation and severe physical abuse. With a civil commitment to Atascadero, however, most of the physical and psychological abuse can be avoided. Atascadero is, at least in contrast to state prison, a relatively tranquil institution in which time can be served with a minimum of harassment. Therefore, another concern of the defense attorney is how to obtain the "easiest time" for his client. This is a further reason for the defense attorney to advocate a civil commitment when the offense is a serious one, and the only realistic alternative is state prison. When all factors are taken into consideration and the various sanctioning alternatives ranked, a sanctioning gradient emerges, in which what happens in practice is in distinct contrast with what happens in theory (see Table 3-5).

When the court decisionmakers are involved in negotiating a sanctioning decision, they do not appear to be overly concerned with general deterrence, rehabilitation, or even punishment. They must focus on the very practical problem of what to do with individuals who are excessively troublesome members of the community. Whether rehabilitation at a prison or treatment in a mental institution is offered, court personnel are skeptical that either will take place. From their perspective, there have been few indications that the offenders sent to the various institutions return greatly improved. A prevalent view is the realization of the improbability of effective behavior change—given the lack of motivation on the part of most defendants, the ratio of professional help to offenders in prison and at Atascadero, and the lack of psychiatric knowledge about the etiology and treatment of behavior problems. Of course, when the court decides to commit an offender to Atascadero, it will be pleased if the limited therapy given

Table 3-5
Sanctioning Gradient

For Minor Offenses (misdemeanors and light felonies)	For Serious Offenses (heavy felonies)
Most Severe	
	State prison
Atascadero (as MDSO)	Atascadero (as MDSO)
County jail (6 months or more)	County jail (6 months or more)
Fine plus less jail	Fine plus less jail
Probation (with supervision)	Probation (with supervision)
Probation (without supervision)	Probation (without supervision)
Suspended sentence	Suspended sentence
Small fine	Small fine
Dismissal	Dismissal
Least Severe	

produces positive results. As a matter of fact, all the decisionmaking participants sincerely hope that the person will be helped in some way, but few seriously believe that any significant change or improvement actually will take place.

The desire to punish or exact vengeance does not appear to motivate significantly the court personnel. After they have witnessed hundreds of criminal cases being processed through the courts, any new case is "just another case" unless it is an exceptionally brutal crime. After a short time on the job, most attorneys no longer become emotionally involved in the cases or enraged at what they see. New cases must be disposed of, and the object of the day's work is to negotiate cases and determine what sanction is most appropriate.

An esoteric theory of general deterrence does not appear to guide the court personnel either. The problems of the Superior Court are too immediate, too direct. The volume of cases that the court handles is enormous, and the amount of work to be done extensive. In such a setting, time for reflection on general deterrence theory is not available, for the primary organizational requirement is that the court personnel clear the Master Calendar so that new cases can be processed.

With the pessimism about treatment and rehabilitation and the lack of concern for both general deterrence and vengeance, what does the court consider when committing an offender to an institution? Institutionalization serves the very practical function of preventive detention. It removes the offender from the community—almost always for a longer period of time than if the offender were sentenced to county jail. Although an institution does not necessarily treat or effectively rehabilitate, it does *sequester*. If nothing else, a civil commitment to Atascadero as an MDSO removes the offender from the community for approximately eighteen months to two years, while prison retains custody of the offender for two or three years.

The Process of Sentencing

When numerous cases of a roughly similar nature are processed through the courts, norms reflecting the appropriate sanctions for different types of cases are generated. All the factors surrounding the case, the offense itself, and the offender are considered by the decisionmakers; a judgment about the seriousness of the case is reached, and a correlation is made between the case and an equally severe sanction. The object for attorneys and for the court is, as one Criminal Master Calendar judge stated, "to figure out the *going rate* for different types of cases." For instance, a forcible rape or a child molest case involving force, when the offender has several similar prior offenses, is worth approximately three years time, and so the offender is sent to state prison. A rape by threat with no priors or a child molest case with priors but no force is worth about eighteen months or two years time, so the offender is sent to Atascadero. An attempted rape or a relatively minor child molest case might be deserving of a year; therefore, the offender would be sentenced to county jail.

The sentencing process involves, then, the classification and ordering of cases and sanctions. Both are very important for court organization, for effective communication, and for efficient processing.

Classification schemes are of particular significance for the program-evoking aspects of communication. When an event occurs that calls for some kind of organization response, the question is asked, in one form or another: "What *kind* of event is this?" The organization has available a repertory of programs, so that once the event has been classified the appropriate program can be executed without further ado.[9]

After numerous cases have been processed through the court organization, and after the classification schemes for cases and sanctions become solidified, the cases are disposed of in a routine way by the court decision-makers.

When a stimulus is of a kind that has been experienced repeatedly in the past, the response will ordinarily be routinized. The stimulus will evoke with a minimum of problem-solving or other computational activity, a well structured definition of the situation that will include a repertory of response programs, and programs for selecting an appropriate specific response from the repertory.[10]

Defense attorneys are fully aware of the classification schemes for cases and sanctions. They are also knowledgeable about what sanction is appropriate for a given case; they know the "going rate" for different types of cases. When a new case comes before the bench, the competent defense attorneys are aware of what they can expect as the most favorable disposition, based on the outcomes of similar cases in weeks past. If a judge attempts to impose a more severe sanction than usual, the defense attorney is very quick to point out that it would be inequitable compared to less severe sanctions imposed by the same judge in the same court. These informal standards that develop in each court organization have a leveling effect on the sentences imposed.

As the norms solidify and the disposition of cases becomes routinized, sentencing patterns emerge. The objective of the social science researcher, as of the court personnel, is to determine the meaningful patterns that emerge from the ongoing social interaction.

A person who has been trained in the observation of organizations can extract by these and other techniques a large part of the program that governs routine behavior. This is such a common-sense fact that its importance has been overlooked:

Knowledge of the program of an organization permits one to predict in considerable detail the behavior of the members of the organization. And the greater the *programming* of individual activities in the organization, the greater the *predictability* of those activities.[11]

What was discovered after an examination of the routinized activities of the court organizations in the three counties was a rather consistent and patterned sanctioning process *within each organization,* although some differences were noticed among the three organizations. Within each organization the classification scheme for cases seemed very consistent, as did the classification scheme and ranking of sanctions. After the subtleties of the court decisionmakers' perceptions of the severity of cases (offense and offender) were identified, it was relatively easy to predict the realistic range of sanctioning alternatives and, in many instances, the actual sanction that would be imposed.

The pattern that emerged in all three jurisdictions concerning the civil commitment to Atascadero was very similar. Atascadero seemed to be the midpoint on the sanctioning gradient—less severe than state prison, but more severe than county jail. With such a pattern, a peculiar paradox has resulted in the administration of the MDSO civil commitment statute. Namely, the offenders most mentally disordered in a psychiatric sense, the offenders most dangerous in a physical sense, and the offenders most in need of psychotherapy by any psychiatric standards are the least likely to be committed to a mental institution (Atascadero), since this disposition is viewed by the court personnel as too lenient. In contrast, the offenders who are less mentally disturbed, less in need of psychotherapy, more passive, and less dangerous in a physical sense are the most likely to be subject to the civil commitment, since this type of offender is considered as not deserving such a severe sanction as state prison.

Notes

1. James G. March and Herbert A. Simon, *Organizations,* New York: John Wiley and Sons, Inc., 1958, pp. 140-141.

2. Abraham S. Blumberg, "The Criminal Court as Organization and Communication System," in Richard Quinney (ed.), *Crime and Justice in Society,* Boston: Little, Brown and Company, 1969, p. 275.

3. March and Simon, *Organizations,* pp. 164-165.

4. Robert K. Merton, *Social Structure and Social Theory,* Glencoe, Ill.: The Free Press, 1949, pp. 151-152.

5. Thomas J. Scheff, *Being Mentally Ill,* Chicago: Aldine Publishing Co., 1966, p. 178.

6. David Sudnow, "Normal Crimes," *Social Problems* 12:3 (1965): 255-276.

7. Robert M. Emerson, *Judging Delinquents,* Chicago: Aldine Publishing Co., 1969.

8. Scheff, *Being Mentally Ill,* p. 179.

9. March and Simon, *Organizations,* p. 163.

10. Ibid., p. 140.

11. Ibid., p. 143.

4

The Negotiation of Mental Disorder: The Perspective of the Attorneys and the Judge

Plea bargaining is the process that disposes of about 90 percent of the cases at the Superior Court level. Since plea bargaining with cases involving mental disorder is of central importance to understanding the work of the court, it will be the subject of this chapter. However, before a detailed discussion of the plea bargaining process is undertaken, the pressures under which all the participants in the bargaining process must function will be described.

Organizational Pressures on the Court

The work of an organization does not take place in a vacuum. Rather it is conducted within a set of requirements and constraints that have consequences for the activities of the organization's members; the sources of the organizational requirements and constraints may be either internal or external. The internal sources consist of such things as statutory provisions or rules with which the organization must comply or limitations in resources or technology necessary to carry out the volume of work facing the organization. The organization's response to and interaction with its environment provides the external restraints. A conception of the nature of these provisions and limitations is of crucial importance for understanding the court's functioning, which, in a general sense, is no different from that of any other formal organization.

These pressures will not be analyzed in detail, for this has been done many times in the past.[1] Instead, a description of some of the pressures facing the court and court personnel will be presented, and their importance for the disposition of sex-related cases will be assessed and reaffirmed.

Calendar Pressures

An organizational pressure repeatedly mentioned in the literature on court functioning is the enormous volume of cases that the courts must process in a relatively short period of time. As a result, the strict adversary proceedings and the classical model of Anglo-American criminal law procedure have been replaced by guilty plea bargaining as the primary mode of settling cases. The current system would collapse if trial by jury were demanded in even 25 percent of the criminal cases.[2] Because of this, the manner in which the court personnel tend to evaluate their performance is not by the quality of justice administered but by the efficiency with which they can dispose of cases. This pressure is summarized by Jacob:

The principal criterion by which the dispositional process is evaluated is efficiency defined in terms of number of cases disposed per dollar of resources expended. Hence speedy dispositions are highly valued because they do not strain available resources. Alternative criteria of the adversary process, such as the proportion of defendants or the correctness of judicial findings are not pertinent. Indeed, proceedings which found many defendants innocent would be considered highly inefficient; court personnel instead seek high proportions of convictions and guilty pleas as indicators of their efficiency.[3]

The type of adjudication in each of the three counties is illustrated in Table 4-1, as well as the number and percentage of cases for each type of adjudication. The high rate of guilty pleas should be noted as well as the fact that the percentages would be somewhat higher if the convictions alone were calculated. The pressure on the district attorney (and to a lesser extent on the judges in each county) to plead out cases had some effect on the "going rate" for different types of cases in each of the three counties.

Law-and-Order Pressures

External pressures, exerted primarily on district attorneys and judges, to secure relatively harsh sentences for certain offenders are also present.

Table 4-1
Type of Adjudication (All Sex Cases)

	Contra Costa		San Francisco		Orange	
	N	Percent	N	Percent	N	Percent
Guilty plea	151	86	163	85	149	75
Jury trial–guilty of at least 1 offense	10	6	20	10	23	12
Jury trial–not guilty	9	5	3	2	13	7
Court trial–guilty of at least 1 offense	1	0.5	1	0.5	6	3
Court trial–not guilty	0	0	1	0.5	3	2
Not guilty by reason of insanity	1	0.5	1	0.5	0	0
Not guilty plea (too insane to stand trial)	3	2	2	1	6	3
No information	0	0	0	0	0	0
Total	175	100	191	99.5	200	102

These pressures appear most often in the form of law-and-order rhetoric, encouraging a tough, vindictive attitude toward criminals, and they arise from several related groups: (1) newspaper reporters, (2) organized law-and-order groups, and (3) the victims themselves, including friends or relatives of the victim.

It is very difficult to assess the degree to which these pressures to secure severe penalties are actually felt and acted on by district attorneys and judges. During interviews with court personnel, it was frequently stated that these pressures were operative. Although the deputy district attorneys and judges generally minimized the effect of these pressures on them, the defense attorneys, and less often the probation officers, agreed that these concerns were in fact considered when the bargaining was being conducted and the sentence determined.

The defense attorneys stated that the judges[4] and district attorneys[5] were concerned that they might appear too lenient, and that, if publicized, this might have an adverse effect on their reputations and careers. Although losing an election is relatively rare for judges and uncommon for district attorneys, such electoral concerns do exert some influence over the bargaining policies of the district attorneys and the formal sentencing policies of the judges.

The direct reporting of cases in the newspapers exerts some pressure on the court personnel. Newspaper reporters, frequently present in court, are especially interested in publishing sensational details of very sensitive cases. The court personnel, therefore, feel that the sentence in a sensitive case, particularly involving a sex crime, will most likely appear in print if the sentence is too lenient. Although these pressures were felt in all three counties, there was some county variation, with court personnel in Orange County being the most concerned and those in San Francisco being the least concerned.[6]

Private law-and-order groups, such as Citizens for Justice, generally compile their own statistical data on sentences imposed for various types of offenses and on the judges who do the sentencing. Armed with these data, they often publish monthly summaries in the newspaper or save the data until an election and attempt to use them to defeat a lenient judge or district attorney.

A third source of pressure comes from the victim or relatives of the victim. Those involved in a sex-related case are generally concerned that justice be done, i.e., that the offender is severely punished. Although strict vengeance might not be the motivating factor, victims feel that the offender should at least be incarcerated to prevent further harm to the community. The victim's or the victim's family's desires can be communicated directly to the district attorney or the judge or indirectly through the probation officer's presentence report.

During interviews with the deputy district attorneys, several mentioned that victims or relatives do make such demands. A good example of this can be found in the presentence probation report. In one case, for example, an adult male was found guilty of unlawful sexual intercourse (California's version of statutory rape). The male in the case had sexual relations with his foster daughter on numerous occasions and the daughter became pregnant. The mother of the girl was interviewed by the probation officer. The following statement appeared in his report:

Mrs. (*wife of defendant*) threatened that if Mr. (*defendant*) is not sent to state prison and if "they give him a pat on the wrist and turn the maniac loose again to harm young girls," then she will have no recourse than to bring legal suit against all parties involved.

The very distinct possibility that the victim or the parents of the victim will go to the newspapers certainly is considered. This concern is one of the elements that increases the "going rate" in certain cases, for such pressures undoubtedly influence the plea bargaining process.

A less prevalent concern is that a disposition might be considered too severe. Several interviews revealed that the judges and district attorneys feared the adverse publicity of being labeled "racist" or worried that the charge of racial discrimination would be leveled against the court. Therefore, there was pressure to avoid giving uncommonly severe sentences to Black or Chicano offenders. Some public defenders candidly stated that they felt they could secure a better disposition for a black offender, all things being equal, than for a white offender.

Role Pressures

A final general pressure exerted on all court personnel can be classified under the heading of role expectations—something that affects the behavior of the decisionmakers in courtroom interaction as well as in the bargaining and dispositional processes. The role expectations of the court personnel come under two subheadings—theoretical role expectations and routinized role expectations. In the theory of court operations, the court participants have different roles to play, functions to perform, and work to do. For the prosecution and defense attorneys, this means an adversary relationship: both parties concerned with administering justice, as well as trying to win the case. The defense attorney's primary objective is to obtain an acquittal for his client, and, short of this, to secure "the best possible disposition." The prosecuting attorney, on the other hand, seeks the best possible disposition for the "people," which in essence means protecting the community from the offender and his criminal activities by incarcerating him for a substantial period of time. There is nothing inherent in the personalities of the actors that causes them to advocate these various positions; it is an intrinsic part of the role they play.

The judge, too, has a role to play, and in many ways it is a contradictory one. He must consider what is best for the offender (i.e., rehabilitation, treatment, or punishment), for the victim (including the victim's wish for revenge), and for the protection of the community from future dangerous acts of the offender. All the while, he must consider the bad publicity that a lenient disposition might generate. If an offender is returned to the community on probation and commits another crime, the judge must assume the ultimate responsibility; a mistake in judgment may have grave consequences.

Since role pressures are so influential, a change in an individual's role would also mean a change in his behavior. If the district attorney were to become a judge, he would soon, no doubt, alter his behavior and act appropriately. The role itself dictates the behavior patterns of the persons adopting the roles. Kahn et al. summarize this view as follows:

To a considerable extent, the role expectations held by the members of a role set—the prescriptions and proscriptions associated with a particular position—are determined by the broader organizational context. The organizational structure, the functional specialization and division of labor, and the formal reward system dictate the major content of a given office. What the occupant of the office is supposed to do, with and for whom, is given by these and other properties of the organization itself. Although other human beings are doing the "supposing" and the rewarding, the structural properties of organizations are sufficiently stable so that they can be treated as independent of the particular persons in the role set. For such properties as size, number of echelons, and rate of growth, the justifiable abstraction of organizational properties from individual behavior is even more obvious.[7]

In contrast to the theoretical roles the court actors are supposed to play are the actual roles that develop over time within each court organization—roles that may vary somewhat from jurisdiction to jurisdiction. Within each court organization, as was explained in the last chapter, varied perceptions exist about the relative severity of cases, the relative severity of dispositions, and what the "going rate" should be in different fact situations. Also discussed was the fact that, in general, the categorization of cases and the resulting dispositions become a matter of relatively routine work for the court actors. As the work becomes routine, policies, both formal and informal, develop, and a relatively uniform sentencing policy emerges within each county. This routine work has implications not only for sentencing policy, but also for the roles the court personnel play. "Organizations with routine work are more likely to have greater formalization of organizational roles.''[8] As numerous cases of a relatively similar nature pass through the system, routinized role expectations develop, so that each participant in the dispositional process develops an assumptive world about what to expect from the other participants. The greater the degree of formalization,[9] the more difficult it is for the actors to deviate from their roles and to adopt a novel form of behavior.

The reduction of personalized relationships, the increased internalization of rules, and the decreased search for alternatives combine to make the behavior of the members of the organization highly predictable; i.e., they result in an increase in the rigidity of behavior of participants.[10]

The adoption of routinized behavior and role expectations also has an effect on the identification of the participants in the organization. The public defenders take on a certain identification with one another, as do the deputy district attorneys. All this tends to maximize role expectations from one's self (self-evaluation), from one's peers in the suborganization, and from the adversaries or other participants in the court organization. The role expectations act both as requirements and constraints over the actions of the participants in the dispositional process.

The Negotiation of Mental Disorder

Although the standard practice of guilty plea bargaining has frequently been described in sociological and legal studies, those cases in which mental disorder is an additional factor have been relatively unexplored. It might well be assumed that cases involving mental illness would not be administered in the same manner, as say, simple burglary or possession of stolen property. Because of the added factor of mental disorder, there might be less bargaining, greater reliance on a jury to decide the facts of the case, and more credence granted the expert psychiatric testimony and recommendations. It is the contention of this study, however, that the facts do not support such assumptions and that to analyze adequately the disposition of mentally disordered sex offenders, one must fully consider the bargaining process, in part as it compares to the bargaining in other types of cases, and, further, as it forms a unique pattern when mental disorder and psychiatric testimony are contingencies with which the negotiators must deal.

The study showed that bargaining is more prevalent in MDSO cases than non-MDSO sex cases, as an examination of Table 4-2 indicates. Notice that in Contra Costa and San Francisco Counties, 100 percent of the cases receiving the MDSO sanction pleaded guilty, whereas the figure was 84 per-

Table 4-2
Type of Adjudication (MDSO and Non-MDSO Cases)

	Contra Costa				San Francisco				Orange			
	MDSO		non-MDSO		MDSO		non-MDSO		MDSO		non-MDSO	
	N	Percent	N	Percent	N	Percent	N	Percent	N	Percent	N	Percent
Guilty plea	28	100	123	84	11	100	152	84	48	96	102	68
Jury trial—guilty of at least one offense	0	0	10	7	0	0	20	11	2	4	20	13
Jury trial—not guilty	0	0	9	6	0	0	3	2	0	0	13	9
Court trial—guilty of at least one offense	0	0	1	1	0	0	1	0.5	0	0	6	4
Court trial—not guilty	0	0	0	0	0	0	1	0.5	0	0	3	2
Not guilty by reason of insanity	0	0	1	1	0	0	1	0.5	0	0	0	0
Not guilty plea (too insane to stand trial)	0	0	3	2	0	0	2	1	0	0	6	4
No information	0	0	0	0	0	0	0	0	0	0	0	0
Total	28	100	147	101	11	100	180	99.5	50	100	150	100

cent in both counties for cases that did not receive the MDSO sanction; in Orange County 96 percent of the MDSO cases pleaded guilty, whereas 68 percent of the non-MDSO cases did so.

Issues in Bargaining

There are three closely related issues surrounding the bargaining process. The first issue involves a determination of the category into which the case should be placed, given an understanding of the characteristics of the offense and the offender. No *formal* bargaining takes place to resolve this issue, but there is an informal negotiation process, which will be called the negotiation of the reality of the case. The second issue of concern to the attorneys is the quantity and quality of evidence available in the case at hand. This issue, the triability of the case, will be discussed in a later chapter, for its importance will be more fully appreciated as part of a general discussion about residual cases. The third issue for consideration consists of what sanction should be applied; this is the topic of most studies of formal guilty plea bargaining.

The Negotiation of the Reality of the Case

When imposing a sanction on an offender, the court takes several factors into account. The court examines the entire case, including the specific offense at hand and the characteristics of the offender. In most cases, however, the "facts" are not entirely clear, since the testimonies of the victim and the offender often differ and the information that the court must depend on regarding the offender is sometimes unreliable. The facts about the offense and the offender being rather vague, the attorneys (the two adversaries) and the judge attempt to construct the reality of the case. It is the task of the two adversaries to present information about the offense and the offender[11] that will allow the court to properly categorize the case on the severity scale, so that the appropriate sanction can be imposed.

There are several factors about the reality of any particular case to be negotiated by the attorneys. The first, and perhaps most important, aspect concerns the facts of the offense at hand, as alleged in the complaint or in the information; the court must determine to what extent the facts are accurate. Naturally, the defense attorney would like to convince the deputy district attorney and the judge that his client is innocent of the charges alleged against him. Short of this, he attempts to show that the allegations are greatly exaggerated and thus to minimize the activities in which the defendant is supposed to have engaged.

The deputy district attorney, on the other hand, is quick to point out the number of additional charges that might have been lodged against the defendant. He generally stresses the severity of the offense in order to be in a better formal bargaining position. The judge will listen to both sides and ask a few questions about the facts of the case, during which time he will be comparing this case with similar cases he has heard in the past.

To make a compelling argument for his interpretation of the facts of the offense, each attorney offers information about the offense, mitigating or aggravating circumstances, as well as his interpretation of what actually happened. The object of this is to form a definition of the situation so that the case can be placed favorably on the severity scale—from each adversary's point of view.

One of the tactics employed by the defense attorney is to try to convince the court that the offense was not premeditated but rather the result of circumstances in which anyone might become involved.

The defendant just got drunk one night and fondled his stepdaughters. It's no big deal. He didn't plan and wait for the right moment to strike. The mother was gone; he was drunk; and it just happened. He's learned his lesson and it won't happen again.

At the same time the deputy DA wants to show, contrary to the defense attorney's assertions, that the act was not situational, but planned, or at least clearly intentional: "This man has had sexual relations with his foster-daughters for over two years. We only charged him with ten counts, but he is good for at least fifty." While this reality construction takes place, the judge attempts to determine how much harm was actually done, how much force was used, to what extent the crime was victim-precipitated, and, in general, how to rank the offense in terms of seriousness, as compared with other cases in the past.

The next issue concerning the negotiation of the reality of the case is the prior legal record of the defendant. When the defendant is certified to the Superior Court, each of the participants in the decisionmaking process is supplied with an official "rap sheet" from the Bureau of Criminal Identification and Information (CII), as well as one from local authorities. With these documents, the attorneys try to reconstruct the defendant's prior legal history. This is often a formidable task, since the documents are very general and offer little information about what actually happened; the CII rap sheet merely lists the date, place, charge, and sometimes the disposition of the case. In assessing the defendant's actual involvement, substantial theory building must take place.

The defense attorney seeks to minimize the extent and seriousness of the prior record by convincing the deputy DA and the judge that the defendant was not involved in all the activities outlined on his rap sheet. He points out the weaknesses and inaccuracies in the rap sheet, which could lead to misinterpretation. For example, the CII rap sheet might list several contacts the defendant has had with different police agencies. The defense attorney will quickly point out that few convictions have resulted from these contacts and, therefore, that the rap sheet is not as indicative of a crime-ridden background as it might appear. The defense requests that prior contacts not be considered and will claim that the charges were trumped up or perhaps motivated by racial discrimination. It will also be suggested that the charges listed on the rap sheet were exaggerated, since district attorneys tend to overcharge cases to be in a better bargaining position. The defense cannot credibly deny the various convictions listed on the rap sheet, but it is often suggested that the offense for which the defendant was convicted was not as serious as the rap sheet might indicate.

The deputy district attorney seeks to maximize the seriousness of the rap sheet by attempting to persuade the defense attorney and the judge that the rap sheet actually underestimates the extent of prior criminal activity. The deputy DA will indicate that several charges were dropped in the convictions that were previously secured. The deputy DA might also suggest that in one or more cases the defendant was actually guilty, but the case had been dismissed on a legal technicality. In assessing the likelihood of future criminal activity, the prosecution will claim that such an acquittal should be counted as a regular conviction. The prosecution might explain that the defendant has been picked up as a suspect repeatedly, although there was no formal conviction due to a lack of admissible evidence. The intent of the prosecutor is to convince the court that, in reality, there is a substantial amount of "hidden crime" in the rap sheet.

After weighing the significance of the arrests, charges, and convictions on the rap sheet, the court decisionmakers must also make judgments about the actual dispositions leveled against the defendant, especially if the dispositions were administered in different jurisdictions. The court must determine what the "going rate" would have been if the case had been adjudicated in the current jurisdiction. For example, a five-year sentence to prison for attempted rape in another state might be comparable to one year in the county jail in a jurisdiction in California; the court personnel would not assess it as a state prison disposition, but as a county jail disposition. In this manner the court makes an effort to equalize the rating system it uses to assess the seriousness of the defendant's prior legal history.

The third area of negotiation concerns the defendant's character. In attempting to reach some agreement about the defendant's character, several interrelated issues are discussed by the attorneys: the defendant's social history, his personality, and his attitude. The concern of the court personnel is to find indications about the defendant's character that will help them to reconstruct what actually took place in a given offense and to predict what the defendant might do if not incarcerated.

This negotiation process involves the observations of and the statements by the adversaries about the type of person the defendant is. Recommendations written by former employers, friends, and relatives, which support the position the defense finds most strategic, are submitted by the defense. The deputy DA will then offer an alternative explanation of the defendant's character. The positions of the defense and prosecution vary with the nature of the case, but the central theme of the discussions is to reach a decision about whether the defendant has mental problems or whether he is simply a *bad* person. When the options facing the defendant are state prison or Atascadero, the prosecution will view the defendant's behavior in terms of general criminality, whereas the defense will try to show that the defendant is sick or has behavioral problems.

The prosecution is often skeptical of the "mental problem" view of behavior put forth by the defense and, instead, sees the behavior of the defendant as another manifestation of his criminal life style. One deputy DA put it this way:

There is the type of person who is pushy and aggressive to all persons, but to women especially. If a man asks a woman in a bar to have sexual relations with him and she refuses, then he simply takes the sex he wants. This is simply a genuine lack of concern for other people's rights. This type of person can't be helped down at Atascadero.

In such a serious case the defense attorney will attempt to convince the deputy DA and the judge that the present and past behavior of the defendant is the direct result of the defendant's adverse social background and his mental problems. What this defendant needs, the defense attorney will claim, is treatment, not punishment.

In a relatively minor case, in which the alternatives facing the defendants are Atascadero, as the most severe, and probation, as the least severe, the defense attorney will try to avoid the civil commitment and argue in favor of a minimal amount of punishment. In such a situation, the defense will disparage the "illness" theory of the defendant's behavior and will make remarks casting doubt on the ability of the staff at Atascadero to bring about any therapeutic change. As advocates of one disposition rather than another, the adversaries do not feel uncomfortable totally reversing their ideological and practical positions on a case-by-case basis.

The social history of the defendant is also subject to interpretation—often based on rather sketchy data. Hopefully, the social history will provide an indication about the defendant's character to help determine the appropriate sanction. In an examination of the defendant's social history, no one factor is of overriding importance. The general concerns of the court are the social stability of the defendant, his attitude about his current offense and past behavior, and his motivation to change his ways.

One factor that is usually examined is the defendant's work history, for this will provide the court with an idea about the defendant's stability and his desire to succeed in the community. If one of the alternatives open to the court is to return the defendant to the community, the fact that the defendant has a job or a profession is significant. Given the importance of the work history, the adversaries feel compelled to present arguments about whether the work history of the defendant is "normal" or "responsible," given the social environment from which he comes. Beyond that, the concern of the court is whether the defendant has made a "reasonable effort" to secure and maintain employment.

The marital history of the defendant is also brought under scrutiny. Never marrying is usually viewed as a neutral factor, unless there is evidence submitted by the deputy DA that it is the result of his undesirable character type. In such a case, being unmarried is simply further evidence that the defendant is not the type of person who can survive in the community. A stable family life demonstrates to the court that the defendant has a willingness to confront his problems, to handle the minor forms of frustration, and to assume a certain amount of responsibility for the well-being of other people.

In some cases other social factors might be considered, if they seem relevant in assisting the attorneys to construct a picture of the defendant's character. Military history is an example. In most cases, the defendant has either not been in the military or has received an honorable discharge. Since these facts do not set the defendant apart from the norm, they are often disregarded. In some cases, however, the circumstances surrounding the fact that the defendant did not serve in the military may be of significance, as in one case in which the defendant admitted he had lied to the induction officers to avoid being drafted. The judge considered this a further indication of the defendant's deceptive character.

The military record is also of importance if the defendant had been given a bad conduct or an undesirable discharge for criminal activity in the service. This furnishes the deputy DA with additional information to argue that the defendant is basically of bad character. Finally, the military history might be important if the defendant had been granted a medical discharge for psychiatric reasons. This fact may help the defense prove the point that the defendant needs help, not punishment.

Formal Guilty Plea Bargaining

The basic idea of guilty plea bargaining is for the two adversaries to reach an agreement about the disposition of the case, with each adversary winning some concessions from the opposing side. For the defense attorney, a successful plea bargain would mean obtaining a sanction for the defendant less than what he would have received if he had gone to trial and had been found guilty by a jury. For the prosecution, an acceptable outcome would include securing a conviction, keeping the criminal calendar relatively clear, and, perhaps, prohibiting the defendant from circulating in the community for a significant period of time. If the defense evidences a willingness to cooperate in fulfilling this goal, the deputy DA is more likely to consider a lighter than normal sentence for the defendant. One deputy DA put it this way:

If the defense is willing to plead guilty to a heavy offense such as rape or child molest, then this is a big help to the DA's office, and therefore we are more likely to cooperate with the defense when it comes time to recommend a disposition. Also, if the defendant is willing to plead guilty to a serious offense, this is at least one indication that he may be motivated toward treatment.

In contrast:

The DA's office would recommend state prison if the defendant or the defense has not been cooperative. If the defendant wants to deny everything and make a big problem for the DA's office, especially when it seems clear that he did pretty much what the complaint alleges, then why should the DA's office give him a break and let him go to Atascadero?

In most cases the two adversaries can agree on the terms of a disposition, assuming they have reached an understanding during the rather elaborate "negotiation of the reality" stage. If there remains such substantial disagreement about the case that the adversaries cannot arrive at a consensus about its severity or the appropriate sanction, the case is likely to go to trial.

When examining the plea bargaining process, one must determine what each side offers the other, what concessions are actually made, and what pressures are brought to bear on each side to induce them to reach an agreement. At the center of the negotiations is the length of time, if any, the offender will be incarcerated; other factors that may be involved in the sanction are secondary, although not insignificant. These include the consideration of where the time is to be served and, when applicable, the terms and conditions of probation. These issues will be discussed shortly.

In the formal bargaining process each side has reached an assessment of the reality of the case, classified it, and ranked it on the severity scale. When the ranking has been made, the attorneys have a good idea of what the "going rate" for that case is—that is, the realistic range of acceptable sanctioning alternatives. The defense always strives to secure the least severe alternative and the deputy DA most generally advocates the most severe. It is from within that range, taking all factors of the case into consideration, that the bargain is struck. Offers and counteroffers are made and rejected by both sides, but the bargaining process generally results in an agreement.

Criminal cases go to trial for two main reasons. First, if the defense attorney believes that an acquittal can be won for his client, he will want to argue the case in court. This is so without regard to his belief about the actual guilt or innocence of the defendant. Secondly, if the defense attorney feels that he has nothing to lose, he will take the case to trial. Occasionally the deputy DA will offer only state prison as part of the deal, in which case the defense attorney would take the case to trial, even if he realizes that the chances for an acquittal are as low as 5 percent. Although a state prison sentence is the probable outcome, there may be a few small benefits attributed to going to trial, such as a chance (small though it may be) for gaining an acquittal and the trial experience itself. He also realizes that he will be causing the district attorney's office trouble and this might improve the bargaining position of the defense, since the DA wants to avoid administrative problems.

From the district attorney's perspective, cases go to trial if the defense attorney is asking for something unreasonable, given the circumstances of the case. For instance, if the deputy DA firmly believes that the defendant should be sent to state prison and the defense will not accept the prosecutor's assessment of the situation, the deputy DA will inform the defense that he will not go lower on the sanctioning scale and that the case will go to trial.

One unique aspect of sex cases is their very sensitive nature, especially for the victim of the offense. Regardless of the precise nature of the offense at hand, the deputy DA is generally reluctant to put the victim or victims on the stand in open court because of the traumatic potential of such an event. Whether concerned that the defense will attempt to show that the victim precipitated the offense or was of questionable moral character, or whether the issue is simply the potential trauma of reliving a horrible experience, the deputy DA would like to avoid the situation. Because of this, the defense is in a better bargaining position and can ask for a slightly more lenient sanction than would be possible if the prosecution were willing to have the victim testify. The reluctance to have the victim testify was a concern in all three of the counties studied, especially in San Francisco where the deputy DA in charge of rape cases was female.

As well as being sensitive to the victims involved in various cases, the deputy DA is often sensitive to certain pressures exerted by the community. In some cases the deputy DA is not particularly concerned that the defendant be sent specifically to state prison, but he is eager that the defendant be sent out of the community. This is the type of case in which the deputy DA does not feel strongly about the activities of the defendant but is aware that if the defendant were allowed to return to the community a significant amount of adverse publicity would be directed toward the district attorney's office. In such cases the district attorney does not want to assume primary responsibility for allowing a defendant to return to the community, especially when there is a strong possibility that the defendant will commit another crime.

The final consideration related to the plea bargaining process is the tactic of delaying action on the case at hand in order to enhance an adversary's bargaining position. Depending on the nature of the case, a delay at the Superior Court level may work to the advantage of either the prosecution or the defense. In general, the prosecution benefits if the defendant is incarcerated in the county jail on a minor charge. That is, if the defendant committed a relatively minor crime for which he will most likely be placed on probation, the time served in jail is wasted time; if the case were settled, he would be free. For example, in a statutory rape case in which the victim is close to eighteen-years old and in which no force was used and the defendant has no prior convictions, the defendant would very likely be given probation. If he has to wait in jail for the trial, he will be serving "bad" (possibly unnecessary) time; if he pleads guilty, he will be released from custody as soon as possible.

In most of the cases observed at the Superior Court level, it was the defense that attempted to delay the final disposition of the case as long as possible. In serious cases, the defense believes that the longer the defendant waits in jail, the better his bargaining position. This is so for several reasons: first, there is the general concern of the DA to keep the criminal calendar clear and to avoid a backlog of cases. If the backlog becomes too great, the DA is forced to take action to clear the cases. Second, there is the problem of evidence. The longer the case is delayed before going to trial, the more likely the witnesses are to leave town or forget what happened; the defense attorney would much prefer to question a witness who appears full of doubt about the facts of the case. Third, the emotionalism surrounding the case is important. In a sex offense, especially a child molest, there may be a good deal of publicity, community uproar, and emotionalism on the part of all concerned. The longer action on the case can be delayed, the more the emotionalism and cry for vengeance will subside. This, too, puts the defense in a better bargaining position. These factors are generally operative in a case that is serious and in which the likelihood for a conviction is very great. When the two viable alternatives facing the defendant are commitment to state prison or to Atascadero, he does not usually object to spending six months in jail on the chance that it will ultimately save him a full year or so.

The Subtleties of Plea Bargaining

The formal bargaining that the adversaries conduct over the final disposition can be very detailed and refined. The concessions that each side demands become subtle and are concerned with more than the amount of time the defendant is to be incarcerated. From the perspective of the attorneys and the judge, the long-range goal of the bargaining process is to ensure that the court dispenses relatively equal sanctions for roughly comparable forms of behavior. Since the forms of behavior facing the court can be differentiated by very refined gradations, the sanctioning alternatives, too, become refined. If one attorney seems to have won a substantial concession on the issue of time, the opposing side will demand to be compensated. It would be an error to try to assess the extent of unequal administration of sanctions imposed by the courts unless these minor forms of sanctions are examined in detail.

In charging the defendant, the district attorney seeks to make the charges sufficiently numerous, broad, and serious, so that he will be in a good bargaining position; he wants it to appear that the defendant will spend the rest of his life in prison if he does not plead guilty. To ensure that this point is made to the defendant and defense counsel, the DA will tend to overcharge on the expectation that he will drop many of the charges as soon as the defendant pleads guilty. Certainly, the sanctioning for all the charges, even if proved to be true, could not be carried out. However, they are pressed in the few cases that result in trials, and the defense attorneys are well aware of it. Since the defense goal is to obtain the best disposition for the defendant, the defense attorney must carefully weigh the possible results and ramifications of a trial.

For the most part, neither the prosecution nor the defense is overly concerned with what the defendant pleads to, because almost any disposition can be negotiated between the two parties without regard to the formal label given the behavior of the defendant. Since any one section of the Penal Code (especially concerning sex offenses) is so broad as to encompass numerous fact situations, and any one fact situation might fall into several overlapping sections of the Penal Code, a concern for precision or consistency at this stage in the proceedings is seen as unnecessary. If the adversaries agree that the defendant will spend one year in the county jail, it is not of primary importance whether the man pleads guilty to rape, assault, or false imprisonment—a guilty plea to any one of those three offenses will prove sufficient to invoke the one-year jail sentence.

This is not to suggest that the defense attorney and the prosecution are unconcerned about the actual plea; it is simply not their primary consideration. In some instances, the final plea does make a difference, for example if there were a choice between pleading guilty to a felony or to a misdemeanor. There is the very practical realization that it is legally impossible to place a defendant in state prison if he has pleaded guilty to a misdemeanor. If the case is not extremely serious and if a deal can be made for the defendant to do suitable jail time, the deputy DA may not oppose the defense request for a misdemeanor.

If it is a strongly held conviction on the part of the prosecutor that the defendant should be sent to state prison, substantial concessions (or what appear to be) must be granted the defense, so that it will not take the case to trial. In seeking to avoid a trial, the prosecutor faces the dilemma of not knowing what concessions must be made to mollify the defense. Several possibilities come to the prosecutor's mind, the first of which involves what might be an acceptable charge. If the defendant has been charged with numerous counts, the prosecutor might suggest that if the defendant pleads guilty to one count, the rest will be dropped. It might also be maintained that the one count pleaded to has the lowest minimum eligible parole date to convince the defense that the defendant might be released earlier than if he were convicted by a jury on one or more serious charges.

While this is being offered, the deputy DA is cognizant of the fact that the nature of the defendant's final plea is not very important if he is going to state prison. There are several reasons for this: first, even if the defendant were to plead guilty to several counts, he most likely would serve them concurrently; only in very rare cases does the court sentence the defendant to state prison to serve consecutive sentences. Also, the deputy DA firmly believes that even if the defendant pleads to one light count, the parole board will be able to analyze the conviction and see that the offense was actually more serious than indicated by the final plea.

The district attorney is not particularly concerned with one-time offenders, unless the offense is an especially heinous one. If it appears that the defendant has a perfectly clean record and that, in all probability, he will not commit another offense, the district attorney does not argue for a lengthy confinement. However, if the defendant has been in criminal court several times and recidivism on his part seems likely, the issue of prior convictions becomes an important factor to the deputy DA and the defense attorney. Both are fully aware that the number and type of prior convictions will have a significant effect on the length of sentence, whether it is determined in court, state prison, or at Atascadero. The matter of priors is also important because of the statutes; for instance in a conviction for exhibitionism, the first conviction is a misdemeanor and the second is a felony.

The deputy DA informs the court, both formally and informally, that the defendant has prior convictions. Besides informing the judge in chambers, he makes it official by announcing the alleged priors in open court and having them admitted into the official court records. If pleading not guilty to the charges, the defendant often denies in open court that he has any prior convictions and the judge says: "The priors are deemed denied at this time."

Another issue in bargaining, then, is the number of alleged priors that will remain on the official court record. If the defendant pleads guilty, the deputy DA might be willing to drop the allegations of prior convictions; if he does not, they will remain. The deputy DA realizes that the defendant's not guilty plea will lead to the allegations being proven in court and admitted into the official evidence. If the defendant is not sent to state prison at the time, his record—with an official conviction and priors—will influence the court in any future proceedings.

The issue of priors, similar to the other factors discussed in this section, is an additional negotiable item in the bargaining process. It can be utilized when an adjustment is sought concerning the appropriate sanction. The deputy DA might think that the defendant had been involved in activities "worth" nine months in jail, based on several similar cases and dispositions. If for some reason the defense attorney has been able to convince the judge that a six-month jail term is sufficient, the deputy DA will request that one or more of the priors be retained on the record. Such maneuvering contributes to a situation in which sanctions are equalized and "going rates" become the standard.

Another tactic of the district attorney's office is to add allegations about the offense to the regular charges to increase the gravity of the total charge. In the information (prepared by the district attorney) filed in the Superior Court charging the defendant with a crime, there also may be, among other things, the allegation of great bodily harm. This allegation, if proved, would be extremely detrimental on the defendant's record if he were sent to state prison or to Atascadero, or if he were to appear in court in the future.[12] If the defendant exercises his right to a jury trial, the deputy DA will try to prove the allegation. If, however, the defendant decides to plead guilty, the prosecutor will generally drop the allegation. Although this situation may arise in almost any case, it occurs most frequently when a state prison sentence is likely, for the prosecutor seeks to make it appear that substantial concessions are being made to the defense, in order to induce the defendant to plead guilty.

Another allegation that adds to the charges and increases the gravity of the offense is the allegation that a deadly weapon was used. Although this is not a common allegation, it does occasionally appear in the information with the formal charges. As a section of the Penal Code, it is prescribed that the defendant spend a substantial amount of time incarcerated in addition to the original sentence. If the defendant decides to plead guilty, the deputy DA will drop the allegations, and the defendant will serve time for the original charge.

In cases in which more than one defendant was involved in an offense, the deputy DA may include additional charges of "acting in concert," which is more serious than being an accessory to a crime. Such a charge can be alleged for three sex offenses: "Acting in Concert to Commit Oral Copulation," "Acting in Concert to Commit Sodomy," or "Punishment—Defendant Acted in Concert with Another Person to Commit (Rape)." Again, if the defendant will plead guilty, the "acting in concert" charge will probably be dropped.

Whether or not the offender will be required to register as a sex offender is also an important point for negotiation. The Penal Code states that if a person is convicted of any one of numerous sex offenses, he *shall* register as a sex offender with the police chief of the city in which he resides, and such registration shall follow the person if he changes his residence. The list of offenses for which the convicted person must register is so broad as to encompass most conceivable sex offenses. Legally, therefore, all sex offenders are required to register; in each of the jurisdictions studied, however, the informal policy was that if the offender had not been informed of his obligation to register, he would not be held responsible if he did not do so.

Court personnel are well aware that registration as a sex offender is a very serious matter, a stigma from which there is little possibility of relief. If required to register at every new place of residence, perhaps for the rest of his life, the offender is likely to be the object of police harassment for every new sex offense committed in the community. Because the defense seeks to avoid this sanction, the deputy DA will use it as another bargaining tool to encourage the defendant to plead guilty in exchange for the recommendation that he not be required to register.

Registration thus functions as an additional sanction which can be utilized to equalize an otherwise inequitable sentence. If the deputy DA feels that the defendant should have received a more severe sanction than was imposed, he will request that, as a condition of probation, the offender be required to register. Such a request may well be granted by the court, so that the defendant's sentence will more closely approximate the "going rate" for the particular offense.

In a small percentage of cases certified to the Superior Court, there is the possibility that the deputy DA can dispose of defendants through deportation or parole revocation. If an alien is involved, the deputy DA may be able to secure an agreement to drop or greatly reduce the charges if the defendant is deported to his native land. This disposition would prove acceptable to both sides, since the deputy DA would be pleased to have the defendant leave the community, and the defense would be satisfied that there would be no criminal record for the defendant.

In cases involving a defendant on parole, the deputy DA informs the defendant's parole board of any new charges and inquires whether the parole board intends to revoke his parole. If so, the deputy DA is not concerned with whether the defendant pleads guilty to a serious offense, for a plea to a misdemeanor is sufficient to accomplish the task of returning the defendant to prison. In such cases, what appears to be a lenient disposition by the district attorney actually serves—operationally—as a prison commitment.

If a defendant is found guilty and committed to the Department of Corrections, either the judge or the deputy DA can write a recommendation suggesting an appropriate term. The recommendation can be either favorable or harsh, although it is most often harsh, for it is usually submitted only when the defendant is charged with a serious offense and insists on a trial. If the defendant's actions prove inconvenient for the DA, he might retaliate by suggesting that the offender be incarcerated for a substantial period of time.

Handling Organizational Contingencies

The evidence presented to this point supports the contention that the MDSO designation and the resulting civil commitment are the products of the formal and informal bargaining procedures between the prosecution and defense attorneys. However, even if the two adversaries are able to reach an agreement as to the appropriate disposition for the defendant, various obstacles can prevent them from securing it; this is true whether or not the agreement involves the MDSO sanction. The contingencies faced by the attorneys may take the form of internal organizational policies or statutory provisions that must be fulfilled. Resourceful attorneys, however, generally are able to circumvent the apparent obstacles.

The first contingency to be dealt with is whether or not the MDSO proceedings should be initiated after an agreement has been reached. It is always permissible for the court, at its own discretion, to initiate MDSO proceedings whenever there "is probable cause to believe that the defendant is a Mentally Disordered Sex Offender." This is so after the defendant has been formally convicted of any offense, not necessarily a sex offense. (For instance, if a defendant is charged with burglary and rape, he may plead guilty only to the burglary, having the rape charge dismissed.) Cases in which the attorneys do not want to start the proceedings are usually relatively minor ones, for in serious cases the defense attorney will want them to commence. The most frequent situation in which the proceedings are requested is a moderately serious rape or child molest case in which the defense attorney can convince the deputy DA that a commitment to Atascadero is more appropriate than a commitment to state prison. In such a situation the defense attorney simply makes a motion to the judge to start the proceedings and have the psychiatrists[13] appointed; the motion is summarily granted.

The reverse situation, in which it is mandated by statute that the MDSO proceedings begin and the attorneys object, is a bit more complicated. It should be recalled that when a defendant is convicted of a felony sex offense involving a child under the age of fourteen or when the defendant is convicted of a misdemeanor sex offense involving a child under the age of fourteen and the defendant has a prior conviction for any sex offense, the MDSO proceedings are mandatory. In such cases, if avoidance of the proceedings is the desired strategy, the attorneys are confronted with the necessity of circumventing certain charges.

To accomplish this, the best general strategy is for the deputy DA to construct the original charges in so broad and general a manner that the defense attorney is likely to find one of the charges sufficiently appealing to induce a guilty plea. With several broad charges, including lesser included offenses, the defense attorney and the deputy DA are usually able to reach an agreement.

A guilty plea to a sexually oriented offense defined as a misdemeanor might accomplish the same end. For example, rather than having the defendant plead to a charge of felony child molest, he could plead to misdemeanor child molest. If he does so and has prior sex offense convictions, it might be part of the agreement to strike the priors from the record to prevent the mandatory initiation of the proceedings.

In cases involving children under the age of fourteen that can be considered less serious than the classical child molest situation, the object may be to encourage a plea to an offense that does not seem to be of a sexual nature. One such case involved an adult male who had paid some young boys for sexual favors; the boys told the man that they were over fourteen years of age. When the matter came before the deputy DA, he found that the boys were actually under fourteen, but had a history of participating in acts of prostitution. Legally, if the defendant had been found guilty of child molestation, a felony, the MDSO proceedings would have been mandatory. However, the defense attorney and the deputy DA agreed that the defendant would plead guilty to "Causing a Minor to become a Ward of the Court," which is a misdemeanor.

The Right to a Hearing and a Trial

It was asserted earlier in this chapter that the MDSO sanction is inextricably related to the plea bargaining process. As evidence for this, it was shown that in the adjudication pertaining to the criminal charge, a very high percentage of the defendants who were designated as MDSOs pleaded guilty. The plea to the criminal charge is only one aspect of the adjudication proceedings for MDSOs. Not only does the defendant have a right to a trial by jury on the criminal charges, but he also has the right, after the MDSO proceedings have been initiated, to a hearing on the psychiatrists' reports and a jury trial on the civil commitment.

An example of the bargaining of mental disorder can be inferred from the conspicuous absence of formal hearings and civil jury trials. Although the official records are not entirely clear on this, interviews, observations, and court records revealed that there were no more than a few formal hearings in each county over the five-year period. Furthermore, there was not one jury trial on the civil commitment in any of the three counties during the five-year period covered in this book.

The primary reason for the consistent waiver of these rights guaranteed by statute is the fact that the waiver is part of the advance agreement. Generally, the attorneys have reached an agreement about the specific sanction to be imposed on the offender, and in some cases, a deal is made to stipulate to the contents of the psychiatrists' reports before they have been presented to the court.

This is not to imply that there are no cases in which either adversary is displeased with the reports and seeks to challenge the psychiatrists' diagnoses and recommendations. Such incidents occur occasionally; as a result, a formal hearing at which the doctors are required to testify is requested. The hearings vary somewhat in duration, but they generally last several hours. At the hearing the attorneys ask the doctors questions about the specific wording of the submitted report and seek their admission that the process of diagnosis and recommendation is unreliable; the goal of the dissatisfied attorney is to expose the doctor's ignorance about the facts of the case and the defendant himself.

The outcome of the hearing is generally negligible; nothing new is disclosed which the attorneys have not already mentioned to each other and to the judge in chambers. The attorneys ask direct questions about the technical provisions of the MDSO statute, but the psychiatrists, uninterested in the details of the law, generally give vague, and what appear to be meaningless, answers. It is often an experience in frustration for the attorneys and the judge to query the psychiatrists, because their answers are not as accurate and precise as desired. Except in special cases, then, the attorneys feel that they can communicate their agreement or skepticism of the doctors' reports without the formal hearing.

If disagreement about the psychiatric reports persists after the hearing, a jury trial on the civil matter is not used to resolve the problem. There are various reasons for this, depending on the effect of the psychiatric reports on either adversary's position. It must first be recalled that the vast majority of MDSO cases involve rather serious cases in which the two principal alternatives facing the defendant are a commitment to Atascadero or to state prison. If the reports conclude that the defendant is an MDSO and recommend a commitment to Atascadero, the defense will forego a civil trial because the type of report desired has been obtained, and the defense attorney is pleased with the result. If, however, the reports state that the defendant is not an MDSO, the court is likely to send the defendant to state prison. The defense attorney would definitely want to challenge such reports through a jury trial, but he has no legal right to do so. The right to a jury trial exists only for those who are designated MDSO and do not want to be so labeled—not for those persons who are *not* designated MDSO, but, for purposes of their defense, would like to be. If the defense had the right to trial to prove the defendant was an MDSO, the number of trials would increase greatly.

From the perspective of the prosecution, there is considerable objection when the psychiatrists find the defendant to be an MDSO and the deputy DA feels that the defendant should be sent to state prison. There could be a challenge to this finding, but there usually is not. The reason for this is that, in general, the district attorneys do not believe it is worth the trouble. In a criminal trial in which the difference between winning and losing one's position might be the difference between having the defendant incarcerated for a long period of time and having him set free in the community with no sanction at all, the district attorney's concern would certainly be heightened. On the civil matter, however, the defendant has previously been found guilty on the criminal charges and the least that could happen is that the defendant will go to Atascadero instead of state prison. Recognizing the time, trouble, and expenditure of resources involved in challenging such a commitment, the district attorneys in each county seem to find it not worth the effort.

The Selection of Psychiatrists

One standard for judging a good attorney is his skill in predicting the outcome of the case at hand. The good attorney knows what is going to happen before it happens, and he knows the answers to questions before they are asked. Criminal cases, in general, and MDSO cases, in particular, are no exception to this rule. In MDSO cases the attorney prefers not to attend the MDSO proceedings without knowing what the psychiatrists will say in their reports; he wants to know exactly what will be written before the reports are submitted.

When there is some question about the mental state of the defendant in the early stages of the criminal proceeding, psychiatrists are retained in each of the three counties to examine the defendant and to submit a private psychiatric report to the defense attorney. In San Francisco and Contra Costa Counties, the defense attorneys—private and public—hire private psychiatrists to write separate reports on the defendant before the defendant pleads guilty and before the psychiatrists are appointed by the court. If the defense attorney wants the MDSO civil commitment for his client, he hires a psychiatrist to write a report that indicates the defendant is an MDSO; he submits this report to the judge, the deputy DA, and the probation officer before the MDSO proceedings are ever initiated. In this way some information is offered in the hope that an agreement can be reached before the MDSO proceedings start.

In Orange County the same basic strategy is employed, but the defense utilizes court-appointed psychiatrists instead of psychiatrists hired from a private fund. At the Municipal Court level, the defense attorney begins to plan his strategy for the case. The defense attorneys, particularly the public defenders, utilize two provisions in the Evidence Code to maximize their control over the outcome of the case. The first provision allows the judge to appoint a psychiatrist recommended by the defense. The defense attorney selects a psychiatrist based on two criteria: that he have a generally favorable attitude toward the defense and that he will be subject to influence when the implications of the case are set before him. The second provision permits the defense attorney to maintain the confidentiality of the psychiatric report until he chooses to disclose its contents. Having selected the psychiatrist and seemingly aware of the diagnosis, the defense attorney can feel more secure about taking the case to the Superior Court.

If the MDSO proceedings are begun, the attorneys must speculate about the content of the psychiatric reports and the effect the reports might have on the future of the defendant. If, for example, the defense attorney desires to have his client designated an MDSO and sent to Atascadero, the psychiatrists' reports, or at least one report, must make that diagnosis and recommendation. However, the converse is not true. If all the appointed psychiatrists find that the defendant is an MDSO, the court may still disagree and send him to state prison, especially if he is perceived to be dangerous as well as mentally disordered. But in either case, the attorneys find it helpful to their cause to have psychiatric reports confirming their positions.

In selecting court psychiatrists, there are significant differences in county policies, which result, in part, in the county variation in commitment rates. As with the actual variation in the MDSO commitment rates, the frequency with which the courts appoint psychiatrists to examine defendants varies. The figures in Table 4-3 illustrate the significant variation. Of the total number of cases in which one or more psychiatrists were appointed to examine the defendant, the percentage of cases ranged from a low in San Francisco County of 18 percent to a high in Orange County of 61 percent, while in Contra Costa County it was 52 percent.

There are several reasons for this, although the relative importance of each is difficult to determine. In all three counties there is an approved list of psychiatrists from which the court is to choose two or more. In Orange

Table 4-3
Cases in Which Psychiatrists Were Appointed to Examine Defendant

	Contra Costa		San Francisco		Orange	
	N	Percent	N	Percent	N	Percent
One or more appointed	91	52	34	18	122	61
None appointed	82	47	156	82	65	33
No information	2	1	1	0.5	13	7
Total	175	100	191	100.5	200	101

County, the two advocates are allowed to select the psychiatrists to examine the defendant. In the other two counties, they are not permitted to do so; the judge simply appoints the psychiatrist next on the list. In those two counties there is no way to minimize the uncertainty over the type of psychiatric report the court will receive. Since the adversaries view this as playing "Russian roulette" with psychiatric testimony, they are reluctant to accept the risk.

In selecting a psychiatrist in Orange County, the attorneys base their decision in part on the extent to which they consider the psychiatrist to be either prodefense or proprosecution. They must also contend with the fact that psychiatrists differ in the extent to which they find mental disorder in the defendants they examine. Some psychiatrists seem to find mental disorder and dangerousness in almost every case, while others rarely do. The attorney's selection generally reflects what he wants the reports to recommend.

The court attorneys, defense attorneys in particular, are of the opinion that psychiatrists can generally be subjected to a certain amount of influence. The defense attorneys assume that the psychiatrists have a genuine concern for the defendant as a patient and are less concerned with legal technicalities, such as the legal definition of dangerousness, etc. Therefore, if the defense attorney explains carefully the details of the defendant's situation, the psychiatrist will most likely support the defense position when making the diagnosis and recommendation for disposition. For instance, if the defense attorney explains to the psychiatrist that a non-MDSO recommendation will mean that the defendant will go to state prison where little or no therapy would take place, the psychiatrist will often find that the defendant is an MDSO and recommend a commitment to Atascadero. In a very real sense, the defense attorneys are guilty of manipulating the psychiatrists to provide testimony that supports their particular strategy; the impulse to find a psychiatrist who will submit an objective diagnosis is seldom present.

A further reason why defense attorneys state that psychiatrists can be influenced is that, in general, a court appearance to present testimony in a formal hearing is not enthusiastically received by the psychiatrists. They prefer to avoid this situation for two reasons: first, the psychiatrists generally resent leaving their professional practice, especially when the occasion demands waiting for long periods in a courtroom and when the net accomplishment in terms of assistance to the defendant is relatively meager; second, psychiatrists do not like to be interrogated by hostile attorneys, particularly when the questions are extremely difficult for them to answer. The attorney who disagrees with the reports will try to make it very unpleasant for the psychiatrist by pointing out inconsistencies and by trying to embarrass him; few people can be expected to appreciate such an experience.

Although some attorneys are noted for the behavior previously described, attitudes toward psychiatrists and psychiatric testimony vary. Some attorneys and judges (certainly the minority) are in awe of psychiatrists and impressed by their testimony. These same court personnel often decide that certain defendants have definite mental problems and that specialized medical help is required. Because the subject of mental illness is a mystery to them, they withhold judgment about what is best for the defendant. Within such a vacuum, the psychiatrists—reputed specialists in this field—are granted considerable latitude in making recommendations and persuading the court that their expertise should be accepted.

The vast majority of lawyers and judges, however, is skeptical of psychiatrists, of their methods of obtaining information, and of their recommendations. In general, the court-appointed psychiatrists are not perceived to be as qualified as psychiatrists in private practice, though this would be difficult to verify. As mentioned in Chapter 2, of the two psychiatrists appointed by the court, at least one must be associated with a state or county mental health facility. In practice, however, most of the psychiatrists involved in the proceedings work at least part time for such facilities.

A further cause for skepticism is that the court personnel believe the psychiatrist could not possibly make an adequate diagnosis and recommendation following a short psychiatric examination. In the average case the psychiatrists spends approximately one-half hour talking with the defendant—usually in his jail cell. Furthermore, all the court personnel, especially the probation officers, are fully aware of the fact that much of the information contained in the psychiatric report—the early history and the mental history of the defendant—is taken directly from the probation report submitted to the psychiatrist before the examination is conducted.

During the examination, the psychiatrist relies on what the defendant says to be true about himself and about the facts of the case. Since the psychiatrist generally does not try to verify the information garnered from the interview, the court personnel feel that the defendant's lies may be accepted by a naive psychiatrist. Therefore, it is very possible, according to the court personnel, for the psychiatrists to make an invalid diagnosis of and recommendation for the defendant's disposition. The court personnel have had enough experience with errors in factual information to reinforce their basic skepticism about psychiatrists and their reports.

The general attitude pervasive in all three counties was that the attorneys should use the psychiatrists and the psychiatric testimony as a tool to obtain the type of disposition desired. An example of the manner in which this attitude is expressed was cogently, although crudely, provided by a public defender during the course of an interview. Discussing the use of psychiatrists in court, he said: "None of this has anything to do with justice; they [the DA's office] have their whores and we have ours." The task of the attorney is to get a job done—to secure a desired disposition for or against the defendant; if it is necessary to manipulate psychiatrists, then it must be done.

The judge at the Superior Court is in a slightly different position from the adversary attorneys, but attitudes toward psychiatrists are much the same. The judges are equally skeptical, but they employ psychiatric testimony to rationalize what they had intended to do. For example, such judicial rationalization occurred during a case in which the judge faced the dilemma of finding an appropriate disposition for an offender who had been returned from Atascadero with a "B" (unfavorable) recommendation. The judge had the choice of sending the offender to prison under either a criminal or civil commitment. It was recommended by the doctors at Atascadero that the offender be sent to prison on the civil commitment for further treatment. Of course, the prospect that prison would provide therapy was viewed with cynicism by all court personnel. The judge in this particular case had voiced his criticisms of psychiatrists in the privacy of his chambers on several occasions. But he felt, given the persuasive opinion of the deputy DA, that the offender was still quite dangerous and should be incarcerated for a long period of time. Consequently, at the time of the formal disposition in open court, the judge informed the offender:

I'm no psychiatrist; the deputy district attorney is no psychiatrist; and the defense attorney is no psychiatrist. Therefore, it is my duty to follow the recommendations of the experts in this area and sentence you to the Department of Corrections on a Department of Mental Health commitment.

The judge was able to accomplish the end sought by ostensibly granting credence to the psychiatric recommendations from Atascadero. Had those same psychiatrists recommended the opposite disposition—that the defendant be released and receive outpatient therapy—the judge undoubtedly would not have accepted their recommendation.

The mental health ideology is not always utilized as a rationalization for increasing the severity of the defendant's sanction. A further example of judicial rationalization in Orange County allowed the courts to grant a less severe sanction than would have been possible if the MDSO commitment did not exist. Several attorneys, including public defenders, mentioned that there are several judges in Orange County who are more liberal (that is, less punitive) toward offenders than the prevailing county standards dictate. The press and the public in Orange County are very concerned about whether judges are sufficiently tough on crime, especially when sex offenders are involved. Since judges see so much crime, they utilize a different scale in measuring its seriousness. What may be serious to the layman is not equally repugnant to judges and attorneys involved daily with offenders.

When a sex case is transferred to the Superior Court, there is pressure from the press and the public to take strong action and to incarcerate the defendant for a long period of time—hopefully in prison. Since some judges feel that this is not an appropriate sanction, the mental health and therapy rhetoric is used to commit offenders to Atascadero. The judge might say: "This is what the experts believe is the best for the defendant." With measured restraint, he can satisfy the community's cry for vengeance and prevent some of the offenders from receiving an unnecessarily punitive commitment.

There is one final note about attorney's attitudes toward psychiatrists, which must be mentioned. This is the attitude toward the doctors at Atascadero State Hospital, who make the recommendations for the further disposition of the defendant after he is ready to leave the mental institution. The view, especially prevalent among the deputy DAs, is that the quality and reliability of recommendations and psychiatric care and therapy at Atascadero are not of the highest caliber. This attitude is related in part to a staffing problem at Atascadero common to every public institution in California—there is not sufficient money to hire top quality or a sufficient number of staff members. For instance, at the time the research for this book was being conducted (1973), there was only one Board-certified psychiatrist at Atascadero, even though there were approximately 1200 patients. There were other doctors on the staff, but none was certified with a specialty in psychiatry. Without adequate staff and quality personnel, it is assumed by the court decisionmakers that there exists a margin of error beyond the bounds of acceptability.

Another cause for skepticism toward the medical staff involves the role and identity of the psychiatrist as helper and healer. The feeling prevails among the deputy DAs that there is a tendency on the part of the medical staff to "imagine" they have cured someone and to recommend a release, when, in fact, the "cure" is based on professional optimism and the need to believe that they are actually accomplishing the goals of therapy. Because of this tendency, it is claimed that the medical staff releases offenders while they are still dangerous. This is one more reason why the deputy DAs prefer to send the most dangerous offenders to state prison rather than to Atascadero. At state prison the Adult Authority (parole board) members tend to be more realistic about "cures," and they have a heightened concern for the community, rather than for the offender.

Notes

1. See Donald J. Newman, "Pleading Guilty for Considerations: A Study of Bargain Justice," *Journal of Criminal Law and Criminology* 46 (1956):781-790; Arthur Rosett, "The Negotiated Plea," *The Annals of the American Academy of Political and Social Science* 374 (November 1967):71-81; David Sudnow, "Normal Crimes," *Social Problems* 12, no. 3 (Winter 1965):255-276; Jerome H. Skolnick, "Social Control and the Adversary System," *The Journal of Conflict Resolution* 11, no. 1 (1967):52-70; Abraham S. Blumberg, "The Practice of Law as a Confidence Game," *Law and Society Review* 1 (June 1967):15-39; D.R. Vatri, "Guilty Plea Bargaining: Compromise by Prosecutors to Secure Guilty Pleas," *University of Pennsylvania Law Review* 112 (1964):865-895.

2. See Albert W. Alschuler, "The Prosecutor's Role in Plea Bargaining," *University of Chicago Law Review* 36 (1968):50-112. One prosecutor states in the Alschuler study, "Our office keeps eight courtrooms extremely busy trying 5 percent of the cases. If even 10 percent of the cases ended in a trial, the system would break down. We can't afford to think very much about anything else." (p. 55). The problem of case overload is as true for the Municipal Courts as it is for the Superior Court. See: The President's Commission on Law Enforcement and Administration of Justice, *Task Force Report: Courts,* Washington, D.C.: U.S. Government Printing Office, 1967, pp. 30-33.

3. Herbert Jacob, *Urban Justice,* Englewood Cliffs, N.J.: Prentice-Hall, 1973, p. 101.

4. For pressures on judges and a review of their perspective, see Richard Watson and Rondal Downing, *The Politics of the Bench and the Bar,* New York: John Wiley and Sons, Inc., 1969; Kenneth N. Vines, "The Selection of Judges in Louisiana," in Kenneth N. Vines and Herbert Jacob (eds.), *Studies in Judicial Politics,* New Orleans: Tulane University Press, 1962, pp. 99-119; Jack Ladinsky and Allan Silver, "Popular Democracy and Judicial Independence," *Wisconsin Law Review* (1967):128-169; John E. Crow, "Subterranean Politics: A Judge Is Chosen," *Journal of Public Law* 12 (1963):274-289.

5. For a review of the concerns of and the pressures on the prosecutor,

see George F. Cole, "The Decision to Prosecute," *Law and Society Review* 4, no. 3 (February 1970):331-343; "Prosecutor's Discretion," *University of Pennsylvania Law Review* 103 (1955):1057-1081; Albert W. Alschuler, "The Prosecutor's Role in Plea Bargaining," *University of Chicago Law Review* 36 (1968):50-112; Brian Grossman, *The Prosecutor: An Inquiry into the Exercise of Discretion,* Toronto: University of Toronto Press, 1969; Richard L. Engstrom, "Political Ambitions and the Prosecutorial Office," *Journal of Politics* 33 (1971):190-204; Duane P. Nadrud, "The Career Prosecutor," *Journal of Criminal Law and Criminology* 51 (1960-1961):343-353.

6. For basic information about the salient characteristics of each county, see the section on the Selection and Description of Counties in the Appendix.

7. Robert L. Kahn, Donald M. Wolfe, Robert P. Quinn, J. Diedrick Snock, and Robert A. Rosenthal, *Organizational Stress: Studies in Role Conflict and Ambiguity,* New York: John Wiley and Sons, Inc., 1964, p. 31.

8. Jerald Hage and Michael Aiken, "Routine Technology, Social Structure, and Organizational Tools," *Administrative Science Quarterly* 14, no. 3 (September 1969):369.

9. See Richard H. Hall, *Organizations: Structure and Process,* Englewood Cliffs, N.J.: Prentice-Hall, Inc., 1972, Chapter 6. Hall uses the term formalization instead of routinization. He defines formalization as, "The organizational technique of prescribing how, when, and by whom tasks are to be performed." (p. 196). In one part of the chapter Hall discusses "Role and Formalization" and points out that "it should be clear that the degree of formalization of the expectations about how a particular role is to be played is an important component of how the role is played and how the individual reacts to his situation in the organization." (p. 194).

10. James G. March and Herbert A. Simon, *Organizations,* New York: John Wiley and Sons, Inc., 1958, p. 39.

11. An example of a related process can be found in Robert M. Emerson, *Judging Delinquents,* Chicago: Aldine Publishing Co., 1969. In Chapter 4, Emerson discusses "Presentation Strategies: Pitches and Denunciations," describing how the interested parties make statements for or against the delinquent, trying to influence the court concerning the delinquent's "moral career." (p. 102).

12. The proof of the "Great Bodily Harm" allegation also means that the statutory sentence for conviction of rape increases from five years to life to 15 years to life. For this section to be legally binding, the district attorney must charge it in the information and prove it in court.

13. In some jurisdictions, usually in more rural areas, doctors who are not board-certified in psychiatry conduct the psychiatric examinations.

5

The Perspective of the Court Assistants: The Probation Officer and the Psychiatrist

To make informed and intelligent decisions concerning the disposition of criminal cases, the court often utilizes the information provided by court assistants. The Probation Department, for instance, supplies background information about the offender in routine criminal cases. When the mental or physical characteristics of the offender are at issue, other experts are called upon to aid in diagnosing the offender's malady and in recommending the appropriate disposition. The experts referred to are court-appointed doctors, generally psychiatrists, who examine the offender to determine whether or not he can be categorized within the legal definition of a Mentally Disordered Sex Offender; they then recommend a disposition.

The primary conclusion of Chapter 4 was that the formal guilty plea bargaining agreement between the prosecution and defense attorneys is the main determinant of disposition. The court assistants' role is secondary. However, for several reasons their perspective and influence should not be disregarded. First, it is provided by statute that the offender has the right to a presentence probation report in all felony convictions, which comprise the majority of convictions at the Superior Court level. Second, it has also been required by statute that doctors examine the offender before he is committed to Atascadero as an MDSO. Since both reports are available for public inspection for a minimum of thirty days after submission to the court, the judge is often compelled to grant token acceptance of the findings.

It should be remembered, however, that in most instances the psychiatrist and the probation officer perform their duties knowing full well that the disposition of the offender has been essentially determined *prior to* the submission of their reports and attendant recommendations. Evidence for this assertion can be found in the formal psychiatric and probation reports, which frequently state an awareness of the bargain struck by the adversaries.

In most instances, when a probation officer receives a request for a presentence report and the disposition already decided upon is noted on the front of the request, the probation officer simply tailors the report to agree with the stated outcome of the case. Occasionally, he will refuse to submit a recommendation, and it is not uncommon to see a statement similar to the following in a probation report:

Recommendation: Inasmuch as this report is prepared after the fact of the granting of probation, no recommendation is made.

The Perspective of the Probation Officer

Almost every probation officer interviewed said that when considering the seriousness of the offense, the primary concern was with the amount of harm to the victim; this factor weighed very heavily in determining the going rate for the offense. In general, the more suffering, the more likely the probation officer is to recommend a commitment to state prison or some other form of prolonged incarceration. This can be partially explained by the going rate for any particular offense and by the real possibility—in the eyes of the probation officer—that the offender may commit a similar act if released on probation.

Compared with the attorneys and judges, however, the probation officer is more concerned with the characteristics of the offender than with the facts of the offense. The rationale for this is a belief in the "individualization of justice." Among the probation officers, it is a commonly held belief that the "appropriate" disposition for two offenders might be very different, even if they have committed similar crimes.

With the greater emphasis on the individualization of justice, the probation officer makes more divergent recommendations for disposition than do others involved in the case. The probation officer emphasizes that offenders who commit similar crimes may vary significantly in such areas as legal history, social history, current mental attitude, and likelihood of future criminal activity; since the needs of the offender vary, it would be expected that dispositions differ as well. The resulting variation of recommendations is not evidence that the probation officer is capricious or inconsistent, but that the criteria employed differ from those implied in a "standardized justice" model.

When probation officers discuss offenders in general and sex offenders in particular, one theme consistently expressed is that it is very difficult to generalize about those who have been convicted of the same offense (as defined by the same section of the Penal Code). This can be explained by the probation officer's belief that the formal legal categories are too broad and encompass too wide a range of differing offenders to be useful for these purposes. Consequently, probation officers claim that every case is different and that there is a great need for the individualization of sentences.

More than any other member of the court organization, the probation officer is concerned with the future behavior of the offender—whether he is likely to engage in further criminal activity or to become a productive member of society. The probation officer therefore collects detailed information about the offender on which to base his judgments and recommendations. Whether it be in analyzing the prior legal history of the offender or in conducting a personal interview with him, the probation officer, because he is involved in making predictions about the behavior of the defendant, will attempt to make his decisions about individualizing the sentence as reliable as possible.

There are several means by which the probation officer can infer "what type of person" the offender is. First, there is the written information provided to the probation officer in the police reports, the rap sheet, and the letters from interested parties. These official records are not considered sufficient to appraise the offender and his chances for future success. Therefore, a second, very important means of deriving information is used—a personal interview with the offender. The probation officer firmly believes that such an interview is necessary to provide him with knowledge about the offender's personality and general character.

From the interviews and from a close examination of the case, very subtle facts about the offense and offender emerge, which influence the probation officer's attitude toward the offender and the appropriate sanction. An example, described to me by a probation officer, demonstrates this. The male in the case picked up a female hitchhiker, took her to an isolated place, and threatened her with violence if she did not submit to his sexual advances. At first she vehemently protested, so the male began to exert force. Noting the seriousness of her position, she submitted for fear of great bodily harm. After the rape, the male wanted to rid himself of the victim. He could have abandoned the victim in the isolated area, but instead he did something quite unusual. He asked her where she lived and drove her to her front door. The probation officer commented: "That tells you something about this man. It gives you an idea about the man's character. It tells you something about whether or not this man can be saved."

Because of the details of the case, the probation officer felt that even though the offender had used some force, he should not be sent to prison. Since the defendant had exhibited some guilt about the offense and some concern for the victim's welfare, the probation officer contended that the offender was of sufficient moral character to succeed on probation and that he should not be given a severe sanction, which might increase the probability of future criminality.

As noted in a previous chapter, all court personnel scrutinize the prior legal history of the offender. However, the probation officer assumes a slightly different attitude. First, rather than examining the prior record to determine how severe the sanction for the current offense should be, he looks for signs of possible future criminal activity. Second, the probation officer, more than other court personnel, is concerned with assessing the extent of "hidden crime" in the offender's past. Unproven charges will be considered if the activities seem relevant for making inferences about the character of the offender and about the likelihood of future criminality.

The attorneys and judges may well have their suspicions that the offender has participated in criminal activities for which he was not convicted, but the defense attorney will certainly try to dissuade them from considering these unproven charges. Likewise, the deputy DA has some compunction about judging the offender for activities that have not been proven in court. The probation officer does not feel the same constraint—rooted in the legal tradition—to limit consideration to formal convictions.

The probation officer can estimate the amount of "hidden crime" in various ways. At the outset, he may "read between the lines" of the official rap sheet and conclude that many of the police contacts probably did not result in convictions because of a legal technicality or lack of evidence. Furthermore, hearsay evidence—obtained from reliable sources who report that the offender has been involved in numerous criminal activities, which have either gone undetected or were not proven in court—aids the probation officer in reaching his conclusion. And finally, the probation officer may claim that the offender himself admitted various undetected activities in one of the candid interviews. Although none of this is admissible in a jury trial, the probation officer considers all such information so that he can calculate the chances for successful probation.

The most important decision that the probation officer must make is whether or not to recommend probation for the defendant. The officers generally feel that to be granted probation is a privilege and that probation should be denied if the offender is not motivated to change or if he is not sincere in wanting to participate in the programs offered by the probation department. The following recommendation and evaluation of a defendant considered unmotivated attest to this.

In view of the defendant's steadfast denial of guilt in the present offense, it is difficult for the Probation Officer to evaluate the defendant's true feelings regarding the offense. It is not felt that probation can be recommended at the present time, in view of the defendant's stated innocence; however, were the defendant to change his attitude, it is felt that he could benefit from probation under the normal terms and conditions, with 90 days in the Orange County Jail plus psychotherapy. However, it does not appear to be feasible to attempt to rehabilitate a defendant who feels he has done nothing wrong in the first place. Therefore, the following recommendation is made:

Recommendation: It is respectfully recommended that probation be denied.

The probation officers, however, are often frustrated; although they consider probation supervision and probation department programs a scarce resource, the attorneys and judges use probation as a dumping ground for all offenders who do not become institutionalized.

The probation officer is always confronted with the problem of making accurate assessments based on rather sketchy information. Hearing the offender state openly that he does not want to become involved with the probation department, even after he has pleaded guilty to one or more charges, makes the decision easy. In such a case, the probation officer feels he has no choice but to recommend that probation be denied.

The task becomes more difficult when the offender expresses his desire to change his behavior and to be placed on probation. The dilemma is that the defense attorney often instructs his client to behave in a remorseful manner and to seem highly motivated to improve himself while on probation. To identify those persons who are truly motivated is a difficult task. There are a few indicators, however, on which most probation officers rely. The more criminality in the offender's past, the more likely the probation officer is to infer that it will continue in the future. Related to this, the probation officer considers the claims the offender has made previously. If the offender has said repeatedly that he was willing to change but has never lived up to his promises, the probation officer will be very skeptical. Finally, the probation officer must resort to "sensing" the sincerity of the offender and his espoused motivation.

If the probation officer concludes that the offender is insincere about changing his behavior, a description of his questionable motives for cooperation would be included in the presentence report.

There is a distinct possibility that the defendant's confession and his present request for treatment as a mentally disordered sex offender may be motivated simply by a desire to obtain the minimum possible sentence in this case.

When the offender's insincerity has been exposed, the probation officer's general response is to recommend the most severe of the viable dispositional alternatives: state prison for a serious case and Atascadero for a relatively minor one.

The cases in which the probation officers would most consistently oppose a commitment to Atascadero are those involving excessive force and violence. Some of the opposition is derived from the belief that such an offender does not "deserve" a lenient sanction. Also, there is the fear that if committed to Atascadero, the offender will be returned to the community too soon and inflict more harm on innocent victims. Thus, the probation officers contribute to the paradox that the most passive and least dangerous offenders are the ones given the civil commitment to a mental institution for care and treatment.

Variation in Probation Department Policy and Influence

Even though probation officers in all three counties exhibit a high degree of uniformity in the criteria they use in making their recommendations for disposition, their impact on the final disposition in each of the three counties is not similarly uniform. In comparing each of the three counties, variation can be seen both in probation department policy internally prescribed by the department's administrative decisions as well as in policy externally imposed by the uncontrolled nature of the environment in which the probation department must function. The variation in policy and influence is found not only in routine sex cases, but in MDSO cases as well.

Several aspects of probation department policy were analyzed to clarify its role in the administration of justice in each of the three counties. To assess variation in probation policy and influence, a variety of methods was used. Observations were made of the interaction between the probation department representatives and other members of the court organization, and interviews were conducted with probation officers, both those on the administrative staff and those writing presentence reports. In this process an examination was made of the role of the probation department representative to the Superior Court. An assessment of the extent to which the judge was willing to consider and follow the recommendations set forth in the report was attempted. Related to the judge's reliance on the presentence report is the extent to which the two adversaries attempt to influence the probation officer writing the report to reflect a certain position.

Of the three departments studied, the Contra Costa County Probation Department seemed to exert the most influence over the disposition of cases. The first indicator of relative power and influence was derived from an analysis of the activities of the probation department representative to the Superior Court. In each of the three jurisdictions, there is one probation officer who spends most of his time at the Superior Court, performing various tasks for the probation department and the court. For example, the probation representative may answer questions posed by the judge or the attorneys about probation department policy; he is responsible for the probation department's administrative forms regarding the persons granted probation (noting the terms and conditions of probation), and in some instances, he may venture an opinion about a particular case or defendant before the court. This latter function may occur on a formal basis in open court, but it is usually informal and takes place in the judge's chambers.

Through an analysis of such basic structural features as the physical position of the probation representative in open court and in the judge's chambers, inferences can be drawn about his role in the court organization. In open court in Contra Costa County, the probation representative sits at the same table as the deputy DA and the defense attorney. In the judge's chambers as well, the probation representative sits directly in front of the judge between the two adversaries. Thus, in Contra Costa County, the representative's physical position suggests that he is of equal importance to the other decisionmakers.

The tasks the probation representative performs and the communication channels that develop between him and the rest of the court decisionmakers are also important indicators of his role in the administration of justice. In Contra Costa County, the representative does not simply perform clerical and administrative duties for the probation department. He also assumes a more active role in the decisionmaking process. In open court, for example, the probation representative offers comments and opinions about various defendants, on the request of the judge. During any one of the several appearances that the defendant makes in court, the judge will ask the deputy DA and the defense attorney if they have anything to say; he will then ask the representative the same question. In this situation the representative does not generally have anything significant to add, except perhaps a comment concerning the terms and conditions of probation.

In the judge's chambers, however, the situation is different. The judge again will ask the two adversaries for an opinion and a position statement about the case at hand. When the judge turns to the probation representative and asks for a comment, he is much more likely to venture one. He may say something either favorable or unfavorable about the character of the defendant or the appropriate disposition, and thus he may tend to irritate one of the two adversaries. The attorney against whose position the representative has spoken will accuse the representative of being biased or misinformed and will attempt to silence him. At that point the judge usually defends the representative and grants him the opportunity to conclude his remarks. All evidence indicates that the judge is interested in hearing the representative's opinion.

In addition to the comments by the probation representative, the judge may be influenced by the recommendation of the presentence probation report. In Contra Costa County the presentence report appears to be of some significance to the judge, since he is generally rather reluctant to agree to a bargained plea before he has had a chance to examine the report. Although he does not usually rely on the report in forming an opinion about the appropriate disposition, he wants to avoid gross errors in judgment resulting from a lack of factual information about the defendant's prior legal history, current mental attitude, or potential dangerousness to the community.

In Contra Costa County there is additional evidence that the presentence report is important to the judge. It is not uncommon for a defense attorney, almost always a public defender, to write an additional presentence report for submission. Certainly the public defender's "probation report" is of no legal consequence, but his purpose is to indicate to the judge that there are several reasonable recommendations that can be made utilizing the same "factual" information about the offense and the offender. The public defender emphasizes that it may be unwise to lend too much credence to the presentence report, since it is, by its very nature, subjective.[1]

To further examine the extent to which the judge relies on the presentence report, one must look at the maneuvers of the two adversaries as they plan their strategies. Because both attorneys realize that the presentence report is of considerable importance, they try to influence the probation officer to reflect their respective positions. This takes place in two ways. First, there is the direct influence exerted on the investigating probation officer by the two attorneys. Both adversaries phone the probation officer to relate their positions in the case and try to explain the consequences of various dispositions for the defendant and for the community. The second means of influencing the investigating probation officer is indirectly through the probation representative. Both attorneys are aware that the probation representative has a minimal degree of power to persuade the investigating probation officer. Therefore, in addition to the direct tactics, they will attempt to encourage the representative to modify the report in a way they consider favorable.

The adversaries, at the same time, want to know the judge's attitudes on any given case, so that they can best plan their strategies and bargaining positions. The defense attorney is particularly interested in being aware of the judge's inclinations, since the defendant must be consulted about, and approve of, the deals proposed by the deputy DA. Obviously, the defense does not want to plead guilty to any offense if the judge will not approve of the bargained disposition.

The situation in San Francisco County in no way resembles that which exists in Contra Costa. There, the probation department has almost no influence over the disposition of cases, and the least amount of influence of the three probation departments analyzed. To begin, the probation department representative in San Francisco played no significant role in the functioning of the Superior Court. Physically, as well as in terms of his influence, the representative was detached from the mainstream of court activities. In open court the representative sat away from the rest of the decisionmakers at his own table (situated behind and to the side of the table used by the attorneys), and he was not invited into the judge's chambers. When he entered, it was for minor business, not for the purpose of discussing cases with the judge and the adversaries.

The tasks of the probation representatives were also much more limited than those of his counterpart in Contra Costa County. He merely attended to clerical matters for the probation department; this included maintaining records of the terms and conditions to be fulfilled by the new probationers or advising them on how to contact their newly assigned supervisor. At no time did the judge ask the representative for an opinion about the disposition of a particular case, nor did the representative volunteer an opinion in open court or in the judge's chambers.

As a general rule, the Superior Court judges in San Francisco did not pay much attention to the content or recommendations of the presentence report. Of the three jurisdictions, San Francisco County placed the greatest emphasis on the negotiated plea, and, consequently, the probation report seemed almost superfluous. The judge would encourage the deputy DA and the defense attorney to reach an agreement on the disposition of the case and would be more likely than the judges in other jurisdictions to rubber-stamp the agreement. Unless the probation report provided some startling revelations about the offense or the offender that had not previously been disclosed by the two adversaries, the judge would abide by the agreement the two attorneys had reached previously.

To gather evidence that the presentence report was of little importance to the judge, the communication channels between the investigating proba-tion officer and the attorneys had to be examined. I found that in Contra Costa County the attorneys constantly phoned the investigating probation officer to try to influence the presentence report; this rarely happened in San Francisco. During an interview with a public defender, I asked him how often he talked to probation officers about the cases he handled. He said that he never talked to the officers. In fact, he stated that he had not talked to a probation officer during the three years he had been a public defender in San Francisco. When asked why he did not try to influence the probation officer, he replied: "Why should I? I can get what I want for my client without talking to one." This statement was echoed by other defense at-torneys, both public and private. All agreed that almost any case could be settled between the two adversaries with the almost automatic consent of the judge. They felt that the probation report was of little importance to the judge and, therefore, of little concern to them.

Interviews conducted with probation officers in San Francisco sup-ported the opinions of the attorneys. The probation officers certainly have the feeling that they are ignored by the attorneys and the judges; this feeling is manifested by a relatively high degree of dissatisfaction with their role in the administration of justice. The probation officers believe that there is too much reliance on the negotiated plea—the logical corollary being that there is too little emphasis placed on the presentence probation report. They stated that they were acutely aware of the desire on the part of both the district attorney and the judges to keep the criminal calendar clear—a goal with which they could sympathize. Nevertheless, the probation officers were dismayed by the fact that the judges seemed to follow the recommen-dations of the deputy DAs with greater regularity than they did the recom-mendations of the probation department.

In Orange County the relative power and influence of the probation department can be considered between that of its counterparts in Contra Costa and San Francisco Counties. With reference to the probation representative, his function is much the same as it is in San Francisco—at least in open court. The representative simply fills out probation department forms on the new probationers and helps answer questions they might have about complying with the terms and conditions of probation. The representative does not supply the court with opinions or comments about the cases before the bench, nor does he say anything except in response to a technical question about probation department policy. The representative is physically separated from the rest of the decisionmakers as well; his desk is located in the court gallery behind the railing.

The probation representative does not enter the judge's chambers when the judge and the attorneys are conferring about the disposition of cases. This particular court policy emerged in a rather curious manner. When the probation department originally sent a probation representative to the Superior Court several years ago, he was allowed to enter the judge's chambers and to comment on the cases. It seems that the comments about the defendants were usually negative, and that the defense attorneys therefore became very displeased with his presence in chambers. Because of the peculiar organization of the Orange County Superior Court, the defense attorneys (an organization of public defenders) were able to have the representative removed from the chambers. When a motion is made in the criminal court that requires more than a minimal amount of research and consideration, the entire case is transferred to the "Law and Motions" court, to be heard and decided on. The public defenders informed the Criminal Master Calendar judge that if the probation representative were not removed from chambers and told to refrain from commenting on cases before convictions had been secured, they would file a "motion of prejudice" involving every case in which the representative expressed an opinion. Operationally, this meant that hundreds of cases would be transferred out of the criminal master calendar court temporarily, which would have been an embarrassment to the master calendar judge as well as a great inconvenience for routine court functioning. Therefore, the criminal master calendar judge ordered the representative to remain out of the chambers and to attend only to the administrative matters that directly concerned the probation department.

With reference to the presentence probation report *per se,* the judges in Orange County were closer in attitude to the judges in Contra Costa County; they tended at least to consider the report before making the final determination of disposition. Although the judges in Orange County were more willing to express the probable disposition to the attorneys than the judges in Contra Costa County, they were also more involved in the actual negotiations of cases than the judges in San Francisco County. Specifically, they would take more time to sit down with the attorneys and talk over the facts of the case, the characteristics and needs of the defendant, and the appropriate disposition for the case. Therefore, although a tentative agreement was generally reached before the guilty plea, the judge would typically read the presentence report to see if any additional facts about the case would necessitate noncompliance with the agreement.

Because the presentence report is of some consequence in Orange County, the attorneys were compelled to become familiar with the content of the reports. The result was the same as in Contra Costa County—the attorneys would phone the investigating probation officer and try to influence his recommendation. To a less obvious extent, the indirect method was also employed: the attorneys would speak to the representative in the hallways and seek his help in persuading the investigating probation officer to write the report reflecting a certain position.

Variation in Probation Policy in MDSO Cases

The preceding discussion of the relative influence of the probation departments in each of the three jurisdictions applies to sex cases in general and not specifically to MDSO cases. When the MDSO proceedings are initiated, there is a slightly different response from each of the probation departments. The variation in policy in each of the departments is based both on attitudes toward psychiatrists and psychiatric testimony and on organizational pressures facing the departments.

The probation department in Contra Costa County, again, has the most influence in the disposition of MDSO cases. The general policy there, as with all cases, is active participation at all stages of the criminal and civil proceedings. The Welfare and Institutions Code is rather vague about what the role of the probation department could or should be in the MDSO civil proceedings; in fact, the probation department is mentioned in a very limited way. Therefore, there is wide latitude for interpretation of the proper role of the department by the court and by the department itself. The court's interpretation in Contra Costa County is that the department should do more than meet the minimal requirements of presenting factual data about the case and recommendations for disposition, as specified in the Welfare and Institutions Code.

When the MDSO proceedings begin, the role of the probation department is minimal. The only statutory requirement is that the department supply some form of probation report to the psychiatrists appointed to examine the offender, so that the psychiatrists will have information concerning the offender's background. The probation department in Contra Costa County complies with this provision by supplying a special form devised exclusively for MDSO cases, a short form that supplies factual data.

With the submission of background information, the probation department's involvement could be complete. Through its own interest and the court's request, however, the department continues to play a significant role in the proceedings. The most important reason for this is the belief held by the judges and by most probation officers that the psychiatric reports and recommendations are not to be trusted. The probation department asserts that if the judges blindly follow the psychiatric recommendations without a probation report for verification, the margin of error would be significantly increased, and poor decisionmaking would result.

The probation department and the judges share this skepticism about psychiatric reports for a variety of reasons. First, the probation officers know that the psychiatric interviews take a relatively short period of time, probably an average of one-half hour, and they do not believe it is possible to arrive at a reliable diagnosis and a valid recommendation in that period of time. Secondly, the probation officers maintain that psychiatrists merely copy the probation reports submitted to them and that they do not attempt to verify the factual information on which they base their inferences. In one sense the probation officers are not overly concerned with this shortcoming of the psychiatrists, since they feel that the information supplied is relatively accurate. What irritates the probation officers is that the psychiatrists would *consider* writing a report or testifying in open court without a thorough knowledge of all aspects of the case. Furthermore, the probation officers believe that the psychiatrists place too much reliance on what the offender claims to be true. There is strong doubt among probation officers that an offender will admit the truth to anyone when the potential consequences are grave. Under such conditions, an offender can be expected to lie for self-serving reasons; the probation officers believe the psychiatrists do not grant this possibility serious consideration.

For these reasons, the general attitude of probation officers is that the psychiatric reports may be based on inaccurate information, resulting in invalid recommendations. Since this may lead to costly mistakes, the probation officers prefer to supply their formal presentence report to the judge. This report contains not only factual details but also a thorough evaluation and recommendation for disposition. The judges readily accept these presentence reports, and request them if they are not submitted.

In San Francisco County, the probation department policy concerning MDSO cases is entirely different—the probation department there makes a concerted effort to not become involved. There are several explanations for this attitude—mainly because the department is overworked and understaffed. San Francisco County probation officers have the largest caseload, compared with the other jurisdictions studied. Whenever it is possible to reduce the amount of work required, the time-saving alternative is adopted. In MDSO cases, when the probation department has the opportunity to shift the burden of writing reports and recommendations from its own deputies to court-appointed psychiatrists, the opportunity is seized. This general attitude is reinforced by the knowledge that most of the MDSO cases are disposed of by a guilty plea during the pretrial negotiations. Consequently, any recommendation will fall on deaf ears. The resulting policy of doing as little as possible is evidenced in the extreme by the fact that the probation department does not even supply the court appointed psychiatrists with a probation report, as required by law.

The attitude toward psychiatrists and psychiatric testimony is, however, much the same as in Contra Costa County. The probation officers in San Francisco are skeptical of the psychiatric reports not only for the same reasons as those of the probation officers in Contra Costa County, but also for an additional reason. Since the probation department in San Francisco does not supply the psychiatrists with a probation report containing background information on the offender, the psychiatrists must obtain all their information about the offense and the defendant from the offender himself or from the district attorney's office. The probation officers feel that the information obtained from either source is unreliable and biased. Since the probation officers believe that the psychiatrists do not attempt to verify this information, they consider their reports suspect. This problem would be reduced if the probation department supplied the psychiatrists with background information, but the deputies in the department seem to feel that the return would not be worth their investment in time and energy.

In Orange County the probation department adopted a policy of having nothing to do with MDSO cases, although the department was very much involved in other sex cases. Once the judge suspends the criminal proceedings and initiates the civil MDSO proceedings, the probation department consistently withdraws and allows the court-appointed psychiatrists to make their diagnosis and their recommendations for appropriate disposition.

The primary reason for this policy seems to derive from the probation department's attitudes toward psychiatrists and psychiatric testimony. In contrast to the skepticism toward psychiatric testimony shown in Contra Costa and San Francisco Counties, the Orange County probation officers, both administrative and investigative, expressed respect for the court-appointed psychiatrists and confidence in their ability to submit a competent report to the court. The psychiatrists in Orange County seem to take more time and trouble in preparing the report, and the probation officers feel that the recommendations are never blatantly unjustified.

A further reason for the probation department's deference to the psychiatrists in Orange County can be called "expertise by default." The probation department administrators and the investigating officers do not feel that they have the knowledge and expertise needed to make diagnostic statements and recommendations in cases in which mental disorder seems present. They tend, therefore, to believe that the psychiatrists are the experts in this area and should have the responsibility for examining the offender and making the recommendation for disposition. The following statement made by an Orange County probation officer summarizes the prevalent feeling about sex cases and psychiatric testimony. "Most of us [POs] view sex offenders like you'd view someone with the measles—we're not experts in this case, and so you need doctors to figure out what they've got."

If preparation of the presentence report has begun and the probation officer feels that the offender is a possible candidate for MDSO proceedings, he will not offer a recommendation for disposition in the report but rather a recommendation that MDSO proceedings be initiated. The probation officer believes he is not qualified to assess the mental health of or to provide a recommendation for such defendants, since he does not have the expertise required to make such judgments. As a result, the role of the probation department in Orange County in the disposition of MDSO cases is minimal.

The Perspective of the Psychiatrist

The role of the psychiatrist is, in theory, the same as that of any other expert witness—supplying the court with technical information that it cannot obtain from other sources. As was demonstrated in the last chapter, however, the attorneys attempt to use the psychiatrist not as a valuable source of knowledge but as a tool to gain a desired disposition for a defendant. In general, psychiatists are utilized by the court personnel only because the procedure is mandated by statute or because it is seen as the most effective strategy for securing support for a desired disposition.

The psychiatrist finds himself in a predicament when he becomes involved in MDSO proceedings. On the one hand he is aware that the attorneys are taking advantage of him; at the same time he understands the situation of the attorney. He realizes that any recommendation he makes may result in major consequences for the offender. In some ways the psychiatrist feels the pressure to comply with the attorney's requests, since he sees himself acting with the offender's well-being as the prime consideration.

On the other hand, not being a lawyer and not overly concerned with "justice," the psychiatrist tends to reject the legal "games" played in court and to maintain an allegiance to his professional identity. Why should the psychiatrist, he asks, be constrained by the legal technicalities with which he is confronted, when these legal details make no sense in psychiatric terms? He finds it unreasonable that he has to make a diagnosis of a "mentally disordered sex offender," when the statutory definition of an MDSO is vague and so open to interpretation as to render the definition practically meaningless. The psychiatric recommendations, partly for these reasons, do not show the degree of uniformity or precision that is expected according to strict legal standards.

One further observation should be made about the psychiatrist and the variation in psychiatric reports (both the diagnosis and the recommendation). The psychiatrist should not be considered part of the court organization, and he does not work in a close social or professional network within the court. Consequently, there is less chance to standardize the diagnostic criteria or terminology employed in MDSO cases. This situation confounds the problem, and the variation in psychiatric reports seems to be unnecessarily wide.

Problems of Psychiatric Diagnosis

When the MDSO proceedings are initiated, the court appoints psychiatrists to prepare reports, which are to contain the following: a diagnosis of the offender, an assessment of the offender's dangerousness, an evaluation of his amenability to treatment, and, ultimately, a recommendation for disposition. In writing his report and recommendation, the psychiatrist must not only consider the effect of the recommendation on the offender and the effect a commitment might have on the institution, but he must also be concerned with fulfilling the statutory requirements set forth in the Welfare and Institutions Code. This latter requirement is extremely difficult, since the tasks to be accomplished are ill-defined by the Code, the legal definition of a Mentally Disordered Sex Offender is vague, and there are no standardized criteria available in the Code to provide the psychiatrist with guidelines. Consequently, any thoughtful psychiatrist understandably feels a certain degree of frustration in attempting to complete competently so uncertain a task.

Diagnosis has always been a thorny problem for psychiatry,[2] but the problem is greatly amplified when the psychiatrist must abandon his professional environment for a legal setting that insists he perform tasks that he considers psychiatrically unsound. The provisions of the MDSO statute offer a good example of this, for in many instances it is simply impossible to provide the court with a diagnosis and recommendation when the information about the offense and the offender is insufficient.

Some psychiatrists will state in their reports that it is very difficult to make a proper diagnosis and recommendation in MDSO cases. The reasons for the difficulty vary, but they include both insufficient knowledge about the offender and his specific offense and insufficient psychiatric knowledge about sex offenders in general. The following two statements by psychiatrists exemplify this:

Psychiatrically there is no way to determine the presence of a sex drive for children or young girls in a person who will not admit such an affliction. Hence, there is no approach possible to a psychiatric understanding of why this man becomes involved with young girls, even allowing that he may not have any sex urges toward them. In view of his consistent denials, no psychiatric opinion can be rendered.

Unfortunately, psychiatry is not able to determine whether or not a man is a sexual psychopath except by previous behavior indicated by court conviction or his own admissions. In as much as he denies any sexual crimes and there is no court conviction of such, I would not be able to diagnose him as a sexual psychopath.

It is interesting to note why an offender might not cooperate with a psychiatrist—a common situation, noted in the previous quotations. The least important and least prevalent reason is a general recalcitrance on the part of the defendant. In such cases, the defendant is unwilling to involve himself or cooperate with any person associated with the criminal justice system. This type of person often refuses to be represented by an attorney in the initial phases of the proceedings and, if found guilty, refuses to cooperate with the probation officer or any other person related to the court organization. He adamantly rejects all offers of help, although it would be in his own self-interest to accept them.

The most prevalent reason for noncooperation by the offender is that such a tactic is in his own best interest. In serious sex cases the defense attorney will instruct the offender to verbalize a recognition of mental problems and a desire for therapy; in minor sex cases the opposite strategy is employed. In a situation in which a commitment to Atascadero would be the most severe sanction, the defense attorney tries to avoid all contact with psychiatrists. If, however, psychiatrists are appointed, the defense attorney instructs the offender not to cooperate with them, so that the psychiatrists will be unable to arrive at a diagnosis and recommendation. If the diagnosis is not available, Atascadero would be eliminated as a dispositional alternative.

This situation occurs most frequently in cases in which the offender has pleaded guilty to a misdemeanor at the Municipal Court level but has been certified to Superior Court for the MDSO proceedings. If the offender is found to be an MDSO in Superior Court, it could mean a commitment to Atascadero for a period of approximately eighteen months, even if he had originally been convicted of a misdemeanor. If the offender is found not to be an MDSO, he is certified to the Municipal Court for sentencing on the criminal matter; the most severe sanction that could then be imposed is a one-year commitment to the county jail. Obviously, given these two alternatives, the defense attorney will try to convince the offender that it is in his own best interest not to talk or cooperate in any manner with the psychiatrist.

In cases in which the offender does cooperate with the psychiatrist (the majority of cases), there remains the difficult task of reaching a diagnosis and recommendation based on the criteria set forth in the Welfare and Institutions Code. Some of the confusion is derived from the unique history of the MDSO statute itself. As will be remembered, the MDSO law was originally called the "Sexual Psychopath" law, when it was formulated in 1939; it was given its present title in 1963.

Some of the psychiatrists who are currently writing reports for the courts were doing so before the law was changed and see the current law merely as an extension of the old one, although the change was technically quite significant. Consequently, some psychiatrists still employ the terminology of the original law (sexual psychopath) in their written reports and verbal statements at the court hearings.

The use of this diagnostic category, "sexual psychopathy," is not sound legally or psychiatrically. Legally, the statute was changed to remove the concept, since this category had caused the courts so many problems in the past. Even if the diagnosis of "sexual psychopath" could fall within the legal meaning of "mentally disordered sex offender," the term is no longer psychiatrically acceptable.[3] The term "sociopathic personality disturbance" was substituted for "psychopathic personality," although the two terms are used interchangeably by both the legal and psychiatric professions. It is not uncommon, therefore, to find the term "sociopathic personality" in the psychiatric reports, as in the following quotation:

Opinion: In my opinion the defendant is a Sociopathic Personality Disorder [sic] and has had a variety of sociopathic behavior. I do not feel that he is a Mentally Disordered Sex Offender, but that his behavior is a manifestation of his sociopathy.

Although it is used repeatedly, this terminology also is out of date, since the American Psychiatric Association abolished its usage in the 1968 revision of the *Diagnostic and Statistical Manual.*[4]

For a variety of reasons, then, there is quite an array of terminology and diagnostic categories in the reports submitted to the courts. Because of the varying and ill-defined psychiatric jargon, the attorneys often have a difficult time comprehending the submitted reports. For example, note the two following psychiatric reports offered by psychiatrists who examined a child molester.

Summary: The history and examination reveals that the defendant has failed to attain the mature adult level of psychosexual adaptation. Unable to engage in sexual experimentation with adult mature females, he experiments with the immature minor female. He identifies himself as objectivist, as unique, of above average intelligence and denies any form of inadequacy. He responds to attempts at discussion of his failures with hypersensitivity, rigidity, suspicion, excessive self-importance and the plausible rationalization that the cause of the offense was a desire to experiment. His objectivistic attitude coupled with an unconcern with altruistic motives prevents him from experiencing empathy with the victim which for him becomes reduced to some form of experimental animal. The material presented by the defendant indicated that he is close to be [sic] overwhelmed by a paranoid psychosis.

Diagnosis: Adjustment reaction of adolescence, paranoia with sexual deviation associated with failure to attain adult sexuality manifested by grandiosity, ominiscience, omnipotence, excessive self-importance and female pedophilia, exhibitionism, erotic masochism, onanism. A latent schizophrenic process is not ruled out. Defendant is in urgent need of a period of observation in an institutional setting to arrive at a definite diagnosis.

Diagnosing the same defendant, the second psychiatrist stated:

My diagnostic impression of this defendant is that of Inadequate Personality (with Schizoid Traits), for I feel defendant has been unable to utilize his "intellect" in a meaningful manner. His schizoid traits are manifested primarily through interpersonal relation [sic] concept he has re: his fellow students and grandiosity. I feel that he has a mental defect which predisposes him to the commission of sexual offenses to such a degree that he is dangerous to the health and safety of others.

These and similar reports are generally incomprehensible to the legal mind: it is not uncommon to find the judge's copy of a psychiatric report covered with question marks that call attention to the vague phrases and unfamiliar vocabulary.

The interpretation of what the Welfare and Institutions Code prescribes as an appropriate diagnosis and recommendation varies, and the psychiatrist often has a very difficult time deciding whether or not an MDSO diagnosis should be made based on the fact that the offender has more than one sex offense in his past. That is to say, does a series of sex offenses constitute *prima facie* evidence that a mental disorder exists in the offender and that he is predisposed to the commission of further offenses, or must some more clearly identifiable mental problem be shown before the MDSO designation is applicable?

A closely related problem for the psychiatrist is the extent to which the sexual problems of the offender can be examined exclusively, as was possible under the old "Sexual Psychopath" statute. An alternative way of posing the problem might be the extent to which the new law is open to a broader, more encompassing interpretation. If the broader interpretation is chosen, a wider range of persons comes under its scope. If the narrow interpretation prevails, a severe limitation will be placed on the labeling of different types of persons as MDSOs from a psychiatric point of view. A quotation from a psychiatric report confronting this dilemma of interpretation should make this more clear.

In my opinion, he was a borderline case as a mentally disordered sex offender. I thought he was definitely mentally disordered, suffering from a severe personality disorder, or what amounts to the same thing, a borderline mental illness. I believe that the psychiatric diagnosis of simple schizophrenia could apply in this case. His failure to learn in school, his apparent mental subnormality (but with adequate street knowledge), his great pressure of speech, his intense emotionality, his poor judgment, and his boastful assertions (he told me he could hit a running jackrabbit with a thrown knife) indicate a severe disorder but without delusions or hallucinations.

But his disorder did not dispose him to sexual offenses exclusively. With his admitted practice of burglary and "selling dope," his sexual aggressions appeared as part of a general tendency to aggressiveness and antisocial conduct.

The key issue facing the psychiatrist in the case was whether the mental problem of the offender had to be specifically of a sexual nature. In other words, can a person be classified an MDSO if he has a mental disorder and if his commission of sex offenses merely seems to correspond with his behavior in committing other offenses? Does the sexual problem have to be at the core of the mental disorder, and should the MDSO designation be applied only to persons whose problems are primarily of a sexual nature?

A more specific example of this psychiatric quandry is the relationship of alcohol or alcoholism to the MDSO designation. If the narrow interpretation of the statute is applied, alcoholism would not constitute a mental disease, defect, or disorder sufficient to warrant the MDSO label. However, if the broad interpretation prevailed, and the offender is predisposed, because of his alcoholism, to commit sexual offenses that would endanger others, then alcoholism could be considered a mental disease and the MDSO designation applied.

Within the three counties studied, there seemed to be some variation in the psychiatrists' interpretation of the relationship between alcoholism and the MDSO designation. In general, the psychiatrists in the two northern counties adopt the narrow interpretation of this issue, whereas the psychiatrists in Orange County adopt the broad interpretation. That is, the psychiatrists in Orange County were much more likely to use the MDSO classification for a person seen as being basically an alcoholic who committed sexually oriented offenses. An example of this perspective is to be found in the following Orange County psychiatric report:

Summary: Although, consciously, the man probably does not have an awareness of any perverse sexual drives, he has a mental disorder manifested primarily by a serious addiction to alcohol. This pattern of repeatedly drinking to a point of psychotic intoxication, with aggressive and unpredictable sexual activity occurring in these states, would indicate a mental disorder predisposing him to commit sexual offenses that are potentially dangerous to others.

The psychiatrists in the two northern counties (San Francisco and Contra Costa), using the narrower interpretation, generally feel that a commitment as an MDSO to Atascadero is appropriate for persons whose behavior problems are basically sexual in nature. If the offender is both an alcoholic and a sex offender, these psychiatrists are not likely to diagnose him as an MDSO. They would be inclined to use the MDSO diagnosis, however, if the offender were viewed as primarily a sex offender who also had an alcohol problem. Since Atascadero is considered a hospital at which therapy for sexual disorders is the primary concern, the northern psychiatrists feel that the sexual nature of an individual's problems should take precedence over his drinking problems for purposes of sentencing.

For these reasons, some disagreement among psychiatrists in diagnosis and recommendation can be expected in MDSO cases. The extent of psychiatric disagreement has always been of interest to those concerned with the role of psychiatry in the criminal justice system. Critics of psychiatry and psychiatric testimony have pointed to the high degree of conflict among psychiatrists as evidence that psychiatry is not a science and that therefore it should not be accepted in the courtroom.

In this study, the analysis of psychiatric reports revealed a rather high degree of disagreement among psychiatrists over the appropriate diagnosis of the offender and the recommendation for disposition. Table 5-1 indicates the extent of disagreement of psychiatric diagnosis and Table 5-2 illustrates the extent of disagreement in the recommendations for disposition. It will be noted that there were conflicting opinions in psychiatric diagnosis in 18 percent of the reports in Contra Costa County, 32 percent of the reports in San Francisco County, and 30 percent of the reports in Orange County. In terms of recommendation for disposition, there was conflict of opinion in 24 percent of the reports in Contra Costa County, 32 percent in San Francisco County, and 34 percent in Orange County.

Although evidence of conflict in psychiatric opinion is apparent from the data, it is not clear why the disagreement exists to such a significant extent. The opportunity to select a psychiatrist, especially in Orange County, undoubtedly enables the adversaries to choose doctors who will represent

Table 5-1
Unanimity of Psychiatric Diagnosis

	Contra Costa		San Francisco		Orange	
	N	Percent	N	Percent	N	Percent
No diagnosis made	0	0	0	0	16	13
Unanimous not MDSO	41	45	17	50	25	20
Unanimous MDSO	34	37	6	18	36	30
Conflicting opinions	16	18	11	32	36	30
No information	0	0	0	0	9	7
Total	91	100	34	100	122	100

Table 5-2
Unanimity of Psychiatric Recommendation

	Contra Costa		San Francisco		Orange	
	N	Percent	N	Percent	N	Percent
No recommendation given	0	0	0	0	16	13
Not MDSO, no recommendation	41	45	17	50	25	20
MDSO but no danger, so outpatient therapy	5	5	0	0	2	2
MDSO, mixed recommendations	22	24	11	32	41	34
MDSO, unanimous to Atascadero	23	25	6	18	29	24
No information	0	0	0	0	9	7
Total	91	99	34	100	122	100

their best interests, and this situation would clearly lead to variety in psychiatric opinions. Elsewhere, the attorneys' active lobbying for a certain diagnosis and recommendation would reasonably result in diverse opinions reflecting the attorney's varying interests.

Professionally, there are further reasons for the disagreement in diagnosis and recommendation of cases. First, as was mentioned, there is no organization or forum for the psychiatrists to attempt to standardize the criteria used in the MDSO cases. Since there is no tendency toward the standardization of terms and criteria, the psychiatrists must rely on their professional training. Since schools of psychiatric thought, rooted in varying theoretical orientations, are so divergent, it logically follows that there will be disagreement about a subject area that is vague in its own right.

The disagreement of professional opinions is illustrated by the following case involving a forty-one year old man with a minimal prior record. He had been convicted of four counts of child molest and exhibitionism for fondling two young females, who were aged seven and nine. The first psychiatrist found the offender to be an MDSO.

As a result of psychiatric evaluation I conclude that the defendant, _____ , is a mentally disordered sex offender in that he is predisposed by virtue of a character defect to the commission of sex offenses dangerous to the health and safety of others. Specifically he appears to have a predilection for exhibitionism and sexual molestation of immature females. He continues to deny any responsibility for his acts, attempting to recreate the illusion that he had been wrongly convicted. Such an attitude augurs poorly for the future. The defendant is in need of therapy for his sexual disorder and I recommend commitment to Atascadero State Hospital for an initial 90-day period of observation and treatment. At the present time the defendant shows no evidence of any psychotic disorder. He understands all legal procedures and his relationship to them. He is able to confer rationally with counsel in all proceedings affecting his future.

The second psychiatrist did not agree, although his opinion was advanced without a reasoned explanation.

> In my opinion, _____ , will benefit by this experience. It is my further opinion that he is not dangerous. It is my further opinion that there are insufficient findings to justify a diagnosis of mentally disordered sex offender at this time. He does have an inadequate personality and could benefit by some psychiatric help which he could obtain on an outpatient basis.

In this case the probation officer also made an evaluation of the defendant and suggested that the defendant be removed from the community and held for a period of observation at Atascadero State Hospital.

The experts involved disagreed on several issues: the criteria utilized to determine whether or not the offender was an MDSO, the operational definition of dangerousness, and the question of whether the offender could benefit from treatment in the community or whether the setting at Atascadero would be required. This disagreement among the psychiatrists is difficult to interpret or explain. There is no way of discerning, on the basis of official records, whether the disagreement was the result of the invalidity of psychiatric classification schemes, the inherent vagueness of the MDSO statute, or the extent to which the psychiatrists in any particular case serve as extensions of the adversary system.

The Problem of Dangerousness

The statutory definition of an MDSO includes the element of dangerousness. To be so defined, a person must be predisposed to the commission of sexual offenses to such an extent that he is dangerous to the health and safety of others. However, the statute does not include guidelines indicating what constitutes dangerousness. Does *dangerousness* mean immediate physical danger, general physical danger, or does it include the concept of psychological danger to the victim—as may occur when an exhibitionist exposes himself to a child? Since the criteria for assessing dangerousness are a problem for psychiatrists,[5] it is reasonable to expect that it will be an even greater problem when the statute to be interpreted is itself lacking in specificity.

In certain obvious cases, all psychiatrists could agree whether a person constitutes a danger to the health and safety of others. For instance, if a person were convicted of child molest involving force and the person had several similar prior arrests and convictions, every psychiatrist in each of the three jurisdictions would be able to agree. In such a case there is not only the element of immediate physical danger, but also the fact that since such acts had occurred several times in the past, they would be likely to continue in the future. The problem facing the psychiatrists and the courts is not how to evaluate the obvious cases but what to include at the lowest levels of the spectrum representing degrees of danger. Should legally defined "dangerousness" include cases of psychological harm or merely those involving physical danger to others?

As evidenced, there was some variation among the three jurisdictions regarding the psychiatric conception of dangerousness. Although there was some variation *within* the counties, the two northern counties, in general, tended to limit their definition to the concept of physical danger to the victim. A psychiatrist from San Francisco County stated:

Furthermore, the victim in the present offense appears to be over the age of 14, and the evidence does not seem to be overwhelmingly convincing that force or violence or threats were used. It is not clear, therefore, that the defendant's offense represented a physical danger to the health and safety of the victim, and with respect to possible psychological danger, there appears to be very poor consensus among psychiatric experts with respect to the psychological danger, if any, following such incidents.

Therefore, the psychiatrist could not find that the person was an MDSO.

Although the psychiatrists in Orange County might agree that there is little consensus among psychiatric experts about the psychological consequences of nonviolent child molestations, they are, nevertheless, more likely to include the concept of potential psychological danger in their interpretation of the MDSO statute. Consequently, the psychiatric reports from Orange County often read like this:

Opinion: In my opinion, the defendant is a sexual deviate, associated with pedophilia. He sees his sexual activities with young children as a problem for him, and verbalizes the need for some sort of psychological help. Although he has never apparently been any physical threat to anyone, I do feel that he is a threat to the psychological health of his victims and I feel he should be considered a mentally disordered sex offender.

Again, the psychiatrists in Orange County have adopted a much broader interpretation of the MDSO statute than is used in the two northern counties. The result is that a greater variety of offenders is subject to this classification. This raises the question of the extent to which conceptions of "dangerousness" are based on standardized psychiatric criteria or on community norms.

The psychiatrists in the three counties similarly disassociate the perception of the dangerousness of the offender from the MDSO diagnosis. Although it clearly states in the MDSO statute that the offender be dangerous to the health and safety of others, the psychiatrists in all three counties occasionally state that a person can be an MDSO without being dangerous. In one case an exhibitionist was certified to the Superior Court specifically to be examined by psychiatrists. The first psychiatrist stated:

He is essentially a dependable husband, successful citizen, and well-motivated, insightful person. Although he is classifiable as a mentally disordered sex offender (sexually predisposed to young girls), under his present regime I do not consider him to be a present social danger. I recommend, therefore, that he be adjudged a mentally disordered sex offender (diagnosis: Personality Disorder, Sexual Deviation, female pedophilia), but that he would not benefit from state hospitalization and would benefit from out-patient psychiatric counselling and therapy.

The second psychiatric report also states that the offender is not a danger, yet classifies him as an MDSO.

It is my opinion that while the defendant must be categorized as a mentally disordered sex offender because of his pattern of sexual interest in pre-adolescent girls, with on two occasions giving in to his impulse, he does not represent a danger to the community and could best be treated by allowing him to remain in the community and continue with out-patient therapy.

In both of these reports the psychiatrists' statements that the person is an MDSO but not dangerous constitute a legal impossibility. One of the necessary requirements of the MDSO designation is the element of dangerousness; if that element is absent, the designation cannot properly be applied. It is as if they were stating that a murder, in the legal sense of the word, had taken place when the element of intent was absent—nonsense to anyone with legal training. These legal technicalities are of no great concern to the psychiatrists, since the statute itself is seen as defective. The position often expressed by the psychiatrists is that they should not be compelled to comply with a rule that makes very little psychiatric sense.

In conclusion, it has been shown that the manner in which psychiatrists in each of the three counties interpret the MDSO statute and the criteria they use to assess dangerousness and mental disorder vary. The variation that exists, moreover, contributes to differential commitment rates of MDSOs to Atascadero. Specifically, since the psychiatrists in Orange County employ a broader definition of the MDSO statute than do the psychiatrists in the two northern counties, the number and type of offenders to which the MDSO designation might be applied is significantly greater in Orange County. For this reason, the attorneys and judges in Orange County have available a greater range of sentencing alternatives for a wider variety of cases.

Notes

1. It should be mentioned that in Contra Costa County, as opposed to

the other two jurisdictions, there was considerable discussion of instituting a "Pre-plea Report" so that the facts of the case and recommendation of the probation officer could be utilized by the court decisionmakers *before* the guilty plea. This also confirms the assertion that the probation department exerts more influence in Contra Costa County than in the other two jurisdictions.

2. For a review of the problems of psychiatric diagnosis, see H.O. Schmidt and C.P. Fonda, "The Reliability of Psychiatric Diagnosis: A New Look," *Journal of Abnormal and Social Psychology* 52 (1956):262-267; Benjamin Pasamanick, Simon Dinitz, and Mark Lefton, "Psychiatric Orientation and Its Relation to Diagnosis and Treatment in a Mental Hospital," *American Journal of Psychiatry* 116 (1959):127-132; Thomas Szasz, "The Problem of Psychiatric Nosology: A Contribution to the Situational Analysis of Psychiatric Operations," *American Journal of Psychiatry* 114 (1957):405-413; P. Hoch and J. Zubin, *Current Problems in Psychiatric Diagnosis,* New York: Grune and Stratton, 1953.

3. In 1952 the American Psychiatric Association revised the *Diagnostic and Statistical Manual* and abolished the term psychopathic personality. In its place was substituted the term sociopathic personality disturbance. See *Diagnostic and Statistical Manual: Mental Disorders,* prepared by the Committee on Nomenclature and Statistics of the American Psychiatric Association, Washington, D.C.: American Psychiatric Association, 1952, pp. 38-39.

4. In 1968 the American Psychiatric Association again revised the *Diagnostic and Statistical Manual* and deleted the term sociopathic personality disturbance. The new *Manual* provided two diagnostic categories that might be used instead of either psychopathic personality or sociopathic personality disturbance. The first possible category, subsumed under the general heading of Personality Disorders, is "Sexual Deviation." The second possible diagnostic category, subsumed under the heading Conditions without Manifest Psychiatric Disorder and Non-Specific Conditions, is called "Dysocial Behavior."

5. For a general discussion of the problems facing psychiatrists in defining dangerousness, see Bernard Rubin, "The Prediction of Dangerousness in Mentally Ill Criminals," *The Archives of General Psychiatry* no. 3, (September 1972): 397-407. The general conclusion reached by Dr. Rubin is that there is no standardized psychiatric criterion for the prediction of dangerousness in anyone.

6

The Imposition of Sanctions in Three Jurisdictions

It was asserted in Chapter 3 that there was general variation in the sentencing policies of the three jurisdictions, but that within each jurisdiction the sentences were administered in a rather uniform manner. Chapter 6 will examine this assertion in detail, concentrating on several key issues: first, the variation in sentencing among jurisdictions (with a focus on the problems of comparing official statistics); second, the results of the "residual case analysis"; and third, the relationship of these factors to the varying commitment rates of MDSOs to Atascadero.

Variation in Sentencing Policy

Jurisprudential and scholarly concern for the equal distribution of justice is manifested by an interest in the variation in sentencing policy. Before the results of the current study are presented, a brief review of the polemics of the issue is in order.

There are basically two types of issues in the study of variation in sentencing policy—the jurisprudential and the empirical. Jurisprudential theorists have long held that arbitrary sentences are both intolerable under a rule of law and invalid under the broadest interpretation of the due process clause of the Constitution. There is virtually no disagreement with this view, for it is generally felt that the potential for abusive discretion should be limited so that individual rights will not be violated. We are now witnessing a nation-wide return to standardized justice models in which the goal is similar sentences for comparable crimes. But it is with the second, the empirical issue, that this study will take exception.

There have been numerous studies indicating the lack of uniformity in judicial sentences for roughly similar acts, although few studies have presented compelling data.[1] These works are generally composed of more rhetoric than data. For example, a recent book written by a Federal District Court judge contains descriptions of sentencing as "a wild array of sentencing judgments," "wildly unequal sentences," or "the capricious unruliness of sentencing."[2]

Words such as capricious, whimsical, idiosyncratic, and arbitrary abound in these works, which are generally devoid of empirical evidence to support their claims. However, it is not the purpose of the present study to criticize directly such characterizations of sentencing policies for two reasons: first, they may be an accurate portrayal of decisions in the judicial jurisdictions in which the studies took place; second, it would be extremely difficult to criticize the methodology employed in such studies, since their descriptions of the methodologies are generally inadequate. What must be stated is that in the jurisdictions examined here, there appeared to be no "widely varying sentences" within a given jurisdiction for comparable cases.

Some variation in the sanctions imposed by the courts on defendants who had committed roughly similar criminal acts will be revealed in the "residual case analysis." The decisions to impose different sanctions were, however, in no way capricious or whimsical. Although the decisions may have been "unjust," they were rational and well-calculated if the "rationality" of the court organization is considered. There are several possible explanations for the uniformity in sentencing policy in the three jurisdictions examined. Some of the reasons may be explained by the unique organizational structure of large criminal justice systems in California.

One such explanation rests on the type of court organization called the "Criminal Master Calendar System." In this system, all criminal cases certified to the Superior Court are sent to the Criminal Master Calendar Judge. This judge handles *all* criminal cases except those that go to trial. Since most defendants plead guilty, and a large number of cases are dismissed at this level, the result is that one judge in each jurisdiction disposes of about 95 percent of all criminal cases. Whereas in other jurisdictions there may be many judges hearing a shared percentage of the cases, California's system is likely to increase consistency and reduce the element of "judicial independence" in the imposition of sanctions.

One of the explanations for the variation in sentences in other areas was that the judges infrequently met to discuss the sanctions imposed for comparable cases. For instance, Steele and Barlett claim: "The disparity arises because of the diverse ways individual judges, each operating in a vacuum without much knowledge of the kinds of sentences imposed by fellow judges, view criminals and certain types of crime."[3] The jurisdictions studied avoided this problem. Even if a case is presented to a new judge and a conviction is secured, both court adversaries are quick to inform the judge what the "going rate" has been in the Criminal Master Calendar Court. With some exceptions, this awareness of the "going rate" seems to influence the judge's decision, resulting in the standardization of sentences.

While the judges do not seem to associate with one another to share opinions about appropriate sanctions for similar cases, the deputy DAs and the defense attorneys do. They frequently hold meetings to discuss any new developments in the "going rate" for different types of cases. If a lighter than normal sentence is meted out, communication channels throughout the court organization spread the word, and new demands are presented by other defense attorneys for similar dispositions for their clients in similar situations. In this manner, the attorneys, who are primarily responsible for deciding what sanctions are to be imposed, tend to develop relatively standard policies for the imposition of sanctions for roughly comparable cases. With these organizational explanations, it is obvious that the description of judicial sentences as "idiosyncratic ukases"[4] is not applicable.

Another factor in the analysis of variation in judicial decisions is the word *judicial*. We found that the role of the judge in determining the sanction is not paramount but that he relies on the two adversaries to furnish him with their decision. There is, of course, some variation in the extent to which judges in each county merely "rubber-stamp" the agreement reached by the adversaries. In San Francisco the Master Calendar Judge does, indeed, follow their suggestions.

In Contra Costa and Orange Counties the judge takes a more active part in the decision. However, he does not *decide* what sanction to impose, but, on those occasions in which he will not accept the decision of the attorneys, he requests that they present alternative agreements until the judge finds one that is acceptable. In so doing, the judge seems to set the parameters within which the bargaining may take place.

There are other, more important, reasons why one might mistakenly overestimate the extent to which sentencing policy is both capricious and arbitrary. These reasons are not unique to California; they are common to most large criminal justice organizations. The primary reason is that the formal offense category for which the defendant is convicted may bear only a slight relation to the circumstances for which he is actually sentenced.

There are two related explanations for this lack of correlation between formal conviction and sentence. The first, equally applicable to all jurisdictions, concerns the nature of the plea bargaining process. If the central concern of the court personnel is to impose specific sanctions for given offenses, then what the court personnel call or label the particular criminal act is of secondary importance; that is, the formal title of the crime is of less concern than the amount of time the defendant will have to spend in an institution. For instance, there might be three different defendants charged with one count of rape, three counts of rape, and six counts of rape, respectively. The dominant concern of all court personnel is the type of institution in which the defendants will be incarcerated and for how long; the number of counts to which the defendant is willing to plead is of secondary concern.

From the perspective of the district attorney, a plea to any one of the counts lodged against the defendant is sufficient to impose any sanction agreed on in the bargain. A plea to one count of rape will send the defendant to state prison, as will a plea to all six. As a result, the defendants often plead guilty to one or two counts from the numerous counts lodged against them. These defendants are then indistinguishable—on official records—from those who originally were charged with only one or two counts. Thus, many defendants responsible for very serious crimes are "officially convicted" of the same number and types of counts as less serious offenders. When a severe sentence is imposed on such defendants, in effect they are being "informally convicted" of the initial counts lodged against them.

When considering the assertion that sentencing policy differs from one jurisdiction to another, one must ask what is meant by the word *policy.* Two meanings of this word are relevant for an analysis of variation in criminal sentences. According to one definition, the sentencing policy may vary from jurisdiction to jurisdiction; if another meaning is intended, there is no such variation.

An examination of a specific situation will clarify the ambiguity surrounding the two meanings of this word. The following is a hypothetical case that could have taken place in any of the three jurisdictions. It involves a defendant charged with four counts in a sex offense: one count each of rape, assault, burglary, and oral copulation. The defendant allegedly entered an apartment, forcibly raped the female occupant, threatened her with a gun to force her to perform oral copulation on him, and finally, beat her to such an extent that she required hospitalization. Furthermore, the defendant had similar priors, and the evidence in the case was strong enough to convince a jury of his guilt.

In one county, the policy of the district attorney might be to plead the case out to the lightest possible offense—in this case, assault, since this offense has the shortest minimum statutory sentence. In the second county, the policy might be to plead the case out to the crime that most resembles the "essence" of the fact situation, in this instance a rape. In the third county, the most punitive, the policy might to be plead the case out to at least two offenses, generally the two perceived as the most severe. Each of the three counties can therefore be described as having a different policy, which results in a different configuration of official statistics.

However, in another, and perhaps more important, sense, the policies were exactly the same. Although the formal conviction might differ in each jurisdiction, the sentence would be the same—a commitment to state prison. No matter what the offense might be *called* in each jurisdiction, the result would be consistent. To understand sentencing policy, the distinction must be made between the act of labeling something as different and actually *doing* something different. Much of what appears to be variation in sentencing policy, based on an analysis of the official records, is really nothing of the kind. Although the sanctioning policies vary among different jurisdictions, the difference is not as great as one might infer from the official data; in situations with similar facts, what actually differs may be only the plea.

A further explanation of why the formal offense for which the defendant was convicted has little relation to the situation for which he was sentenced lies in the nature of the formal Penal Code sections. In general, they are so broad and so vague that any number of different situations can fall within one particular formal section. When criminal justice researchers suggest that widely varying sentences are meted out for the same offense, they may be relying on the formal Penal Code sections as the operational definition of the "same offense." For example, under the section dealing with oral copulation, the fact situation can vary from a case involving consenting adults to a case in which an adult forces a child to submit to his advances. As a result, there will naturally be variation in the sanctions imposed for a conviction under the same Penal Code section, since the facts differ so dramatically.

The conclusions about the variation in sentencing policy depend in large part on the classification system used. If the formal code sections are utilized, there will seem to be a high degree of variation in the sentence imposed—not only within each county but also among counties. A valid judgment about such variation requires a different approach to classifying cases. The focus of attention must be on the "constellation of factual elements" if one is to compare sentences accurately, either within or among counties.

To continue the comparison of the three counties in this example of an oral copulation offense, the formal Penal Code Section and the "constellation of factual elements" approach will be used. Table 6-1 shows all convic-

Table 6-1
Dispositions for All Convictions of Oral Copulation

Disposition	Contra Costa		San Francisco		Orange	
	N	Percent	N	Percent	N	Percent
Dismissal	0	0	0	0	0	0
Suspended sentence	0	0	0	0	0	0
Small fine	0	0	0	0	0	0
Probation (court)	0	0	0	0	0	0
Probation (supervision)	5	29	49	78	7	32
County jail (6 months)	2	12	1	2	2	9
Atascadero State Hospital	7	41	3	5	5	23
State prison	3	18	10	16	8	36
Total	17	100	63	101	22	100

tions for oral copulation. It can be seen that the variation in sentences for a conviction is clearly quite extensive. It might be inferred that the sanctions imposed are "wildly unequal" or that they represent a "wild array of sentencing judgments."

By employing the "constellation approach," one can examine and compare all homosexuality cases involving the following constellation of facts: two males (adult and consenting) are discovered in a public place by a police officer, neither files a complaint nor is considered a "victim," and the police officer acts as the complainant. When this constellation of facts is plotted, the results look quite different, as shown in Table 6-2; the conclusion to be drawn from this table is markedly different: within each jurisdiction the administration of justice is quite uniform.

It will be noticed that there were no homosexuality cases involving the constellation of facts described above in Contra Costa and Orange Counties. In fact, in the sample used for this book, there was not one such case certified to the Superior Court during the five-year period in either of the two counties. Interviews with a number of deputy DAs and defense attorneys who had worked at the Municipal Court level in Contra Costa and Orange Counties revealed that a substantial number of such cases are settled at the Municipal Court level. The attorneys explained repeatedly that when such cases come before the Municipal Court, they are pled to a misdemeanor—either Disorderly Conduct (lewd vagrancy) or Disturbing the Peace. After the misdemeanor guilty plea has been obtained, a relatively light sanction is imposed by the court—most generally probation and a small fine or a minimal amount of jail time.

From the stratified random sample of cases in San Francisco, a total of

Table 6-2
Constellation of Homosexuality Cases

Disposition	Contra Costa		San Francisco		Orange	
	N	Percent	N	Percent	N	Percent
Dismissal	0	0	0	0	0	0
Suspended sentence	0	0	0	0	0	0
Small fine	0	0	0	0	0	0
Probation (court)	0	0	0	0	0	0
Probation (supervision)	0	0	42	100	0	0
County jail (6 months)	0	0	0	0	0	0
Atascadero State Hospital	0	0	0	0	0	0
State prison	0	0	0	0	0	0
Total	0	0	42	100	0	0

forty-two cases were certified to the Superior Court in the five-year period. Of those, all received the same general sanction—probation. Since probation is a general category, there can be substantial variation. An examination of Table 6-3 will reveal that such variation did not result. In the forty-two cases of consenting adult male homosexuality during the five-year period, there were four different judges imposing the sentences, and the range of sanctions is shown in Table 6-3.

It appears from the data that the imposition of sanctions for cases with this constellation of facts is quite uniform. In fact, of the forty-two cases, thirty-three, or 78 percent, received *exactly* the same sanction, while the variation in the rest of the sanctions was negligible—especially considering the range of sanctioning alternatives available to the court (from dismissal of the case to a commitment to state prison for a period of one year to life).

Consideration of the cases that received sanctions either below or above the norm will indicate that, while the variation may be the result of judicial discretion, it is, nevertheless, not based on capricious or whimsical decisions. In the few cases receiving a less severe sanction, that is, probation costs of less than $250, the defense attorney was able to convince the judge that the defendant was indigent and that the additional $100 would be an unnecessary hardship. Since being placed on probation was the significant punishment, the judge agreed that no purpose would be served by requiring indigent defendants to meet the same standards as others.

Table 6-3
Sentences in Homosexuality Cases

N			
33	Probation, 2 years	$250 probation costs	Deemed misdemeanor pursuant to Section 17 PC
1	Probation, 2 years	$150 probation costs	Deemed misdemeanor pursuant to Section 17 PC
3	Probation, 2 years	$5/month probation costs	Deemed misdemeanor pursuant to Section 17 PC
1	Probation, 2 years	$302, probation costs	Deemed misdemeanor pursuant to Section 17 PC
1	Probation, 2 years	$250, probation costs	Remain felony
1	Probation, 2 years	$10/month probation costs	Remain felony
1	Probation, 2 years	3 months county jail	Remain felony
1	Probation, 2 years	3 months county jail	To be deemed a misdemeanor upon successful completion of probation
42 Total			

The cases that received the more severe sanctions are also illustrative of common court decisionmaking processes. In the cases in which the conviction remained a felony or the defendant was sentenced to jail, the salient and common variable was that the case was taken to trial and the guilty plea secured after the trial was in session. It is certainly an abuse of judicial discretion to penalize a defendant for exercising his constitutional right to a trial, but this variation is in no way capricious. It is a calculated, rational policy to induce defendants to conform to the requirements of the court—to process a large number of cases in a relatively short period of time. This procedure is used primarily by judges and district attorneys in cases in which the facts seem rather obvious, and a conviction appears routine. According to one defense attorney who specializes in this type of case, "They [the judges] state flatly that the defendant will go to jail for thirty days and it [the charge] will remain a felony if he is found guilty at a jury trial." In this manner, instances of judicial discretion are shown to stem not from the idiosyncratic judgments of the judges but from rational policies of organizational life.

Depending on who is asked, there are competing explanations for the policy of certifying homosexual cases to the Superior Court in San Francisco County. The policy is especially puzzling since the Municipal Court judge has the power to reduce the offense to a misdemeanor, and, as one defense attorney put it, "It is a foregone conclusion that the offense will be reduced to a misdemeanor at the Superior Court." The deputy district attorneys maintain that the policy serves the private defense attorneys, since they can charge the client more if the case is certified to Superior Court. At the same time, the defense attorneys claim that the deputy DAs are responsible for the policy, since it increases their felony case count and therefore enables them to request more money and manpower. Neither of these two explanations seems adequate considering San Francisco's basic interest in reducing the caseload at the Superior Court level.

This policy concerning consenting male homosexuality cases does seem arbitrary in nature, in that its rationale is not apparent and, seemingly, a different policy would serve more effectively. One would think that the same policy as that utilized in Contra Costa and Orange Counties (that is, having the case concluded with a misdemeanor conviction with probation and a small fine) would serve San Francisco as well; certifying the case to the Superior Court benefits neither the defendants nor the criminal justice system.

Residual Case Analysis

The method of "residual case analysis" employed in this book is similar to the "negative case analysis" used by Becker et al.[5] In their study, they applied the label to cases that did not conform to the analytical model they had constructed with qualitative methods. Here, a case in which the observed variation is either positive or negative will be considered a residual. A *positive* residual is a case in which the sanction imposed on the defendant is more severe than what would be expected—all predictive factors considered. A *negative* residual is one in which the defendant was given a sanction that is less severe than what would be expected. By closely examining both types of extreme residual cases, a researcher can discover the important factors for the disposition of the case—factors that were *not* originally included in the analysis.

Concerning the negative residuals, the primary explanation for the occurrence of sanctions less severe than expected is the problem of evidence. If the deputy DA has a "strong case," i.e., a case with good and compelling evidence, the standard bargaining procedures can be conducted with the defense attorney, and a routine disposition will result. If, however, the deputy DA has a "weak case," i.e., poor or unconvincing evidence, his bargaining position is weakened, and he must make more concessions to the defense in order to secure a conviction. At the same time, the defense attorney's position is enhanced when the evidence is bad, so a relatively light sanction can be demanded in exchange for cooperation with the prosecution. An example of a case should make this more clear.

The case involved a male arrested and charged with five counts of rape and three counts of kidnap, involving five different victims. The male used the same method of operation in each of the incidents. He would sneak up behind the victim and place a weapon at her throat. Before she could identify him, he would blindfold her, transport her to another area, and rape her. At the police station a confession was secured for all five rapes, and, consequently, the prosecution was in a very good bargaining position. When asked by the public defender what sort of deal might be made in the case, the prosecutor laughed and announced that the defendant was going to state prison.

Soon thereafter, the public defender discovered that the confession was of questionable constitutionality, because the police had made improper promises to the defendant in exchange for the confession. The public defender introduced a motion in court to suppress the confession because of its alleged unconstitutionality. When the motion was granted, the prosecutor's position was totally different: he had no confession and no witnesses. The probability of conviction by a jury was greatly reduced, and the plea bargaining took on a different character. Instead of insisting on state prison, the DA was willing to settle for six months in jail. Since the public defender did not want to risk the possibility of a jury conviction, which would probably entail a prison commitment, he agreed to the jail sentence—thereby securing what he considered to be the best possible disposition for his client.

This case illustrates the importance of the quantity and/or quality of evidence in a criminal case. When the prosecution and defense attorneys make their evaluations, they do so on two separate levels. First, they consider the facts of the case as alleged in the complaint, the information, or the police report. Second and more important, they evaluate these facts in terms of whether they can be proven in court; that is, they immediately make judgments about the triability of the case. If it is fairly obvious to the court personnel that the defendant did what he is alleged to have done and yet the case "cannot be made" in court, the deputy DA finds himself at a distinct disadvantage. At such times, the defense attorney takes advantage of the situation by demanding a lenient sanction for the defendant. Confronted with this undesirable reality, the deputy DA concedes that a conviction and light sanction is preferable to no conviction and no sanction. Therefore, an agreement is generally reached, allowing the DA to secure a conviction and the defense attorney to obtain a lenient sentence.

The inevitable conclusion reached in analyzing the evidence factor in criminal cases is that an outcome that looks capricious or whimsical may not be. When the word *capricious* is used by certain critics of judicial sentencing policy, various connotations are intended. In the common understanding, capricious behavior (or in this instance decisionmaking) is based on a sudden change of mind caused by a whim or impulse. Nothing about the sentencing process revealed in this book even remotely resembles this definition. It is true that there are some cases (residuals) that do not conform to the standard of routine sentencing policy of a jurisdiction, such as cases in which the evidence is lacking. This does not indicate that the decisionmakers are capricious. Rather, the disposition of most cases that vary from the norm can be understood because the conditions on which the decision rests, namely evidence factors, are fortuitously distributed. For example, in two cases with similar fact situations (with two witnesses in one case and no witnesses in the other), the second case will receive a less severe disposition, because, merely by chance, there are no witnesses, and the case, therefore, cannot easily be made in court. If the evidence in both cases were the same, the sanction most likely would be the same.

Negative residuals can also result for other reasons. One situation that can be subcategorized under the evidence factor involves the availability of testimony. If, for some reason, the victim of an offense is reluctant to testify in open court, the deputy DAs bargaining position is weakened, and the defense attorney's is enhanced. For instance, if the victim of a rape or a child molest has been highly traumatized by the offense, the deputy DA must consider his weakened bargaining position and the concessions he will have to make. For if the defense attorney discovers that the victim does not want to testify in court and the testimony is vital for conviction, the defense will be able to apply pressure for a favorable plea agreement.

The deputy DAs response at that point depends on the degree of reluctance exhibited by the victim and the nature of the concessions demanded. If, in a serious offense, the defense were to ask for a commitment to Atascadero as an MDSO rather than state prison, the deputy DA might well agree, thinking that a conviction would be secured, the offender removed from the community, and the victim spared another traumatizing experience. If, however, the defense attorney were to demand probation, the deputy DA would feel compelled to insist that the victim testify so that a state prison commitment could be secured. In any event, the victim's reluctance to participate in the trial damages the deputy DAs bargaining position; often, a lighter than expected disposition is imposed and a negative residual case results.

In other situations, what appears to be a light sentence in the official records is actually a severe sanction. Such situations involve cases in which the defendant has his parole revoked, is deported, or is transferred to another state where a more severe sanction is to be imposed. In a case that would normally demand a state prison commitment, the deputy DA is often willing to settle for a plea to a minor offense and a resulting light sanction, if he firmly believes that the defendant will have his parole revoked and be returned to prison. Since the deputy DAs objective is to return the defendant to state prison, he will want to do so with a minimal expenditure of time and energy; a simple misdemeanor conviction will accomplish this goal in some cases.

There appear to be two primary determinants of positive residual cases (cases in which the sentence imposed is more severe than would be expected). The first concerns the potential dangerousness of the defendant. If the court personnel, especially the judge and the deputy DA, believe that the defendant may commit another crime in the immediate future and seriously injure an innocent victim, the court is likely to impose a sanction that is more severe than the fact situation of the immediate offense would explain.

A case example related to me by a Superior Court judge explains the court's position. The case involved a middle-aged man who was arrested and charged with one count of statutory rape. Specifically, the man had picked up a sixteen-year-old female hitchhiker and made sexual advances toward her. The man evidently used nothing beyond a "strong suggestion" that the female have sexual relations with him, and she consented to do so.

Compared with other felony sex cases in Superior Court, this appeared to be a relatively minor one. The defendant did not use force, did not exhibit a weapon, and did not make any threats of grave bodily harm. The victim admitted that the defendant employed something between a "strong suggestion" and "slight coercion" to convince her to have sexual relations with him. The victim in the case did not show any signs of physical abuse nor did she exhibit any form of psychological trauma. She did not seem to be particularly outraged that the offense had taken place. However, she was certainly angry enough to press charges and stated that her goal was to prevent the defendant from committing a similar offense in the future.

Such a case generally would warrant a relatively minor sanction, such as county jail time in conjunction with probation. In this case there was one additional and very important element—the defendant was on parole from prison, to which he had been sentenced several years earlier on a murder conviction. In the murder offense, the defendant had stabbed a young female hitchhiker who had resisted his sexual advances. The judge, considering these details, realized that the appropriate sanction would not be the typical one for the type of case at hand. Rather than being placed on probation and serving time in jail, the offender was sentenced to state prison.

This case dramatically illustrates the court's concern with the possibility that defendants will commit future dangerous acts. When the judge and the district attorney believe the probability is high that an offender will commit another serious crime, they are likely to impose a more severe sanction than would be warranted if the current offense were considered alone. This position is taken by the judge and the district attorney not only because of their fear of adverse publicity in the event that a new offense is committed but also out of genuine concern for unsuspecting and innocent citizens in the community.

A further explanation for positive residuals is related to the concern for dangerousness and the lack of evidence in previous cases involving the defendant. Some cases receive more severe dispositions than would be expected, because there is a significant amount of "hidden crime" that does not appear on the official records. Specifically, if the deputy DA and the judge believe that the defendant has been responsible for criminal offenses in the past for which he has not been convicted and sanctioned, the sentence in the current case will be more severe.

This situation may arise in one of several ways. The first possibility is that the defendant in a current case has actually been convicted of a serious crime in the past, but, because of a lack of evidence, the defense attorney was able to secure a very lenient disposition. The previously cited case of the kidnap/rapist who received six months in jail is a perfect example of this. At the time the defendant received a light sentence, everyone in the courtroom felt that he was very lucky. At the same time however, the judge and the deputy DA were undoubtedly thinking, "If that man ever comes into this court again and is convicted of even a relatively minor offense, we are going to throw the book at him and send him to state prison." Cases in which such a background is relevant do occasionally occur in Superior Court, and the official records will show a conviction for a minor crime with a severe sanction (a positive residual).

The second example of a positive residual explained by the presence of "hidden crime" also focuses on the evidence factor. If the defendant is suspected of one or more crimes that cannot be proven in court, the deputy DA must concentrate, for purposes of conviction, on the offense for which a conviction can be secured. Even if the evidence is sufficient to guarantee a conviction on only one offense, the deputy DA will encourage the judge to consider all criminality in the defendant's background when determining the sanction to be imposed.

In one case involving a series of rapes, the authorities thought they knew who was responsible, but the evidence was inconclusive, and the chance for conviction was questionable. At one point, the person suspected of the rapes was arrested on a relatively minor assault charge, for which a conviction could easily have been secured. In deciding what sanction to impose, the deputy DA convinced the judge that this defendant was the rapist they sought, and the judge committed the defendant to Atascadero as an MDSO. This relatively harsh sanction was based, as one deputy DA stated, on "an informal conviction for rape." Since "informal convictions" are not in evidence as part of official records, this case can be designated as a positive residual.

Variation in MDSO Commitments

The explanations for variation in the disposition of general (non-MDSO) sex cases can be applied to MDSO commitments as well. The variation among counties is viewed as a result of different but consistent sentencing policies; the variation within counties can be comprehended when one takes residual cases into account.

At the beginning of this book, it was asserted that there is variation among counties in commitment rates of MDSOs to Atascadero, as shown by the Bureau of Criminal Statistics data. Before an explanation is given for this variation, data from this study will be presented confirming those of the Bureau. To begin, Table 6-4 presents the county variation in formal designation of offenders as MDSOs and commitment to Atascadero; this is not the rate per 100,000 persons in the population in each jurisdiction, but the number and percentage of sex offenders granted the MDSO designation from the aggregate of all convicted sex offenders certified to the Superior Court. It will be noticed that there is, indeed, a significant variation in the MDSO commitment rate, varying from a low of 6 percent designated MDSO in San Francisco, to a high of 27 percent so designated in Orange

Table 6-4
Court Designation of MDSO or Not MDSO

	Contra Costa		San Francisco		Orange	
	N	Percent	N	Percent	N	Percent
Designated MDSO	28	17	11	6	50	27
Not designated MDSO[a]	138	83	176	94	134	73
No information	0	0	0	0	0	0
Total	166	100	187	100	184	100

[a]All cases except those found not guilty.

County, with the rate in Contra Costa County 17 percent. Accordingly, the number of offenders receiving the MDSO commitment in Orange County is 4.5 times greater than in San Francisco.

To understand this variation, two other tables should prove valuable. Table 6-5 presents the "levels of sentencing," which show the most general categories for which an offender could be sentenced. There are several things of note in this table that explain the variation in commitment rates. First of significance is the absence of any misdemeanants sent to Atascadero from San Francisco County, while the other two counties do make such commitments. Further, San Francisco had the lowest percentage of cases certified to the Superior Court as misdemeanants for the purpose of the MDSO hearing. In general, these data indicate that San Francisco County does not consider relatively minor cases as potential MDSO commitments and, instead, disposes of them at the Municipal Court level. It should be mentioned, however, that data on commitments of misdemeanants to Atascadero can be misleading. Although in general these cases are less serious than those that result in felony convictions, it is entirely possible that the deputy DA might have been able to obtain a felony conviction in these cases but bargained the case down to a misdemeanor conviction on the condition that the defendant be committed to Atascadero as an MDSO. In cases in which it appears that a commitment to Atascadero is likely, the defense attorney believes that it is preferable to be sentenced on a misdemeanor conviction rather than a felony conviction.

The next item of note in Table 6-5 is the large number and percentage of cases in San Francisco that are reduced from a felony to a misdemeanor status; this is a rare occurrence in the other two counties. The primary reason for this reduction is that such a motion frequently involves consenting male homosexuality cases (of which there is a large number in San Francisco, as discussed in a previous section). And finally, Table 6-6 presents the general disposition of both MDSO and non-MDSO cases in

Table 6-5
Levels of Sentencing

| | Contra Costa | | | | San Francisco | | | | Orange | | | |
| | MDSO | | non-MDSO | | MDSO | | non-MDSO | | MDSO | | non-MDSO | |
	N	Percent	N	Percent	N	Percent	N	Percent	N	Percent	N	Percent
None	0	0	14	10	0	0	7[a]	4	0	0	22[a]	15
Felony	23	82	94	64	11	100	93	52	44	88	91	61
Felony reduced to misdemeanor	0	0	3	2	0	0	49	27	0	0	6	4
Misdemeanor to Atascadero	5	18	0	0	0	0	0	0	6	12	0	0
Misdemeanor to Superior Court, then back to Municipal Court	0	0	25	17	0	0	7	4	0	0	10	7
Misdemeanor	0	0	11	7	0	0	24	13	0	0	21	14
No information	0	0	0	0	0	0	0	0	0	0	0	0
Total	28	100	147	100	11	100	180	100	50	100	150	101

[a]Includes Not guilty, Not guilty by reason of insanity, and Too insane to stand trial.

Table 6-6
Disposition

Disposition	Contra Costa MDSO N	Percent	Contra Costa Non-MDSO N	Percent	San Francisco MDSO N	Percent	San Francisco Non-MDSO N	Percent	Orange MDSO N	Percent	Orange Non-MDSO N	Percent
None[a]	0	0	38	26	0	0	11	6	0	0	26	17
Dismissal	0	0	0	0	0	0	0	0	0	0	0	0
Small fine	0	0	11	7	0	0	1	0.5	0	0	8	5
Suspended sentence	0	0	0	0	0	0	0	0	0	0	0	0
Probation, no supervision	0	0	3	2	0	0	1	0.5	0	0	1	0
Probation, supervision	0	0	19	13	0	0	91	51	0	0	45	30
Fine plus jail	0	0	5	3	0	0	0	0	0	0	0	0
Jail (6 months or more)	0	0	44	30	0	0	35	19	0	0	34	23
Atascadero State Hospital	28	100	3[b]	2	11	100	5[c]	3	50	100	7[d]	5
State prison	0	0	24	16	0	0	36	20	0	0	29	19
No information	0	0	0	0	0	0	0	0	0	0	0	0
Total	28	100	147	99	11	100	180	100	50	100	150	99

[a]Includes Not Guilty, and back to Lower Court as non-MDSO.
[b]Includes 1 NGI and 2 CRC.
[c]Includes 1 NGI, 2 CRC, and 2 1370 PC.
[d]Includes 1 CRC and 6 1370 P.C. (NGI = Not Guilty by Reason of Insanity; CRC = civil commitment as heroin addict; and 1370 PC = Too Insane to Stand Trial.)

each of the three jurisdictions; the significance of this table will be referred to shortly.

The variation in MDSO commitment rates can be explained primarily by the variation in the "going rates" for different types of cases. As was mentioned in Chapter 3, norms develop in each county about what constitutes the "appropriate" sanction for different types of cases, considering both the offense and the offender. The salient fact for this analysis is that on several levels, the "going rate" differs in the three jurisdictions. With the exception of consenting adult homosexuality cases, the "going rate" is slightly higher for comparable sex offense cases in Orange County than in San Francisco. There have to be more negative factors in a case in San Francisco—either in the offense itself or in the offender's background—to merit as severe a sanction as is meted out in Orange County.

This affects the MDSO commitment rate in two ways. First, consider the most serious cases—the state prison commitments. It will be noted in Table 6-6 that the commitments to state prison are approximately equal in the three counties, with 16 percent in Contra Costa, 20 percent in San Francisco, and 19 percent in Orange County. There are some cases for which the "going rate" would clearly be state prison in any of the three jurisdictions, such as rape or child molest with extreme violence, especially if the offender has priors. The presence of such cases in San Francisco was noticeable; there were several rape/homicide cases, but there were none in the other two counties. However, the cases that affected the MDSO rate were slightly less serious. In San Francisco County six of the eleven MDSO commitments, or 55 percent, were rape cases, whereas the percentage of rape cases that resulted in commitment to Atascadero from either Orange County or Contra Costa County was much smaller. One can conclude that San Francisco drew its MDSO cases from the most serious types of cases certified to the Superior Court.

The type of case that explained the real difference in commitment rates, however, was that of medium severity. When the alternatives facing the court were commitment to Atascadero or something less—either county jail or probation—Orange County was more likely to choose Atascadero, while San Francisco generally would select county jail and/or probation. For instance, in a case of mid-range seriousness such as a child molest case with no force or threat, or a rape case with no priors, the defense would bargain the case down to county jail time in San Francisco. But in Orange County where the "going rate" is somewhat higher for comparable cases, the offender would probably receive a civil commitment to Atascadero—where he would spend approximately two years, instead of a year or less in the county jail.

Support for the assertion that defense attorneys bargain down in this manner can be found in the interviews in each county. When the defense attorneys in San Francisco were asked why they did not utilize the MDSO civil commitment more often, one defense attorney summarized the consensus of opinion by saying, "Why should I, when I can bargain the case down without being forced to resort to it?" When defense attorneys in Orange County were asked why they seemed to use the MDSO commitment so frequently, one public defender answered quite clearly, saying, "Probably the most important reason why we use the civil commitment so much is that it is so hard to bargain cases any lower." The public defender meant that when the choice was between state prison and Atascadero, the defense would choose Atascadero. If the public defenders had the choice of bargaining the cases down to county jail, they would undoubtedly do so. Since the "going rate" is relatively high, they must use the MDSO commitment in a comparatively high percentage of cases—cases that might well have meant county jail sentences in San Francisco.

It should be reiterated that official data can be deceptive and that the best way to evaluate the "going rate" for different types of cases is to become thoroughly familiar with the offense severity gradient and the sanctioning gradient in each county. A qualitative approach must be utilized: the researcher must attempt to "know" the "going rate" in much the same way that a good defense attorney knows exactly what to ask for and what he can expect for various types of cases. This was essentially the method used here—that is, the researcher immersed himself in the value system of each of the three counties and acquired a thorough knowledge of the cases.

Based on this detailed knowledge of the cases in each county, it can be stated with assurance that Orange County did not have 4.5 times as many "MDSO types" in any clinical or psychiatric sense. What Orange County had was 4.5 times as many offenders for whom, by Orange County standards, the "going rate" was from two to three years of incarceration and sequestering—without regard to any psychiatric abnormalities.

Two final comments must be made before the discussion of variation in commitment rates is completed. First, it is true that the defendant populations compared were not exactly the same: there were more minor cases in San Francisco consisting primarily of consenting adult homosexuality cases. Orange County had a higher concentration of serious cases, since it is their policy to certify to the Superior Court only serious cases. Consequently, there is a greater likelihood of having MDSO type cases in Orange County, which means a higher percentage of commitments to Atascadero, although this does not explain the magnitude of the difference. Furthermore, this would only influence the percentage of sex cases sent to Atascadero as MDSOs and not the commitment rate per 100,000 persons in each jurisdiction.

While it has been asserted that sentencing policies and "going rates" vary among counties, this study found that the similarities in the three counties were certainly greater than the differences. The previous analysis of variation within counties and the presence of residual cases among general sex cases can be applied to the consideration of variation in MDSO commitments within counties. This is of less importance than the variation of MDSO commitment policies among counties, but it should be mentioned.

Not all MDSO commitments are based on the "going rate" for different types of cases in each county. There are some cases in which the MDSO commitment is a residual case, either negative or positive. If the case is considered to merit a state prison commitment, yet the evidence is not strong enough to guarantee conviction at a jury trial, the defense attorney might bargain the case down to an MDSO commitment rather than face the possibility of a state prison commitment for his client. The defense attorney might even try to bargain the case down to county jail, but his success would depend on the deputy DAs perceptions of the weakness of the evidence and the seriousness of the case.

It is possible for an MDSO commitment to be a positive residual as well. For instance, if the court were truly convinced that a person convicted of a minor child molest was a potential kidnapper, that defendant might well receive a commitment to Atascadero even though his current crime would not warrant it.

Before this chapter is concluded, one final point should be made about residual cases and the paradox in the administration of justice that such cases illuminate. A difference in the extent of residual cases among counties was found, with San Francisco having slightly fewer than either Contra Costa or Orange Counties. There are two possible explanations why these two counties, especially Orange County, have more internal variation in sentencing.

In Orange and Contra Costa Counties there is more emphasis on and faith in the "individualized justice model": the courts in these two jurisdictions pay relatively more attention to the characteristics of the offender than does the court in San Francisco. Second, there is a very real economic factor. Orange County, in particular, has more time, money, and resources to devote to a consideration of the "nonessential" elements of the case. San Francisco County, on the other hand, spends less time evaluating the psychiatric reports, presentence probation reports, and other information submitted by the court assistants; there is a tendency in that county to focus directly on the facts of the offense. The resulting paradox is that San Francisco County, the justice organization that is the most overworked and understaffed and spends the least time and money per case, is the organization that dispenses the most fair and equitable justice—if one's conception of justice is the uniform application of sanctions for similar offenses. If one adopts a "standardized justice model" and emphasizes punishing the crime rather than the criminal, the justice administered in San Francisco more closely meets that standard. There, the bargains struck between the two adversaries and agreed to by the judge are more likely to be routinized in policy and administered with efficiency.

Notes

1. For a general review of disparities in sentencing policy, see Peter W. Low, "Inconsistencies within the Sentencing Structure," *National Commission on Reform of the Federal Criminal Law,* (Jan. 8, 1968), pp. 27-36; Edward Green, *Judicial Attitudes in Sentencing,* London: Macmillan and Co., 1961, pp. 8-20; Frank Remington and Donald J. Newman, "The Highland Park Institute on Sentencing Disparity," *Federal Probation* 26 (1962):4-9; Talbot Smith, "The Sentencing Council and the Problem of Disproportionate Sentences," *Federal Probation* 27 (1963):6-9; James Steele and Donald Barlett, "Justice in Philadelphia," *The New Republic* (May 26, 1973):19.

2. Marvin E. Frankel, *Criminal Sentences: Law without Order,* New York: Hill and Wang, 1972, pp. 7, 8, 84.

3. Steele and Barlett, "Justice in Philadelphia," p. 23.

4. Frankel, *Criminal Sentences: Law without Order,* p. 11. He states: "This means we must reject individual distinctions—discriminations, that is—unless they can be justified by relevant tests capable of formulation and application with sufficient objectivity to ensure that the results will be more than the idiosyncratic ukases of particular officials, judges or others."

5. Howard Becker et al. *Boys in White: Student Culture in Medical School,* Chicago: University of Chicago Press, 1961, p. 22.

7

Conclusion: The Criminalization of the Civil Commitment

The primary purpose of this book is to assess and determine the essential distinctions between the civil and the criminal sanction—specifically the civil and the criminal commitment. This assessment and determination is placed against the theoretical positions discussed in Chapter 1, which outlined (1) the procedures employed in the use of either sanction and (2) their substantive effects. This task would have been easier in the early history of civil commitment law;[1] the differences between the two sanctions in both substance and procedure then were quite obvious. The situation became a bit more complex as quasi-criminal commitments emerged and blurred the lines that defined the two legal systems.

Although the use of the civil commitment continues for certain classes of individuals, this book suggests that any presumptions about the procedural and substantive differences between the civil and the criminal sanctions do not hold. Given the current state of civil commitment law, the essential distinctions between the two forms of sanctions are negligible. On both substantive and procedural grounds, the type of commitment formally designated as "civil" has gradually become more "criminal" in nature; in short, there has been a "criminalization of the civil commitment."

These basic changes in the nature of the civil commitment are taking place in the daily operations of the trial court commitment proceedings as well as in the decisions handed down by the appellate courts. With this in mind, the final tasks are (1) to employ the empirical data gathered to draw conclusions about the specific relationship of the two commitments for sex offenders, (2) to discuss policy recommendations that draw from the conclusions, and (3) to correlate the research with current legal trends involving other types of civil and quasi-criminal commitments throughout the country.

The MDSO Civil Commitment

Whether one adheres to the "procedural" or "substantive" school of theoretical distinctions, the MDSO civil commitment has been "criminalized" to such an extent that it is now very difficult to discern the difference between it and the criminal sanction. The proponents of the procedural school argue that the essential distinction is in the nature of the legal procedure; criminal sanctions are governed by criminal procedure and civil sanctions by civil procedure.[2] This study demonstrates that the criminal and civil procedures employed in sanctioning convicted sex offenders are essentially the same. There are several reasons for making this assertion. First, the overall tenor of the MDSO civil commitment is criminal in nature, because the civil commitment proceedings are administered in a court of criminal actions, namely the Criminal Master Calendar Court. Further, the court decisionmakers work almost exclusively with criminal cases—the judge is generally the Criminal Master Calendar Judge, and the participating district attorneys and defense attorneys work primarily on criminal matters.

At the same time there is great similarity between the specific legal procedures used in the disposition of criminal cases and those used in MDSO civil cases. In the first instance, civil proceedings cannot be initiated until the criminal defendant is found guilty of one or more of the charges alleged against him. It is also mandated by statute that a defendant on the civil matter must be accorded most of the constitutionally guaranteed safeguards available to criminal defendants, including the right to confront and cross-examine prosecution witnesses, the right to introduce evidence and testimony on his own behalf, the right to have a defense counsel at all stages of the civil proceedings, the right to an open hearing, and the right to a trial by jury on the issue of whether he is an MDSO. In addition to the statutory guarantees, the California appellate courts have provided additional procedural protections. Not only does the MDSO defendant have a right to a jury trial, but this civil trial is to be conducted according to criminal procedural rules, that is, an unanimous verdict instead of a three-fourths majority, as in other civil jury trials.[3] Moreover, the standard of proof is not a "preponderance of evidence" as in other civil trials, but rather proof "beyond a reasonable doubt."[4] The California Supreme Court has thus held that persons subject to the MDSO proceedings are entitled to the full panoply of the protections of the due process clause.[5]

There are further examples illustrating the similarity between the MDSO proceedings and criminal proceedings. If the Superior Court judge decides to impose a criminal penalty after the civil proceedings have been terminated, and the criminal proceedings are reinstated, the time served by the defendant in the mental institution must be applied to his new criminal sentence. This provision makes little sense if one considers earlier appellate court decisions in this area, for it has been held that the condition of being afflicted with sexual psychopathy should not be considered a mitigating circumstance.[6] In theory, civil commitment for the treatment of an illness in a mental institution should not affect the duration of his criminal *punishment.* Credit for time served has been granted by the legislature which has come to realize that the MDSO commitment to Atascadero is strikingly similar in both nature and operation to its criminal commitment alternatives.

Members of the substantive school offer the proposition that what distinguishes the civil from the criminal sanction is its substantive effect, either formal moral condemnation or punishment. To some theorists in the substantive school, the principal distinguishing issue is blameworthiness.[7] Specifically, the purpose of a criminal sanction is to induce loss of status for the offender by imposing the community's moral condemnation; the civil sanction does not seek to induce a loss of status and is not supposed to be associated with moral blameworthiness. However, a thorough analysis of the Superior Court sentencing practices reveals no discernible difference in the attitudes of the court personnel with regard to the moral blameworthiness of persons subject to the MDSO civil commitment as opposed to the alternative criminal commitments; persons receiving either sanction are viewed in essentially the same way by the court decisionmakers. This general attitude reflects how rarely court personnel make moral judgments about convicted defendants. Instead, their concerns are more practical and mundane, such as sequestering dangerous persons, clearing the court's calendar, securing the "best possible" disposition, and imposing a sanction reflective of the "going rate" in that jurisdiction. As a result, persons under a civil commitment are judged as being no less blameworthy than offenders in state prison or county jail.

Other substantive theorists evaluate the sanction itself and consider whether it is primarily perceived as punishment or treatment;[8] the civil commitment is said to treat while the criminal commitment is supposed to punish. This distinction follows logically from the proposition that the proper focus of the criminal law should be on the *act* perpetrated by the offender, as opposed to the civil concern with the individual's *personal needs*. Thus, the involuntary MDSO civil commitment adopts the medical model; the restrained person is viewed as having an illness, which requires treatment. The restraint, however, is to last only until the illness has been cured or until the individual is no longer a danger to society. The key variable in determining the length of incarceration is supposed to be the extent of the mental illness or the degree of difficulty encountered in obtaining a cure.

Rather than wide variation in the length of incarceration reflecting seriousness of mental illness, courtroom experience reveals a relatively standard amount of time spent at Atascadero for all MDSOs sent there. This finding supports the argument that MDSOs are sent to Atascadero to fulfill the requirement of being incarcerated for a given period of time. Whether or not their illness might be cured with a shorter or longer commitment is not given thoughtful consideration. Pragmatically, the court, responding to the defendant's pathology or degree of dangerousness, prefers to employ a sanction that appropriately corresponds to the amount of time the court thinks the defendant should be incarcerated.

Because the medical model of providing treatment until the illness is cured does not apply in the daily Superior Court sentencing process, one must look elsewhere for evidence of the court personnel's priorities. Countless interviews and extensive statistical analyses have revealed that the length of incarceration is the predominant consideration in imposing sanctions—either civil or criminal. The court personnel employ an identical ranking system to assess the severity of the case by considering the details of the offense and the characteristics of the offender. Concern is initially focused on the quantity and quality of available evidence needed to secure a conviction or an acquittal—the "triability" of the case. After the assessments are completed, identical plea bargaining strategies take place while the court personnel select a sanction that matches the "going rate" for any given case. Whereas the civil sanction is supposed to imply a consideration of the needs of the individual and the criminal sanction focuses on the details of the offense, in practice this distinction is not made.

Finally, an assessment of the substantive effect of the two types of commitments reveals no significant difference, except that the MDSO civil commitment is felt to be a more severe sanction than a criminal commitment to county jail and a *less* severe sanction than a criminal commitment to state prison. These severities are judged mainly by the length of commitment: persons sentenced to the county jail cannot be sent for more than one year; those incarcerated in a state prison are likely to spend three or more years; others committed to Atascadero are generally institutionalized for approximately two years.

Except for the time differential, the court personnel view a civil commitment to a maximum security mental institution essentially the same as a commitment to a maximum security penal institution. Both commitments accomplish the identical purpose—the sequestering of a person in a secure institution to prevent further harm for a certain period of time. The court personnel sincerely hope that some successful therapy takes place at the mental institution, just as they would like it to take place in a penal institution. Most of them, however, are not optimistic about the effectiveness of therapy at Atascadero.

The function of the civil commitment in providing the courts with an additional alternative on the sanctioning gradient has been observed through an intensive study of court records. Situations occurred repeatedly in which an offender received probation upon conviction for his first offense; as the number of new offenses increased, so did the severity of the sanction. After one or two offenses for which probation did not prove sufficient, the offender was committed to the county jail. If new offenses followed, the person was often civilly committed to a mental institution. If offenses occurred after release from Atascadero, the offender was committed to state prison. The cumulative sanctioning effect in sentencing sex offenders became apparent, and the MDSO civil commitment to Atascadero was simply one more stepping stone on the path to state prison. A comparison of the theoretical sanctioning gradient, compared to the everyday operations of the court, is illustrated in Figure 7-1, showing how the two systems are merging within the total sanctioning system of the Superior Court.

Perhaps the most revealing example of the relationship between the MDSO civil commitment and the alternative criminal commitments can be derived from an analysis of recent adaptations in Superior Court organizational policy, principally in Orange County. The adaptation at the Superior Court was initiated originally by a gradual policy change at Atascadero State Hospital. As mentioned above, the MDSOs at Atascadero were generally institutionalized for about two years before being returned to the Superior Court. If the MDSOs were given an "A" recommendation from the hospital stating they were cured or no longer a danger, there was a 92 percent chance that the Superior Court judge would grant probation and impose no further penalty.[9] Gradually, because of the staff's medical and humanitarian efforts to reintegrate the patient into the community as soon as possible,[10] the average length of incarceration declined from two years to approximately one year.

The Superior Court's response to this change in policy confirmed the impression that Atascadero is simply one more penal institution to sequester offenders. Since offenders at Atascadero have had their time reduced, the Superior Court has begun to impose additional criminal penalties. At the present time, if the medical staff at Atascadero returns an offender with an "A" recommendation, the court will impose a criminal penalty and sentence him to county jail for a year to compensate for the year or so that he will no longer spend at Atascadero. Such action tellingly illustrates that if the "going rate" for certain cases is violated because of outside factors, the court feels compelled to maintain its norms by utilizing other resources. If the court feels that certain types of offenders should be incarcerated for approximately two years, any type of commitment or institution is sufficient. The basic consideration is the amount of time served, whether the label is civil or criminal.

When an organization is faced with an uncertain and fluctuating environment, there are alternatives to remaining passive or adjusting internal policy. An organization can take a more active role in its environment and, by introducing structural changes, begin to modify the very nature of that environment. The Superior Court's adaptiveness in this respect indicates that the court is similar to other organizations—it is able to change its policies to fit what appears to be a capricious environment. For the court to fulfill its goals, it must act in a manner that, as Thompson states, is characteristic of all organizations:

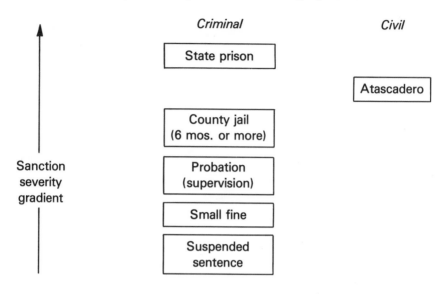

In Theory: Two Separate Sanctioning Systems

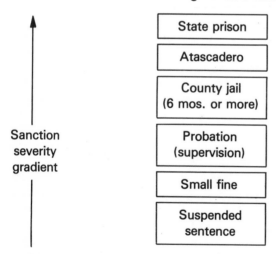

In Practice: One Indistinguishable Sanctioning System

Figure 7-1. Sanctioning Systems.

When the task environment becomes dynamic rather than stable, new complications arise for the organization. Standardized response rules are inadequate, for the organization faces contingencies as well as constraints. It must determine when and how to act, and its cues must be taken from the task environment.[11]

Because the court's goals were not being met by the staff at Atascadero, other alternatives were employed to ensure that the routine sanctioning procedures were not disrupted.

This process is primarily evident at the Superior Court in Orange County. Previously the Superior Court and Atascadero State Hospital were two distinct organizations functioning in an autonomous manner; now they are in a transitional stage toward becoming coparticipants in the meting out of sanctions. Specifically, ties have been established between some of the staff decisionmakers at Atascadero and some attorneys at the Superior Court, particularly public defenders. This communication was established by attorneys who wanted to increase the probability of securing a specific disposition for their clients.

Securing favorable dispositions for their clients is a primary concern of the defense attorneys. When the alternative is a criminal commitment to state prison, the defense attorney will advocate the civil commitment. When, as stated in Chapter 4, the defense attorney is seeking to influence the deputy DA and the judge, psychiatric testimony and recommendations for committing the client as an MDSO are solicited from staff members at Atascadero. The attorneys contact sympathetic personnel and play on their fears that a "patient" is likely to be committed to state prison. Staff members are requested to write letters stating that the prognosis for the defendant is good if he receives treatment instead of punishment and that, in essence, the defendant is a good candidate for the MDSO commitment.

Another situation in which the defense attorney seeks the aid of the Atascadero staff is in securing a release at the "appropriate" time. After a defendant's commitment to Atascadero, the time of his return to court is critical, considering the court's interest in satisfying the normative requirements of the "going rate." If he is returned at an early date, the court is likely to impose an additional criminal sanction. It may be county jail if the release from Atascadero is seen as only slightly premature, or it may be state prison if the release is considered excessively early. To avoid this undesirable consequence, the defense attorney tries to make certain that the offender remains at Atascadereo the "appropriate" amount of time—a period short enough to make the commitment more desirable than state prison but long enough to satisfy the "going rate" standards of the court.

The interaction of the judge and the two adversaries in the judge's chambers provides evidence that the key decisionmakers are very often sensitive to the appropriate level of sanction for each type of case before the sentencing decision is actually made. For instance, in one rape case in Orange County, the defendant could reasonably have expected to be sent to either state prison or Atascadero. The defense attorney had succeeded in convincing the deputy DA to accept the defendant's commitment to Atascadero instead of state prison. However, the offense was a serious one, and the deputy DA felt that the defendant should be incarcerated for a substantial period of time. After reluctantly agreeing to the defendant's commitment to Atascadero, the deputy DA turned to the public defender and said: "You had just better make sure that he doesn't get out too soon." Implied in that statement was the threat that the deputy DA would insist on an additional criminal commitment for the defendant if he were returned too "early," even with an "A" recommendation.

The judge in this particular case was also inclined to send the defendant to state prison. When he saw that the deputy DA was willing to accept the MDSO commitment, he decided not to object. However, immediately after the judge consented to the MDSO commitment, he added, "I want to make it perfectly clear to you [public defender] and to the defendant that if he comes back from Atascadero in a relatively short period of time, even with an "A" recommendation, no promises or no deals have been made about what type of disposition he might get upon his return." The judge insisted that this statement be put on the official record in open court.

To explain the extensive use of the MDSO civil commitment by the Orange County Superior Court, consideration must be given to the reciprocal relationship between two factors. On the one hand Atascadero is utilized more often than in the other two counties because of the requirements of the "going-rate"; that is, there are more cases for which the appropriate sanction is deemed to be two years of institutionalization. A deeper explanation is that Atascadero is utilized extensively because the attorneys have succeeded in eliminating much of the uncertainty of that type of commitment. They are able to influence, within limits, the length of incarceration of some defendants.[12] In the other two counties, the MDSO civil commitment is employed if necessary, but it is avoided whenever possible. The length of stay at Atascadero can be presumed but not with enough certainty to meet the needs of some attorneys. For court decisionmakers, it would be desirable if a commitment to state prison or Atascadero were the same as a commitment to county jail with a fixed length of time determined by the court. The differing use of the MDSO civil commitment, then, is related to another organizational axiom; organizational alternatives are utilized proportional to the capability of the decisionmakers to minimize the margin of error and to decrease the uncertainty of their decisions.

Establishing communication channels between the Superior Court and Atascadero as a strategy for minimizing uncertainty also raises the issue of organizational boundaries. Where to draw a distinct boundary line around an organization, especially when the organizational structure and environment are dynamic, has always been a problem for organizational theorists.[13] It is especially well represented by the relationship of Atascadero State Hospital to the Superior Court, and perhaps other criminal justice organizations: It is difficult to determine whether Atascadero should be considered an organization separate from the Superior Court or an extension of it.

The Superior Court and Atascadero might reasonably be considered totally separate and distinct organizations, maintained by two separate branches of state government, and each with a different set of assumptions about its purpose, and each striving to meet different goals. Yet some of the staff members at Atascadero, because of their compliance with the requests of the Superior Court attorneys, are functioning in such a way as to compromise their professional ethics and goals by assisting the Superior Court in fulfilling *its* goals. By so doing, some of the staff members might appear to be part of the sanctioning process of the Superior Court.

The question of organizational boundaries depends, of course, on which definition is chosen. Certain conclusions logically follow from consideration of Etzioni's definition: "We follow the narrower definition and see as participants [of an organization] all actors who are high on at least one of the three dimensions of participation: involvement, subordination, and performance."[14] If one accepts this view, a transition period in interorganizational boundaries and relationships is being witnessed. For the Superior Court to minimize uncertainty in the consequences of its decisions, it has tried to adjust as any other organization would, by attempting to eliminate the distinction between itself and its environment. Thompson articulates this general organizational theory.

When the purpose and cause/effect understanding are present, the basic threat to organizational success lies in interdependence with an environment which may be uncooperative. Under these conditions, organizations try to achieve predictability and self-control through regulation of transactions at their boundaries—through negotiation, by buffering, or by varying their own activities to match fluctuations in the environment. The location of discretionary positions and the number and nature of the structural units at the boundaries of the organization are determined by the need to regulate boundary transactions. If these cannot be regulated satisfactorily, the organization tries to move its boundaries—to incorporate or encircle unreliable units.[15]

It would be inaccurate to assert and unrealistic to assume that the boundaries of the Superior Court could encompass Atascadero State Hospital as part of the court organization. However, it is fair to state that certain aspects of interorganizational reciprocity are becoming so extensive that the MDSO civil commitment can best be understood as an alternative criminal commitment and that Atascadero can accurately be depicted as an extension of the criminal justice system.

Policy Recommendations for the MDSO Law

Since the empirical evidence has revealed abuses in the administration of the MDSO civil commitment statute, certain policy recommendations are justified. When a policy change for a particular statute is considered, three options are patent: One, repeal the statute because it is not functioning satisfactorily; two, retain it because it is effective; three, revise certain parts of the law, while repealing the abusive aspects. Recommending any of these changes is difficult because of the ramifications that the new policy might have for the defendants, as well as for both the criminal justice and mental health systems. Not only are there legal, social, and ethical issues to consider, but the recommendations should be feasible and desirable. With this in mind, this book supports the third option. Before justifying this recommendation, however, an explanation is in order to discriminate against the other two options.

The primary argument for *not* repealing the law is based on the realization that such an action would result directly in severe physical and psychological harm for several hundred persons currently designated MDSOs, as well as those who might be so classified in the future. The reason for such severe negative repercussions lies in the nature of the MDSO cases. As explained in Chapter 6, the vast majority of offenders receiving the MDSO designation were convicted of felonies, which, according to the "going rate" dictates of the Superior Court, require that they be removed from the community for approximately two years. Since probation is not a likely choice, the sentencing alternatives are therefore limited to Atascadero or state prison. If the MDSO law were repealed, state prison would be the single option for commitment.

A commitment to state prison would be particularly undesirable for MDSOs with generally passive and weak personalities, typified by child molesters, who are at the lowest end of the prison inmate hierarchy. If they are committed to state prison, more aggressive prisoners could abuse them, a circumstance that is less likely at Atascadero. Consequently, a commitment to Atascadero can be seen as a relatively humane sanctioning alternative for the defendant. In this situation, the current MDSO law provides a commitment to an institution with a relatively tolerant atmosphere where these offenders can not only serve their time without threatening their basic rights, but at the same time satisfy the retributive demands of society.

The quality of time served is not the only factor; the quantity of time is also of great importance. Persons committed to Atascadero undergo a shorter period of institutionalization than if they had been sent to state prison for a comparable offense. In most cases, the defendant and the defense attorney will prefer a commitment to Atascadero rather than state prison because of the time saved. In this way, the current law definitely benefits the defendant. For humanitarian reasons, it serves no useful purpose to repeal a law that would spare more persons from being committed to prison for longer periods of time.

Although the MDSO law should be retained, it does not follow that it should remain intact; there are some sex offenders who are not best served by the current statute. There are offenders who would remain institutionalized longer under the MDSO civil commitment than would be the case if they had been processed under the standard criminal commitment. These include misdemeanants whose criminal punishment would be a maximum of twelve months in the county jail, but under the MDSO law, they are subjected to one day to life indeterminate commitments. Even though the civil commitment to Atascadero is theoretically indeterminate, the statistics show that the average length of the misdemeanant's commitment ranges from twelve to eighteen months or even longer in certain cases. The prospect of a longer commitment disguised as therapy offers little consolation to an offender who regards additional time in an institution as punishment, with negligible therapeutic advantages.

Although no incidence of widespread abuse was uncovered here, it is certain that some abuse *has* taken place in the past,[16] *may* take place in the jurisdictions not examined in this study, and *could* take place in the future. Therefore, persons involved in the formulation of policy should be concerned with the potential for abuse and revise accordingly. These revisions should affect those minor cases in which the defendant is committed to a mental hospital for a longer period of time than he would have served if criminally committed. Since the first two policy recommendations have been argued against, the third option to merely revise certain parts of the law serves the conflicting needs of the defendants and society.

Perhaps the best way to revise the MDSO civil commitment would be to make it a "voluntary" commitment, i.e., no person could be committed to Atascadero without his consent. This could be accomplished by restricting the raising of the MDSO issue to the defense just as criminal insanity is raised only by the defense. This statutory change would not inordinately affect the administration of the law, since the vast majority of individuals involved do in fact choose such a commitment. If a person could choose between Atascadero and county jail and felt that time in a hospital was unnecessarily long or the therapy inadequate, he should be able to refuse the therapeutic confinement and opt for the criminal punishment.

If replacing an involuntary commitment with a voluntary one may be too radical a change for some members of the legislature, another alternative is available. It would substantially provide that the duration of the civil commitment could not exceed the statutory maximum of the criminal commitment. This revision would not dramatically change the administration of the law, since the vast majority of the cases are felonies, and most offenders spend less time on the civil commitment than on a comparable felony commitment to state prison. The change in the law would again affect those who might have been required to spend less time in the county jail but find themselves incarcerated for a longer period of time under the civil commitment. Even though a person could still be involuntarily committed to Atascadero as a MDSO, he could not spend more than a year in that institution if he were a misdemeanant. It might be noted that there is some legal precedent for this proposal in the field of juvenile law.[17] If, at the termination of the year commitment, it is feared that the person is still dangerous to others, the standard civil commitment proceedings for the mentally ill would prove adequate to protect the community.

A final recommendation concerns the exit procedure from Atascadero. Under the current statute, the Atascadero staff is not required to assess a patient's recovery or to send a progress report to the committing court. Even with current periodic reviews, a patient can remain there for years without the court learning of his mental state. A personal evaluation should be mandated by statute, as in the case of a person committed to the Department of Corrections. The staff members should review the progress of the patient, and the superintendent of the hospital should submit a required report to the court stating why the person should not be released. If the superintendent cannot justify the commitment, the patient should be returned to the court.

In conclusion, all the policy recommendations flow directly from the analysis of the administration of sanctions at the Superior Court level. The significant findings are (1) that the MDSO civil commitment serves as an alternative criminal commitment, despite its civil designation, and (2) that the main focus of policy recommendations should be to make the statute more reflective of that reality.

Other Civil Commitments

Although this study has been specifically concerned with the sentencing of sex offenders at the trial court level in California, some of the conclusions can be generalized and applied to other civil and quasi-criminal commitment statutes throughout the country. The principal finding is that the MDSO civil commitment has become increasingly similar to, and interchangeable with, its criminal commitment counterparts. This trend can be detected in the functioning of other civil and quasi-criminal commitment statutes and is evident on two levels: through the routine imposition of sanctions at the trial court level and through the decisions handed down by the appellate courts. This will be the subject of the remainder of this chapter.

An analysis of the daily operations of the Superior Court has revealed that organizational pressures on the trial court decisionmakers discourage them from distinguishing between those people who need punishment and those who need treatment. The same is true with the administration of other civil commitment statutes; the civil/criminal dichotomy appears no longer viable. Rather, the court's concern is with *control,* no matter what technical, legal label is applied. Consideration of the individual characteristics of the defendant is not a common occurrence. The theoretical underpinnings of therapy and treatment are overshadowed by considerations of how to dispose of cases while controlling deviants. To meet this end, civil commitments, in all their statutory variations, are being used increasingly as criminal commitment alternatives and play an integral part in the total sanctioning system of the trial court.

In addition to the empirical evidence presented in this study, other data suggest that the civil commitment is interchangeable with its criminal commitment alternatives. For instance, after California revised its civil commitment law for the mentally ill and incompetent (making the criteria for commitment more stringent and therefore more difficult to affect), two studies documented a shift in the attitudes and actions of the legal functionaries, resulting in fewer persons being processed through the mental health system and more into the criminal justice system. One study recorded an increased number of arrests and the introduction of mentally disordered persons into the criminal justice system *after* they had refused a referral to a mental health agency.[18] The other study found that an alternative *civil* commitment was used with greater frequency to control persons who were *first* arrested and *then* found too insane to stand trial on the criminal charges.[19] They subsequently were civilly committed to a mental institution under a different statutory provision with the criminal charges still pending. Both these studies lend support to the assertion that the mental health and criminal justice systems operate as one large and overlapping reciprocal system for the social control of deviant behavior.

This increased use of the civil commitment to replace the criminal sanction at the trial court level can be expected to continue as the civil commitment is transformed from a sanction shrouded in mystery and uncertainty to one for which the consequences are fairly well understood and quite predictable. The most significant reason for this change has to do with the response of the court decisionmakers to certain modifications in the trial court's organization and functioning. Previously, in many Superior Courts, all types of legal actions were randomly assigned to the many different departments of the Court. The judge in each department would have to handle a wide variety of cases, ranging from probate to civil commitment or from personal injury to criminal. One of the effects of this ''Individual Calendar'' system of assigning cases was that the judges, and the attorneys assigned to the courtrooms, were not able to develop a high level of expertise about a particular type of case. The dispositions, particularly criminal and civil commitments, often seemed inconsistent and appeared to reflect the personal biases or idiosyncracies of individual judges.

New developments in court organization and functioning have significantly altered the way sanctions are imposed. First, many trial courts have switched from an "Individual Calendar" system of assigning and hearing cases to a "Master Calendar" system, which allows specialization in each court department. Each judge hears primarily one type of case, e.g., probate, juvenile, or domestic. There is also a special department for criminal matters, called the "Criminal Master Calendar Court," and in many instances there are departments for civil commitments. This specialization has resulted in greater judicial awareness of the numerous sanctioning alternatives available for each type of case as well as greater routinization of the sanctioning process.

A concomitant change pertains to the growing specialization of the deputy district attorneys and the public defenders assigned to the various departments and to their greater role in the sanctioning process. As the two adversaries begin to specialize to a greater extent, they come to understand more clearly the practical consequences of the various sanctioning alternatives and make more informed decisions about the most desirable dispositions. With weekly or monthly meetings in their offices, the transfer of knowledge among the trial deputies about the relative merits of the various sanctioning alternatives, including civil commitments, is certain to take place. As the civil commitment and its ramifications are better understood in the context of the criminal sanctioning process, it will be advocated more often as a criminal commitment alternative to satisfy the refined sanctioning requirements of the court.

In conjunction with the increased knowledge of the consequences of the civil commitment, the deputy district attorneys and public defenders are becoming more instrumental in the sanctioning process per se. As the backlog of cases grows, trial courts have turned more and more to plea bargaining, the consequence of which is that judges act in a supervisory role over the adversaries, who actually decide the sanction to be imposed. As this has occurred, the trial attorneys have become exceedingly interested in the nature and consequences of the full range of sanctioning alternatives. The public defenders have made a particularly strong effort to find sanctioning alternatives to the standard criminal commitment, and the district attorneys have had to respond by seeking out expert information to enable them to argue intelligently against the defense counsel in court. Increased plea bargaining among attorneys has also meant that it is they, and not the judges, who control the sanctioning process; consequently, through routine bargaining procedures, the sanctions meted out are more predictable and consistent.

Finally, as civil commitments become acceptable sanctioning alternatives in the eyes of the court personnel, communication will be improved between the court decisionmakers and treatment "programs," which are technically outside the criminal justice system. As with the MDSO statute, the ties between the attorneys and the program officials are important for two reasons: to gain their clients' admittance and to obtain their release. A substantial amount of time and energy is expended by the court personnel and the program officials in trying to convince the judge of the worthiness of these programs. This is especially true of drug-related programs, which are constantly seeking to expand their operations. Not only do staff people inform the judge that the defendant is a good candidate for "treatment," but also they are quick to point out the requirements for the defendant's acceptance into the program, his responsibilities as a resident, and the specific length of his supervised stay.

The expanding relationship between the court personnel and the treatment programs will also affect the release of the person, once admitted. Since most of the programs outside the criminal justice system seek to perpetuate and to enlarge their operations, concessions are made to the criminal justice personnel, who, in turn, are willing to advocate their usage. The primary concern of the court personnel is either that the amount of time the client is to remain in the program be routinely fixed or that it be subject to the influence of the court decisionmakers. In either case, there will be greater predictability on the part of the court personnel, and, therefore, these programs, whether civil or criminal, will be increasingly used as sanctioning alternatives in the future.

The assertion that the criminalization of the civil commitment is taking place at the jurisprudential level can be supported by a brief review of recent appellate and Supreme Court decisions (at both the federal and state levels). In 1972 the U.S. Supreme Court indicated its surprise at the paucity of cases involving civil commitments that had come up for review and seemed to suggest that more cases should be appealed.[20] Litigants have apparently taken the Court's suggestion seriously, since a greater number of civil and quasi-criminal commitment cases are being appealed and reviewed. As a result, the appellate courts throughout the country have paid significantly greater attention to these types of cases, and some truly landmark decisions have been handed down.

The noticeable trend of granting greater procedural protections and civil liberties to mental patients and criminal defendants under the civil commitment grew out of the same underlying ideology as the civil rights legislation and litigation of the 1960s. Into the 1970s there developed what has become a full-scale effort to secure rights and privileges for persons facing or under a civil commitment. It is probable that this trend will continue, as the courts become (1) more realistic about the limited abilities of institutional psychiatry and of behavioral sciences to treat effectively mental illness and (2) more aware of the lack of adequate resources for treatment.[21] The courts are recognizing that a civil commitment to a mental institution entails a "massive curtailment of liberty"[22] and carries with it a stigma that is equal to, if not exceeding, a criminal commitment to a penal institution.[23]

This last factor has been so crucial in recent appellate court decisions that it can be viewed as the underlying principle on which the courts have granted additional rights to mental patients and criminal defendants subject to the civil commitment. The courts have begun to reject the old civil-criminal labeling game, in which a civil commitment meant the loss of procedural protections and frequently led to additional deprivation of liberty as well. The assumption that being incarcerated in a mental institution for care and treatment is somehow less oppressive than being jailed for punishment finally is being questioned by the courts. As the Supreme Court stated in the famous *Gault* decision: ". . . [C]ommitment is a deprivation of liberty. It is incarceration against one's will, whether it is called 'criminal' or 'civil.' "[24]

Certain trends in appellate and Supreme Court decisionmaking can be detected by comparing the relative proportion of different types of cases decided over time. One obvious trend is the Court's increased interest in criminal law and procedure over the last seventy-five years or so.[25] The thrust of these cases has been to provide more and more procedural safeguards to criminal defendants, particularly through the application of the fourteenth amendment to state criminal proceedings. Casting aside the more narrow legal arguments, the courts subscribe to the principle that the loss of liberty is the most severe sanction in our society (next to capital punishment), and therefore every procedural protection must be accorded to persons threatened with the loss of that liberty through legal action. From this close judicial scrutiny of the inadequacies of the criminal process, the appellate courts have also become aware of that class of persons that traditionally has been proceeded against criminally but that is now proceeded against civilly. Guided by the precedent of criminal law, the courts gradually have begun to accord these appellants the same rights and privileges (both procedural and substantive) as persons proceeding through the criminal process.

To comprehend the court-mandated trend toward the criminalization of the civil commitment, a brief review of some of the leading cases is in order. It is instructive to begin with a review of the quasi-criminal commitment cases pertaining to procedural due process, since these are the cases that have been given the most attention and that were the cutting edge for appellate review of involuntary civil commitment laws. This review is only presented to point out a trend and is not intended to document and analyze appellate court decisions in great depth.

Procedural safeguards have always been of central importance in

Anglo-American law, although the quality of those safeguards varies depending on the level of potential loss to the parties in a legal action. A hierarchy of procedural rights has developed, in which civil proceedings of little consequence have the fewest protections, whereas criminal proceedings involving the greatest deprivation of liberty have the most rigid procedural safeguards. As Justice Brennen has stated: ". . . the more important the rights at stake the more important must be the procedural safeguards surrounding those rights."[26]

The first quasi-criminal commitment legislation reviewed by the courts pertained to juvenile delinquents and the operation of the juvenile justice system, which allowed severe state action against youth while according them few procedural protections. This situation was substantially remedied in the famous *Gault* case, when the U.S. Supreme Court granted some of the basic criminal procedural safeguards to those proceeding through the juvenile justice system. The Court stated in *Gault* that ". . . unbridled discretion, however benevolently motivated, is frequently a poor substitute for principle and procedure."[27] In another landmark juvenile case, the Supreme Court, after discussing the gravity of juvenile confinement, held that it would not allow the juvenile offender to lose his liberty with a lower standard of proof than required for adult offenders. Judicial intervention in the child's life for his own good, said the Court, ". . . cannot take the form of subjecting the child to the stigma of a finding that he violated a criminal law and to the possibility of institutional confinement on proof insufficient to convict him were he an adult."[28] After addressing itself to the abuses that have taken place in the juvenile justice system, with its lack of procedural safeguards and open-ended commitments, the Supreme Court summarized its attitude about juvenile justice as follows: "There is evidence . . . that the child receives the worst of both worlds: that he gets neither the protections accorded to adults nor the solicitous care and regenerative treatment postulated for children."[29] Juvenile cases are being reviewed ever more frequently by the appellate courts, with the result that procedural safeguards gradually are being added to the existing juvenile statutes, and the substantial discretion available to juvenile court officials is gradually being reduced. While these cases are too numerous to detail, the trend obviously remolds the juvenile justice system in the criminal justice model, abandoning much of the theoretical underpinnings (*parens patriae*) of the juvenile court movement.[30]

Another category of quasi-criminal commitment that has received attention by the appellate courts is that involving adult offenders who are proceeded against civilly, most notably sex offenders, heroin addicts, and what are generally described as mentally disordered criminals. The language of the courts in a few of the key decisions is instructive; it expresses an attitude of growing skepticism about the benevolent nature of the civil commitment in its actual operation. In one leading case, the Third Circuit Court of Appeals had to rule on the constitutionality of a statute providing for the commitment of sex offenders to an institution maintained by the Department of Mental Hygiene.[31] The Act in question, Pennsylvania's Barr-Walker Act, provided that if a person is convicted of one of several sex offenses and is found to constitute ". . . a threat of bodily harm to members of the public . . . ," then the trial court may, in lieu of the standard criminal penalty, impose an indeterminate sentence for a period of from one day to life. The petitioner in this case had been proceeded against pursuant to this Act. However, at the hearing of determination, the only evidence admitted against him was a recommendation by the Commissioner of Mental Hygiene, which included the ultimate findings of fact based on reports of a confidential psychiatric examination and a probation investigation. The petitioner had no opportunity to confront either the Commissioner or the others who made reports about him. Procedural due process had been denied, it was claimed, because the proceedings afforded him no right to confront and cross-examine witnesses against him. The Circuit Court agreed, stating in part:

The effort of enlightened penology to alleviate the condition of a convicted defendant by providing some elements of advanced, modern methods of cure and rehabilitation and possible ultimate release on parole cannot be turned about so as to deprive a defendant of the procedures which the due process clause guarantees in a criminal proceeding.[32]

In another leading decision, the U.S. Supreme Court had to decide a case concerning the constitutionality of a sex offender statute in Colorado.[33] The case involved a man who was convicted of a sex offense for which a maximum sentence of ten years could be imposed by the standard criminal commitment. Instead of imposing the standard criminal penalty, however, the trial judge had the offender examined by psychiatrists pursuant to the Colorado Sex Offender's Act, which provides in part that if the offender constitutes a threat to the bodily harm to the public, he can be committed for an indeterminate period of time. That was the finding against the defendant in this case, but he was not granted a right to a hearing on the issue or a right to confront the witnesses against him. He appealed, challenging the constitutionality of the procedure. Justice Douglas, writing the unanimous opinion of the Court, stated, "The commitment proceedings . . . whether denominated civil or criminal are subject to both the Equal Protection Clause of the Fourteenth Amendment . . . and to the Due Process Clause."[34] With reference to the nature of the special sex offender act, the Court said, "The punishment under the . . . Act is criminal punishment even though it is designed not so much as retribution as it is to keep individuals from inflicting future harm."[35] The *Specht* decision thus suggested that the full panoply of relevant protections that the State guarantees in criminal proceedings should be accorded the sex offenders subject to the Sex Offender Act.[36]

The standard of proof was at issue in another sex offender case decided by a State Supreme Court.[37] Since the proceedings pursuant to the special Act were legally designated as civil, they operated according to the rules of civil procedure. But the standard of proof in a civil case, a preponderance of evidence, was viewed as insufficient by the State Supreme Court:

> No less critical is the standard of proof—the degree of persuasion which the plaintiff must achieve in the minds of the judge and jury in order to invoke the coercive powers of the state against the defendant. The law wisely proportions this standard to the gravity of the consequences of an erroneous judgment. . . .[38]

Recognizing that the civil commitment to a maximum security mental institution constituted a deprivation of liberty as grievous as that of the criminal commitment to a penal institution, the Court held that the standard of proof necessary to affect the civil commitment must be the same as in criminal procedure. The procedure thus became *proportionate* to the gravity of the consequences of an erroneous judgment. These cases illustrate the fact that the appellate courts around the country are beginning to recognize that persons subject to quasi-criminal commitment have the ". . . right to avoid a grievous loss of liberty and a lifetime of stigma except under the most rigorous safeguards."[39]

While there may be some valid theoretical distinctions in the civil/criminal law dichotomy, those differences less frequently are considered sufficient to support a separate set of procedural rules for each legal process. Not only does this hold for the quasi-criminal commitment, as we have seen, but it also holds for the standard civil commitment for the mentally ill, for persons not involved with the criminal law. This newest legal trend is based on the same assumption as the revision of the quasi-criminal commitment laws—that the deprivation of liberty in American society is a serious loss, and, therefore, the most rigid procedural safeguards should apply to any proceedings that threaten that liberty. This is the rule of law, even if the commitment proceedings are supposedly designed for the benefit of the individual. In one civil case a person was committed as mentally ill following a jury trial where the standard of proof was a "preponderance of evidence" and not the "beyond a reasonable doubt" standard used in criminal cases.[40] On appeal, the Court overturned the statute, stating that because personal liberty in our society is a "transcending value," those proceedings dealing with the deprivation of liberty should have rigid procedural safeguards. It makes little difference to the person who loses his liberty, said the Court, whether the law that justifies the deprivation is based on grounds of treatment or punishment, whether the law is nominally called civil or criminal.

Procedural safeguards were at issue in the famous case of *Lessard* v. *Schmidt*,[41] involving the involuntary civil commitment of the mentally ill. After a commitment proceeding and subsequent appeal by the committed person, the U.S. District Court found that the same fundamental values are at stake in a civil proceeding as in a criminal one: There is the loss of liberty, the loss of social rights, the loss of future opportunities, and the stigma of being mentally ill. It appeared to the Court, therefore, that the interests in avoiding a civil commitment are at least as high as for those persons accused of criminal offenses. The resulting burden on the state to justify a civil commitment must also be high to correspond to the procedural protections for the persons subject to it. Accordingly, the Court ordered the addition of several procedural safeguards to the statute, safeguards that have been traditionally associated with criminal proceedings. Whereas there are still some areas in which the procedural protections for civil commitments are not as rigorous as in criminal proceedings (most notably in the fifth-amendment right against self-incrimination),[42] this trend toward securing additional procedural safeguards is evident in other cases as well.[43]

Not only is the process by which one is civilly committed beginning to resemble the procedure involved in the criminal commitment, but also the substantive aspects of that commitment have been modified. As the medical model of care and treatment through the civil commitment is no longer operative, alternative means must be devised to determine how long a person could be hospitalized. The nature and duration of the civil commitment is beginning to correspond more directly to the antisocial behavior at issue. The appellate courts' recent decisions in this respect follow the precedents set in the area of criminal law, with its long history of criminal statutes being ruled unconstitutional because confinement in a penal institution was disproportionate to the severity of the offense at hand. The leading case at the federal level is *Weems* v. *United States*,[44] in which it was determined that excessive criminal penalties are unconstitutional on the grounds that they violate the eighth-amendment prohibition against cruel and unusual punishment. ". . . [I]t is a precept of justice," the Supreme Court stated, "that punishment for crime should be graduated and proportioned to the offense."[45] A more recent example of this line of reasoning can be found in a California Supreme Court case in which a statute provided for a life sentence for persons with a similar prior conviction convicted of exhibitionism.[46] The Court decided that such a penalty was simply too severe for that particular crime and declared the statute unconstitutional, stating, "We conclude that in California a punishment may violate . . . the Constitution if, although not cruel or unusual in its method, it is so disproportionate to the crime for which it is inflicted that it shocks the conscience and offends fundamental notions of human dignity."[47]

The substantive due process that has concerned the courts in criminal cases has finally interested them in civil commitment cases as well. While such cases have been too long ignored, allowing substantial abuses in the name of treatment, the courts are beginning to realize that the substantive standards of many civil and quasi-criminal commitment statutes are too broad. The therapeutic model of social control allows sanctions that are too elastic, permitting excessive confinement for relatively minor forms of social deviance. The U.S. Supreme Court has begun once more to address these issues by making comparisons to the standards of criminal law. For example, the Court recently indicated some reservations about the possible consequences of a civil commitment in the famous *Powell* v. *Texas* decision.[48] The Court stated: "One virtue of the criminal process is, at least, that the duration of penal incarceration typically has some outside statutory limit. . . . 'Therapeutic civil commitment' lacks this feature; one is typically committed until one is cured.' ''[49]

The landmark decision at the federal level concerning substantive due process in civil commitments is *Jackson* v. *Indiana*.[50] This case involves a statute pertaining to the civil commitment of persons found too insane to stand criminal trial. The Indiana statute stated that if a trial judge had reasonable ground to believe that the defendant is incompetent to stand trial, the judge must appoint two physicians to examine the defendant, after which a competency hearing is held. If the trial court finds that the defendant is not able to understand the proceedings against him and participate in his own defense, the court has the authority to commit the defendant to a state mental institution until he becomes sane. *Jackson* involved a defendant who was charged with two counts of robbery, the goods being valued at four dollars in one incident and at five dollars in the other. The doctors who examined him said that the prognosis was "rather dim" that he would ever be competent to stand trial, but he was, nevertheless, committed to the mental institution. He appealed, contending that he was in effect receiving a life sentence, even though the criminal allegations had never been proven against him. It was claimed that the law was unconstitutional, because it was a violation of due process of law. The Supreme Court agreed with this reasoning and stated in its decision:

We hold, consequently, that a person charged by a State with a criminal offense who is committed solely on account of his incapacity to proceed to trial cannot be held more than the reasonable period of time necessary to determine whether there is a substantial probability that he will attain that capacity in the foreseeable future. If it is determined that this is not the case, then the State must either institute the customary civil commitment proceeding that would be required to commit indefinitely any other citizen, or release the defendant. . . . *At the very least, due process requires that the nature and the duration of commitment bear some reasonable relation to the purpose for which the individual is committed.*[51] (Emphasis added.)

Thus the Supreme Court is finally concerning itself with the "substantive constitutional limitations"[52] on the power to confine persons on preventive grounds.

150

At the state level as well, there has been some concern shown for the substantive provisions of civil and quasi-criminal commitment statutes. In California, for instance, both the legislature and the appellate courts have begun to recognize the dangers of open-ended civil commitments based on the *parens patriae* philosophy and have also begun to place limitations on the duration of quasi-criminal commitments. The legislature has enacted a civil addict law, for example, that limits the amount of time a heroin addict can remain in the civil addict program to seven years.[53] This provision contends with the theoretical basis of a *parens patriae* civil commitment, because the time would normally expand until the person was cured or rehabilitated. Certainly, from a medical point of view, it might take longer than seven years to "cure" some people of their addiction. But the legislature believed that in the interests of justice and fairness, the commitment should not extend beyond a reasonable period of time, even if it meant releasing persons who were still addicted to heroin.

Finally, California's Supreme Court also decided recently a case concerning substantive provisions of a quasi-criminal commitment, in this instance dealing with commitment to a juvenile institution.[54] The holding in this case has serious implications for the *parens patriae* philosophy as a basis for extending the duration of commitment longer than would have been the case under the standard criminal penalty. The case concerns a juvenile, age nineteen, who was charged and ultimately convicted of the crime of misdemeanor assault, for which the maximum criminal penalty would have been a commitment to the county jail for a period of six months. This juvenile, however, was committed to a Youth Authority institution, California's state level institution for juvenile delinquents. There, because of the *parens patriae* philosophy of juvenile commitments, the defendant could have remained until he was twenty-one. The defendant appealed the commitment, claiming it was unconstitutional to commit him to the Youth Authority for a potentially longer period of time than he would have received had he been sentenced under the provisions of the Penal Code. After reviewing the constitutional aspects of the deprivation of liberty, the Court stated:

No reason has been suggested, nor can we conceive of any, why the concern for personal liberty implicit in both the California and federal Constitutions is any less compelling in defendant's case. We believe that those charters are no less vigilant in protecting against continuing deprivations of liberty than are their due process clauses in protecting against the initial deprivation of that liberty. We conclude that personal liberty is a fundamental interest, second only to life itself, as an interest protected under both the California and United States Constitutions.[55]

The Court then discussed the rationale for the open-ended juvenile commitment, most notably the rehabilitation of malleable offenders. The Court said

There remains as much wisdom in that observation [about the benefits of rehabilitation] today as it held . . . years ago. However, we are no longer able to find such a generalization, standing alone, as sufficient justification for governmentally imposed inequality where deprivations of personal liberty are involved.[56]

The Court noted that whereas youthful offenders may have remained the same over the years, and whereas rehabilitation is still a laudable goal, ". . . constitutional analysis has undergone considerable metamorphosis."[57] The Court therefore concluded that because of the greater interests in individual liberty and the greater necessity for the state to establish a compelling reason for the deprivation of that liberty, youthful offenders could not be committed to the Youth Authority for a period of time in excess of the maximum jail term permitted by statute for the offense committed.

The decisions cited above indicate that many of the appellate courts throughout the country are becoming more realistic about the current and potential abuses of civil and quasi-criminal commitments. With this realization that many civil commitments for care and treatment have essentially the same substantive effect as a criminal commitment, the appellate courts have responded by increasing the procedural protections associated with civil commitment proceedings. Thus, they greatly resemble the procedural safeguards of criminal proceedings. Although this trend may not be advancing as rapidly or as extensively as would be desirable, the cases have laid the foundation for the modification or abolition of civil commitments that are abusive in nature.

For some, the criminalization of the civil commitment may have negative connotations, since civil commitments, particularly quasi-criminal commitments, originally began as a humanitarian substitute for the criminal sanction. The original motivation was to decrease the stigma of a criminal commitment and to provide therapeutic intervention for behavior problems rather than criminal punishment for misdeeds. In light of this, to reinstate the dominance of the criminal process may not seem like a progressive measure. Yet, realistically, the humanitarian motives and concerns of some of the early reformers have never been satisfied. The stigma of being a "mental patient," a "mentally disordered criminal," or a "juvenile delinquent" is probably as great, if not greater, than simply being a "criminal." Upon release, the "ex-con," with all his problems securing employment and establishing a normal lifestyle, seems to have fewer problems than the "ex-mental patient," who may be viewed as both irrational *and* dangerous. Moreover, because of lack of resources or of psychiatric expertise, experience reveals that commitment to a mental hospital with scant hope for a cure has often proved to be as serious a deprivation of liberty as a criminal commitment. Certainly, to those who are committed and forced to be "treated," their therapeutic incarceration is felt to be punishment; the fact that their commitment has a different label does not conceal its punitive nature.

Making the civil commitment more "criminal" should be viewed as a desirable trend—primarily because a greater number of people are served by this process compared to those for whom it is detrimental. Two prime benefits are: First, the modification of the civil commitment laws by the legislatures and appellate courts throughout the country brings the legal standards into theoretical harmony with the actual nature of that sanction in the daily administration of justice at the trial court level. And second, increased procedural and substantive protections in civil commitment law will serve as a check on the government's power to control its citizens. The criminalization of the civil commitment should continue, making it possible to devise legal principles and procedures for subjecting the process of civil commitment to the restraints of law.

Notes

1. For a review of this literature, see Nicholas N. Kittrie, *The Right to Be Different,* Baltimore and London: The Johns Hopkins Press, 1971.
2. See Glanville Williams, "The Definition of Crime," *Current Legal Problems* 8 (1955):107-130.
3. People v. Burnick, 14 Cal.3d 306 (1975).
4. People v. Feagley, 14 Cal.3d 338 (1975).
5. People v. Burnick, 14 Cal.3d 306 (1975).
6. For example, see People v. McCracken, 39 Cal.2d 336, 346. It was pointed out that the statute ". . . was not intended to make sexual psychopathy a mitigating circumstance. On the contrary, the sexual psychopath may be removed from society under the Sexual Psychopath Law until he is cured or until he is no longer considered a menace to the safety of others. The court may thereafter resume the criminal proceedings and impose the punishment allowed by law since the confinement as a sexual psychopath is not a substitute for punishment, the entire statutory procedure being civil in nature rather than penal."
7. For example, see Henry M. Hart, "The Aims of the Criminal Law," *Law and Contemporary Problems* 23 (1958):403.
8. For example, see Robinson v. California 370 U.S. 660 (1962); People v. Levy, 151 Cal. App.2d 460 (1957); Kittrie, *Right to Be Different,* p. 374.
9. See: Ronald Beattie and Virginia Vanich, *The Mentally Disordered Sex Offender in California,* Sacramento, Calif.: Bureau of Criminal Statistics, 1972, p. 39.
10. This shift in policy was in large part because of changes in the staff hierarchy.

11. James D. Thompson, *Organizations in Action,* New York: McGraw-Hill Book Co., 1967, pp. 72-73.

12. Ibid., p. 1. Thompson states: "Uncertainties pose major problems to rationality, and we will argue that technologies and environments are basic sources of uncertainty for organizations. How these facts of organizational life lead organizations to design and structure themselves needs to be explored."

13. For a discussion of the problem of defining organizational boundaries, see Thompson, *Organizations in Action,* pp. 39-44; Richard H. Hall, *Organizations: Structure and Process,* Englewood Cliffs, N.J.: Prentice-Hall, 1972, pp. 6-10; Amitai Etzioni, "A Basis for Comparative Analysis of Complex Organizations," in *A Sociological Reader on Complex Organizations,* 2nd edition, New York: Holt, Rinehart and Winston, 1961, p. 75.

14. Ibid., p. 76.

15. Thompson, *Organizations in Action,* p. 160.

16. People v. Levy, 151 Cal. App.2d 460, 311 P.2d 897 (1957).

17. People v. Olivas, 17 Cal.3d 236 (1976).

18. ENKI Research Institute, "A Study of California's New Mental Health Law," 1972.

19. Marc F. Abramson, "The Criminalization of Mentally Disordered Behavior," *Hospital and Community Psychiatry* 23, no. 4 (1972):101-105.

20. Jackson v. Indiana, 406 U.S. 715, 737 (1972).

21. Wyatt v. Stickney, 325 F.Supp. 781 (M.D. Ala., 1971).

22. Humphrey v. Cady, 405 U.S. 504, 509 (1972).

23. Donaldson v. O'Connor, 493 F.2d 507, 520 (5th Cir. 1974).

24. In re Gault, 387 U.S. 1, 50 (1967).

25. Kittrie, *Right to Be Different,* p. 7.

26. Speiser v. Randall, 357 U.S. 513, 520-521 (1958).

27. In re Gault, 387 U.S. 1, 18 (1967).

28. In re Winship, 397 U.S. 358, 367 (1970).

29. Kent v. United States, 383 U.S. 541, 556 (1966).

30. Breed v. Jones, 421 U.S. 519 (1975); In re Joseph, 30 Cal. App.3d 880, 106 Cal. Rptr. 729 (1973); In re Macidon, 240 Cal. App.2d 600, 49 Cal. Rptr. 861 (1966); In re Rambeau, 266 Cal. App.2d 1, 72 Cal. Rptr. 171 (1968); People v. Burton, 6 Cal.3d 375, 491 P.2d 793 (1971); In re Carl T., 1 Cal. App.3d 344, 81 Cal. Rptr. 655 (1969); In re Dennis R., 19 Cal. App.3d 350, 96 Cal. Rptr. 791 (1971); In re Daniel R., 274 Cal. App.2d 749, 79 Cal. Rptr. 247 (1969).

31. United States v. Maroney, 355 F.2d 302 (1966).

32. Ibid., p. 310.

33. Specht v. Patterson, 386 U.S. 605 (1967).

34. Ibid., p. 608.

35. Ibid., p. 609.

154

36. Ibid., p. 610
37. People v. Burnick, 14 Cal.3d 306 (1975).
38. Ibid., p. 310.
39. Sarzen v. Gaughan, 489 F.2d 1076, 1083 (First Circuit, 1973).
40. In re Ballay, 482 F.2d 648 (D.C. Circuit, 1973).
41. 349 F.Supp. 1078 (E.D. Wisconsin, 1972).
42. Alan Stone, *Mental Health and Law: A System in Transition,* Rockville, Mary.: National Institute of Mental Health, 1975, p. 187.
43. Lake v. Cameron, 364 F.2d 657 (1966); Denton v. Commonwealth, 383 S.W.2d 681 (Ky., 1964); Heryford v. Parker, 396 F.2d 393 (10th Circuit, 1968); Dixon v. Attorney General of Pennsylvania, 325 F.Supp. 966 (M.D. Pa., 1971).
44. 217 U.S. 349 (1910).
45. Ibid., p. 367.
46. In re Lynch, 8 Cal.3d 410 (1972).
47. Ibid., p. 424.
48. 392 U.S. 514 (1968).
49. Ibid., p. 529.
50. 406 U.S. 715 (1972).
51. Ibid., p. 738.
52. Ibid., p. 737.
53. Section 3201 of the Welfare and Institutions Code (California).
54. People v. Olivas, 17 Cal.3d 236 (1976).
55. Ibid., pp. 250-251.
56. Ibid., pp. 251-252.
57. Ibid., p. 252.

Appendix: Methodology

The Perspective of the Book

The author of this book assumes that it is of central importance for a social science researcher to take the role of the other—to comprehend the perceptions of the actors (organizational personnel)—for a proper investigation of how organizations come to define, record, and process persons as instances of certain social categories. This perspective has a long tradition in sociology and has been identified by several names over the years, such as qualitative research,[1] participant observation,[2] the action perspective,[3] field research,[4] ethnomethodology,[5] and phenomenological sociology.[6] Whatever the name, these perspectives have several things in common: They emphasize the importance of "getting close to the data"; they deemphasize the role of detached, quantitative data, which have no correspondence to the observed social reality; they emphasize the necessity for subjectivity on the part of the observer as well as the observed; and they stress the importance of viewing behavior as a process within an ongoing social organization.

Although any one of several developed terminologies would be acceptable for purposes of this study, the terminology used by Garfinkel, Cicourel, and Kitsuse—all of whom based part of their work on the phenomenological perspective of Schutz—is preferred. Each of these theorists stresses the importance of not simply studying static "social facts," such as rates of occurrence of some social phenomenon. Instead they stress the importance of examining the ongoing social action that produces the rates; the focus is on organizational processes.

Schutz and his followers assert that the social sciences must deal with the observed social action in terms of the "common-sense" interpretations of social reality currently accepted by the members of the group, organization, or society under investigation.[7] By common-sense interpretations, these authorities refer to the actors' interpretations of their social world, based on the means by which they try to fulfill their role expectations, given the requirements and constraints of the organization in which they are working.

To determine the common-sense interpretations of the organizational personnel, it is necessary to focus on the practical, everyday decisions that they constantly are forced to make. How do the organizational personnel categorize persons or events in order to process them through the organization? How do they make sense of the vast number of cases to be processed? What relationship do the informal or common-sense categories have to the formal organizational categories? To answer these questions, the researcher must devise a series of approaches to help him understand the everyday rationality of the organizational decisionmakers and, specifically, the vocabulary and premises they use in making their decisions.[8]

The Approaches to the Research

After the theoretical perspective had been determined, decisions were made as to what methodological approaches would be utilized. Since methodological decisions in the social sciences have their theoretical counterparts,[9] some approaches follow naturally from the chosen theoretical perspective. The use of a phenomenological perspective implies that a variety of the now traditional qualitative approaches should be employed.

Two central concerns of a social science researcher are to produce convincing data and ultimately to make a compelling argument. A single methodological approach usually will not suffice; a variety of approaches is required to fulfill such a research goal. No one approach can offer convincing data about the actor's subjective definition of the situation. For example, direct participation in an activity is problematic, since the researcher can only assume that his experiences are the same as those of the other participants. Verification demands diverse approaches.

McCall and Simmons have aptly stated that studies of a qualitative nature have generally employed a variety of methodological approaches, and they offer standardized definitions of the various procedures.[10] The most common approach is simply direct observation of the ongoing social activities; a less common form of observation is participant observation, during which the researchers actually participate in the activities of the actors they are observing. Although these may be the primary tools of the qualitative analyst, they prove insufficient when there are limitations on the researcher's time.

For verification of the researcher's observations, it is necessary that he know what happened when he was not available to observe directly. To compensate for this limitation, the researcher must use what McCall and Simmons call "informants"[11] to provide some of the missing data. These informants or "surrogate observers" may take the form of actors in the organization, who are interviewed, or they may be old records, official or unofficial. In either case, they are to provide the researcher with data that he cannot or did not directly observe.

For the purpose of understanding the actor's perspective, another invaluable tool, utilized in most qualitative research, requires an interview with what McCall and Simmons refer to as a "respondent." A respondent is an actor engaged in the observed activities, who tells the researcher about his thoughts, motives, and intentions while he is engaged in organizational tasks. The report of a respondent minimizes the danger of making invalid inferences about the actor's activities when the researcher cannot perceive the information directly. The same person may be an informant or a respondent on different occasions. When he is an informant, he simply reports directly on the events he observes; as a respondent, he relays information about his personal feelings regarding the organizational activities. McCall and Simmons conclude:

As we have seen, a number of techniques—direct observation, informant interviewing, document analysis, respondent interviewing, and direct participation—are typically and to some degree necessarily involved in a field study of any complex social organization.[12]

The selection of a variety of qualitative techniques by no means solves the researcher's challenge of producing convincing data. Utilizing qualitative methods does not necessitate forsaking some of the standard, scientific procedures such as random sampling and hypothesis confirmation. As one authority states, using qualitative methods does not mean that the researcher is to be unscientific in his data collection. "On the contrary, it merely specifies that it is crucial for validity—and consequently, for reliability—to try to picture the empirical social world as it actually exists to those under investigation, rather than as the researcher imagines it."[13] This research, being no exception, utilizes a variety of qualitative and quantitative techniques in order to "try to picture the empirical and social world as it actually exists to those under investigation. . . ."

Selection and Description of Counties

The actual selection of the three counties (Contra Costa, San Francisco, and Orange) was a relatively simple matter. Official statistics revealed that these three counties had the greatest variation in commitment rates. It was assumed that this fact was related to the differential policies of the justice system of each county, rather than to the clinical characteristics of the defendants processed through the systems. It seemed that a study of these three counties would offer the best opportunities to examine the organizational classification and processing of persons as instances of informal social categories.

All three of the counties could be described as having rather modern, bureaucratic, efficient organizations for justice. Each has some form of Master Calendar system, so that one judge (the Criminal Master Calendar Judge) handles the majority of the criminal cases certified to the Superior Court. At the Superior Court level there are twenty-five departments in Orange County, twenty-six in San Francisco, and eleven in Contra Costa County. In each of these counties, one department handles approximately 90 percent of the criminal cases. Prior to 1973, two departments in Contra Costa County disposed of most of the criminal cases.

The three counties could be described as urban or suburban. San Francisco is the most urban with the greatest population density, primarily because its city borders are exactly the same as its county borders. Orange County was once considered a bedroom community of Los Angeles, but it is now the second largest county in the state, explained in large part by extensive industrial development. Contra Costa County is a curious combination of a middle-class suburb of San Francisco and Oakland and a working-class community surrounding the one industry in the county—oil refining.

Orange County is the largest of the three counties, with a 1970 population of 1,420,386; San Francisco had 715,674 in the same year; and the population of Contra Costa County was 558,389. The largest black population resides in San Francisco and comprises 28.6 percent of the total population; Contra Costa had a 10 percent black population; and Orange County had the smallest black population with 2.7 percent.

It is generally felt that Orange County is one of the most conservative in the state, San Francisco one of the most liberal, with Contra Costa being at neither extreme. Although this belief is difficult to quantify, Orange County is renowned for its conservative politics, especially the activities of the American Independent Party and the John Birch Society, while San Francisco is allegedly tolerant of "deviant" groups, such as the homosexual population, and is reputedly more sympathetic to left-wing causes, such as the antiwar movement. San Francisco is commonly portrayed as a sophisticated, liberal community with a degree of social conscience, while Orange County is seen as a middle-American community, concerned with law and order, rising welfare rolls, and declining moral standards.

Observations

The observations were primarily conducted in two locations—the open court and the judges' chambers of each of the three counties. They were nonparticipant in the sense that I did not take part in the actual discussions or decisions concerning the various cases.

In the open court of Contra Costa County I sat inside the railing that divides the court personnel from the gallery; in San Francisco and Orange counties I sat just outside the railing, in much the same position that would be assumed by a newspaper reporter or a member of a defendant's family. During the initial observations I listened to the discussions of the court personnel, noted where they sat, and observed all the procedures relating to a typical case. I took complete notes of everything heard and observed. At first my observations were of a general nature, but they gradually narrowed as I became more discerning.

Although I was sitting with the rest of the general public, most of the court personnel knew of my interests and were aware of the fact that I was taking notes. Since all utterances of the official participants are transcribed and the presence of reporters taking notes is commonplace, I can only assume that my note-taking did not inhibit the court personnel from spontaneous interaction and expression.

Although the effect of my presence in the judges' chambers would have been difficult to determine, I feel it also did not alter drastically the actors' behavior.[14] This can be accounted for by the fact that originally I was introduced by a friend who had been a probation officer in Superior Court for eight years, who explained my purpose for being there. This set the stage for my being viewed as a neutral observer, rather than as an outsider or "muckraker."

Inside the chambers I noticed that the behavior exhibited was quite different from that observed in the open court setting. The attorneys, and even the judges, seemed much more relaxed; they make jokes and comments, some of an off-color nature, which would never have been acceptable in a public setting. This left me with the distinct impression that my presence was not an inhibiting force on their behavior. Although I had no well-established contacts in the other two counties, this pattern was consistent. That is, the disparity between formal courtroom and chambers behavior was great, and I felt I was accepted as someone in front of whom formal role-playing was not required.

The observations were made during a period of approximately eighteen months, from January 1972 to August 1973. Since the analysis of official records included the years 1968 through 1972, there was some overlap of qualitative and quantitative evaluation of the same MDSO cases.

Interviews

After the initial observations had been conducted, I began to interview the court personnel. At first the interviews were undertaken with all court personnel, including the peripheral actors such as the bailiffs, court recorders, clerks, and clerical workers. The purpose of these interviews was to familiarize myself with courtroom procedures and official vocabulary, as well as with courtroom jargon. I began by asking very general questions about the duties and responsibilities of the interviewee in the court organization and then about his perceptions of the other actors' duties and roles. I also asked the peripheral court personnel about their perceptions of the various defense attorneys, prosecuting attorneys, and judges, especially with respect to those actors' roles in MDSO cases.

After learning the routine of court procedure, my interest focused on those who were considered to be the key decisionmakers in the Superior Court—judges, prosecuting attorneys, defense attorneys, probation officers, and psychiatrists. The primary interview strategy in most instances was to observe one or more of the key decisionmakers in open court or in the judges' chambers and to take note of significant statements. Following the interchange, when the person left the court or chambers, I would privately ask him to amplify what he had said in court. I wanted to know of his strategy, thoughts, and motives, as well as how the particular case at hand compared with other cases with which he might have been involved.

Most of these interviews were rather short, since I casually initiated them. For the most part the court personnel perceive themselves as very busy and having little time to spend on anything not of direct reward to them. However, in some instances I was able to make formal appointments with the decisionmakers and probe at length their attitudes about the use of the MDSO civil commitment in specific cases. My main objective was to gain insight into the types of cases and the circumstances under which a defendant is likely to be classified as an MDSO and sent to Atascadero.

The Questionnaire

A questionnaire was administered to verify some of the hypotheses that were generated by the observations and interviews. The actual questionnaire contained three subsections and was concerned with two general issues. First, how do the key decisionmakers in the Superior Court view the relative severity of various criminal offenses? Second, how do the decisionmakers view the relative severity of the various dispositional alternatives available to them for different types of crimes? The first subsection of the questionnaire, shown in Figure A-1, attempts to establish an "offense severity gradient." The second two subsections, exhibited in Figures A-2 and A-3, seek to establish a "sanction severity gradient." Figure A-2 assesses the relative severity of sanctions for misdemeanor cases and Figure A-3 does the same for felony cases.

When this questionnaire was devised, there were numerous dilemmas to resolve. Naturally, a primary concern was to obtain as accurate an indication as possible of what the court personnel believe to be the relative severity of offenses and dispositions. There was one overriding problem in using questionnaires in general, especially in a Superior Court setting, and that was time. As mentioned previously, the court personnel are very busy and have little time for outside business, especially a private research project.

The consequences of this concern with time took the form of limitations on the material covered, as well as the inferences that could be drawn. The first limitation was on the actual number of items that could be covered. For the offense severity gradient, there were literally hundreds of formal crimes in the California Penal Code and perhaps thirty or more offenses

In the following questionnaire you are asked to rate various offenses in terms of seriousness. In the left hand column you are to indicate the degree of seriousness by writing in a number from 0 to 100; 0 for an offense of no seriousness and 100 for an offense of the most serious kind. For example, murder might receive a rating of 100, whereas jaywalking might be rated at 3.

Rating	Penal Code Section	Nature of the Offense
_____	459	Burglary
_____	288	Molesting child under fourteen
_____	314	Indecent exposure
_____	261.5	Unlawful sexual intercourse
_____	285	Incest
_____	211	Robbery (armed)
_____	261.3	Rape (forcible)
_____	261.4	Rape (by threat)
_____	647a	Lewd vagrancy
_____	288a	Sex perversion
_____	203	Mayhem
_____	220	Assault with intent to commit rape
_____	240	Assault with intent to commit violent injury
_____	653	Tattooing a minor
_____	653g	Loitering about a place where children congregate
_____	311.6	Engaging in obscene live conduct
_____	148	Resisting an officer
_____	281	Bigamy
_____	286	Sodomy
_____	290	Failure to register as a sex offender

Figure A-1. Questionnaire, Subsection 1.

dealing specifically with sexual misconduct. It was not possible to obtain the decisionmakers' opinions on all possibilities, so a select number (twenty) were chosen, including, for the most part, sexual offenses, but also including the most common nonsex offenses. Although no information on some offense categories could be gathered, the most common offenses were covered by the questionnaire.

This questionnaire is concerned with your views of several dispositional alternatives. In the left hand column, please rate from 0 to 100 the dispositional alternatives that, from your agency's point of view, are the *least* severe (0) to the *most* severe (100), for a *misdemeanor* sex conviction, e.g., CPC 314, indecent exposure with no priors.

_____	Small fine
_____	Probation (no supervision)
_____	Atascadero State Hospital (as MDSO)
_____	Dismissal
_____	Jail time (6 months)
_____	Probation (supervision)
_____	Fine and jail
_____	Suspended sentence

Figure A-2. Questionnaire, Subsection 2.

This, too, is concerned with your views of several dispositional alternatives. In the left hand column, please rate from 0 to 100 the dispositional alternatives that, from your agency's point of view, are the *least* severe (0) to the *most* severe (100), for a *felony* sex conviction, e.g., CPC 261.3, forcible rape.

_____	Small fine
_____	Probation (no supervision)
_____	Atascadero State Hospital (as MDSO)
_____	Dismissal
_____	State prison
_____	Jail time (6 months)
_____	Probation (supervision)
_____	Fine and jail
_____	Suspended sentence

Figure A-3. Questionnaire, Subsection 3.

When the offense severity gradient was being devised, a further problem arose because of the time limitation. The dilemma was how to present the offenses so that those questioned could best assess and respond in a short period of time. One possibility was to present cases with a thorough description of the fact situation surrounding the offense. This would have given the respondents the clearest possible choices and would have been the most meaningful; it would also have been a questionnaire that would have required an hour to read and complete. Since it seemed likely that most of the questionnaires would not be completed, a different, less desirable, alternative was selected.

Rather than a complete fact situation, the formal Penal Code number with a brief description of the offense category was submitted. The resultant problem for the respondents was that any number of different fact situations could be subsumed under these very broad, formal, offense categories. An example of this problem is found with oral copulation. A person can be found guilty of this offense if it occurs between two consenting adult males, in conjunction with a child molest, or as a part of a forcible rape. The perceptions of seriousness of these three fact situations can be expected to vary enormously, although the offense category is the same. The assumption had to be made that the responses would be based on the typical case (Sudnow's "normal crime") handled by each agency in each jurisdiction.

A similar problem occurred with the sanction severity scale, since the number of sanctions that a Superior Court judge can level against an offender is extremely high. One of the reasons for this is that there is variability in the size of the units in each sanction. That is, if the court sends the offender to jail, it can be for a period of 1 to 365 days. If the court imposes a fine, it may be from one to several thousand dollars. Therefore, the number of possible sanctions is immense, and the questionnaire cannot deal with all the possibilities. And further, the court can impose almost any combination of the sanctions available. For example, the court can impose either probation, jail, or a fine, or any combination of all three alternatives. The presentation of all these combinations on the questionnaire would be unworkable. To cope with this problem, the most common and general categories of sanctions were used, even though a certain degree of precision was sacrificed.

On examination of the three figures, notice that the respondent was instructed to *rate* the seriousness of the different offense categories and the different dispositional alternatives. The decision was made that the respondents would be asked to *rate* rather than to *rank* the questionnaires for a variety of reasons. First, it was thought that it would be easier for the court personnel to rate, since two crimes might be perceived as being of equal seriousness. Both rape and robbery, for example, can receive a seriousness rating of 95 out of 100, but in ranking, a choice must be made; each item has to be compared to every other item and placed in rank order. This can prove time consuming for the court personnel and, thus, would not have been as acceptable. The most important reason for rating, however, was that if the questionnaires were rated originally, they could then be ranked; the reverse would not be possible.

The rankings alone would not indicate the extent to which the court personnel might differ in their perceptions of the seriousness of offenses. In other words, by using the rating system, the researcher obtains two responses for analysis—the original ratings and the rankings of these same ratings. The researcher therefore has not only the comparisons of differences in rank order of seriousness, but, to some extent, an indication of the degree of the differences among agencies or among counties.

While the actual results of the questionnaires have been presented in the substantive chapters, there is one issue remaining—namely, the extent to which there was agreement among the respondents from each agency in rating the offenses and dispositional alternatives on the questionnaire. There is a statistical technique for testing the extent of uniformity of ranked questionnaires called Kendall's "coefficient of concordance."[15] This formula was applied to rankings of the three parts of the questionnaire for each of the eleven agencies responding; thus there were thirty-three calculations.

Kendall's measure of concordance ranges from 0 for no concordance to 1.0 for perfect agreement, and the value is represented by "W." The W calculations were completed for all sets of questionnaires, and W scores are presented in Table A-1. It should be noted that for the two parts of the questionnaire dealing with the dispositional alternatives, there is a very high

Table A-1
"W" Scores for Concordance of Questionnaires[a]

	Misdemeanor Dispositions	Felony Dispositions	Seriousness of Offense
Contra Costa Co. Judges	.83	.94	.79
Contra Costa Co. Deputy DAs	.90	.89	.73
Contra Costa Co. Deputy PDs	.78	.84	.64
Contra Costa Co. Deputy POs	.85	.88	.63
San Francisco Co. Judges	_[b]	—	—
San Francisco Co. Deputy DAs	.99	.84	.64
San Francisco Co. Deputy PDs	.93	.94	.58
San Francisco Co. Deputy POs	.86	.91	.61
Orange Co. Judges	.87	.85	.72
Orange Co. Deputy DAs	.92	.91	.80
Orange Co. Deputy PDs	.91	.88	.71
Orange Co. Deputy POs	.90	.86	.77

[a]"W" scores range from 0.0 to 1.0.
[b]San Francisco judges refused to answer the questionnaire.

level of agreement. For the offense severity rankings, there is good agreement, although the vagueness of the offense categories—since no fact situation described the offense—undoubtedly contributed to the results. With all such considerations in mind, the results of the questionnaires show a high degree of unanimity of rankings.

Selecting the Sample

The next step, after the counties had been selected and the questionnaires administered, was to choose a sample of sex cases to be analyzed in great detail. The purpose of the detailed and systematic analysis was to allow greater generalizability of conclusions of the qualitative evaluation in each of the three jurisdictions. The process of selecting the sample was essentially the same in each of the counties.

The first step was to go to the office of the county clerk, Superior Court, Criminal Division and locate the "Register of Actions" log. When a case is certified to the Superior Court from the Municipal Court, it is given a Superior Court docket number and logged in the Register of Actions. Each time the defendant appears before the court or a motion is made on his behalf, such motion or appearance is logged in the Register, stating the date and a summary of the purpose and results of the appearance. At the top of the page of each log is the docket number of the case, the defendant's name, and the charges alleged against him.

The next step was to select a population of sex cases from all the cases listed in the Register of Actions. The logs for a period of five years, from January 1968 to December 1972, were examined. Beginning with January 1968, each docket number was examined to see if there were any charges of a sexual nature alleged against the defendant. The different types of sex charges, not the number of counts nor the nonsex charges, were noted on this preliminary list. Table A-2 presents a summary of the entire selection process.

From an examination of the total number of docket numbers in each jurisdiction, there were 178 docket numbers in Contra Costa relating to sex offenses, 561 in San Francisco, and 679 in Orange County. This shows that the volume of sex cases in Contra Costa and San Francisco Counties is about 4 percent of the total, and in Orange County 6 percent.

From the sex-related docket numbers in each county, one can see that there were 192 defendants with charges of a sexual nature alleged against them in Contra Costa County, 713 defendants in San Francisco, and 706 in Orange County. This reveals, obviously, that there were some docket numbers with more than one defendant. To obtain a general idea of group charging policy or of group sexual activities, one must determine what

Table A-2
Characteristics of Total Sample

	Contra Costa	San Francisco	Orange
Total number of docket numbers for all types of cases from January 1968 to December 1972	4500	13,000	11,000
Total number of docket numbers for all sex-related cases from January 1968 to December 1972	178	561	679
Percent of sex related cases to all cases	4	4	6
Total number of defendants for all sex-related cases from January 1968 to December 1972	192	713	706
Percent of docket numbers to defendants (indication of the extent of group crime—the higher the percent, the less group crime)	93	79	96
Total number of different sex charges against all defendants in sex cases	223	875	1008
Percent of defendants to charges (indication of extent of multiple charging by DA—the higher the percent, the less multiple charging)	86	81	70

percentage the total number of docket numbers is of the total number of defendants in each county. The figure is 93 percent in Contra Costa County, 79 percent in San Francisco, and 96 percent in Orange County. The lower the percentage, the more group charging there is and, as the percentage nears 100 percent, the more likely there is to be one defendant for every one docket number.

After a list of the total number of defendants certified to the Superior Court for alleged sex offenses was obtained along with the docket numbers, a frequency distribution of the different types of sex offenses was made. The frequency distribution of sex charges appears in Table A-3. The total number of different sex charges against all the defendants in Contra Costa County was 233; it was 875 in San Francisco and 1008 in Orange County.

By determining what percentage the total number of defendants is of the total number of charges in each county, one can get a crude indication of the extent of multiple charging, although it is not at all clear whether multiple charging represents the actual behavior of the defendant or a tendency on the part of the district attorney to overcharge in order to be in a better bargaining position. In any event, the percentage of defendants to charges in Contra Costa County was 86 percent, 81 percent in San Francisco, and 70 percent in Orange County.

From the frequency distribution presented in Table A-3, a comparison can be made of types and percentages of formal charges in each of the three jurisdictions. It might be noticed that in general there is a great deal of

Table A-3
Frequency Distribution of Offenses Charged (January 1968 to December 1972)

California Penal Code Section[a]	Contra Costa		San Francisco		Orange	
	N	Percent	N	Percent	N	Percent
220	14	6	62	7	85	8
236	2	1	2	0	4	0
261	31	14	23	3	0	0
261.1 (statutory rape)	6	3	30	3	65	6
261.1 (1971 rev.-lunacy)	0	0	0	0	3	0
261.2	2	1	46	5	22	2
261.3	21	9	124	14	97	10
261.4	0	0	31	4	26	3
261.5 (1971 rev. unlaw. int.)	8	4	26	3	34	3
266A	0	0	2	0	0	0
266G	0	0	1	0	0	0
266H	3	1	42	5	7	1
266I	1	0	38	4	2	0
267	0	0	0	0	1	0
272	2	1	3	0	4	0
278	1	0	0	0	1	0
281	1	0	0	0	0	0
285	4	2	5	0	25	2
286	2	1	41	5	41	4
288	39	17	94	11	290	29
288a	31	14	270	31	183	18
290	1	0	1	0	0	0
311.6 or .8	0	0	9	1	3	0
314.1	12	5	7	1	61	6
318	0	0	1	0	0	0
647a	0	0	0	0	54	5
650 1/2	0	0	0	0	0	0
6300 W & I certification	42	19	17	2	0[b]	0
Total	223	98	875	99	1008	97

[a]Based on pre-1970 Penal Code revision unless otherwise stated.
[b]Not recorded.

uniformity in the charges alleged against defendants in each of the three counties. There are, however, some noticeable differences. For example, in San Francisco there is a significantly high percentage of 288a (oral copulation) cases, which resulted from the certification of adult male.homosexual cases to the Superior Court; this same procedure was not followed by either of the other two counties. In Orange County the highest percentage of cases falls within the child molest category (288 PC).

Analyzing the Sample

After the subsample had been selected, it was necessary to carry out a systematic collection of data on the cases chosen. From the total list of defendants, the docket numbers of the selected cases were placed on a new list. If the docket number had more than one defendant, the selected defendant's initials were also listed. No names were used in this part of the analysis, and the original list of names was destroyed. With the new list of docket numbers, the review of one case at a time and the systematic collection of data considered relevant for analysis was begun. Such data were obtained from the assistant county clerks in the form of the complete criminal files. Since all adult criminal files are within the public domain, there generally was no difficulty in obtaining the needed information.

Needless to say, the official court data may be only partially reflective of any objective reality, but they provide valuable clues about the policies, values, and premises on which the court personnel base their final decisions as to the disposition of cases. In any event, to conduct a study involving several hundred cases over a five-year time span, it was necessary to rely on the official court files. Within the official files, there were several places where the relevant information could be obtained. In each folder there was another "register of actions," on which all the official information about the current offense was noted. There were also—depending on the county and on the type of charge—a police report, a probation report, the preliminary examination, the motions filed, psychiatric reports, and in some instances, letters of recommendation.

There were several subject areas for which data were collected from the official files. The first area of interest was demographic data on the defendant, such as age, race, employment status, socioeconomic status, educational level, etc. The second area was the official information about the current offense, such as the number and nature of the initial charges and the final charges, the type of adjudication, the type of defense attorney, the name of the judge, and the disposition of the case. The third area in which information was gathered concerned victim characteristics, such as age, race, sex of victim, person who filed the complaint, and the extent of the relationship between victim and offender. The fourth area was concerned with the recommendations of the court's assistants, the psychiatrists and the probation officers. The final area was the defendant's prior legal history, such as number of prior convictions for sex offenses or for nonsex offenses, the length of time the defendant had spent in prison, jail, or a mental hospital, and the immediate prior disposition.

To gather the data on the current charge, I relied on the register of actions, for this was a fast and reliable way to obtain the information. For the demographic data, I primarily utilized the probation report and, for further information, the police report. Data on prior convictions were obtained from several related sources. The file usually contained an official "rap sheet," provided by the CII (Criminal Identification and Investigation), and the probation report included this same rap sheet plus a survey of involvement with the local police agencies. The data on priors consisted of formal convictions for an offense; contacts that were "arrests and dismissals" were not considered. Parenthetically, I now feel that this was an error, since the court personnel probably use the police contacts involving only "suspicion" as a basis for their dispositional recommendations to much the same extent that they utilize formal convictions.

Besides compiling all the necessary information on a notation sheet, I also summarized the offense that had occurred. A determination was made as to the informal categories used by the court personnel, in much the same way that Sudnow developed his concept of "normal crimes." I would briefly describe the case as a "hitch-hike rape case" or a "senile man fondles young girl" case. With each summary, an indication of the general facts and circumstances surrounding the case was also noted. These capsulizations were used to compare the informal categories in each county and the standard disposition that followed.

Residual Case Analysis

When the variation in one variable is being explained by the variation in one or more independent variables, a particular prediction model emerges. Since not all the variation is explained by the predictor variables, some variance remains unexplained by the model. The unexplained variance can be found in the cases that do not fall close to the prediction model. The cases that deviate from the prediction model, that is, which are not explained by the model, are called residual cases. For example, assuming there is a positive correlation between seriousness of offense and seriousness of disposition, the case of a person convicted of a very serious crime receiving a minor sentence would appear as an extreme residual; the same would hold true in the case of a person convicted of a minor offense and sent to prison. A method for isolating those extreme residuals, which do not fit within the general practices of the administration of justice, would, therefore, be a valuable research technique.

This same approach was taken by Becker et al. in their study of *Boys in White:*

Our analysis would proceed not by establishing correlations but by building tentative models of that set of systematic relationships and revising these models as new phenomena requiring incorporation came to our attention. We did not propose hypotheses and confirm or disprove them so much as we made provisional generalizations about aspects of the school and the students' experience in it and then revised these generalizations as "negative cases"—particular instances in which things were not as we had provisionally stated them to be—showed us further differentiations and elaborations required in our model.[16]

The analysis of "negative cases" proved a valuable heuristic device for identifying factors in the general model that did not explain situations that appeared to be new and anomalous. This analytical technique was used in this research in much the same way, although here it was called "residual case analysis."

The residual cases were isolated and reviewed in a qualitative manner to attempt to determine why such cases were left unexplained by the prediction model. In each county in which the residual case was adjudicated, I was able to interview the court personnel who took part in the sentencing decision for an explanation as to what there was about that particular case that set it apart from the norm. By utilizing the qualitative analysis in this fashion, clarification could be achieved about the manner in which decisions are made regarding the appropriate disposition—in the eyes of the decision-makers.

Notes

1. William J. Filstead (ed.), *Qualitative Methodology,* Chicago: Markham Publishing Co., 1970; John Lofland, *Analyzing Social Settings,* Belmont, Calif.: Wadsworth Publishing Co., Inc., 1971.

2. George J. McCall and J.L. Simmons (eds.), *Issues in Participant Observation: A Text and Reader,* Reading, Mass.: Addison-Wesley Publishing Co., 1969; Howard S. Becker, "Problems of Inference and Proof in Participant Observation," *American Sociological Review* 23 (1958):652-660; Morris S. Schwartz and Charlotte G. Schwartz, "Problems in Participant Observation," *American Journal of Sociology* 60 (1955):343-354; Jiri Kolaja, "Contribution to the Theory of Participant Observation," *Social Forces* 35 (1956):159-163.

3. Jerome H. Skolnick, *Justice without Trial,* New York: John Wiley and Sons, Inc., 1966, Chapter 2; William Foote Whyte, *Street Corner Society,* Chicago: University of Chicago Press, 1964.

4. Joseph Bensman and Arthur Vidich, "Social Theory in Field Research," *American Journal of Sociology* 65 (1960):577-584; Audrey Richards, "The Development of Field Work Methods in Social Anthropology," in F.C. Bartlett et al. (eds.), *The Study of Society,* London: Kegan Paul, 1939, pp. 272-316; Richard Scott, "Field Work in a Formal

Organization: Some Dilemmas in the Role of Observer," *Human Organization,* 23, no. 2 (1963):162-1168; Morris Zedlich, Jr., "Some Methodological Problems in Field Studies," *American Journal of Sociology* 67 (1962):566-576.

5. Harold Garfinkel, *Studies in Ethnomethodology,* Englewood Cliffs, N.J.: Prentice-Hall, Inc., 1967.

6. Based on the work of Alfred Schutz, "On Multiple Realities," *Philosophy and Phenomenological Research* 5 (June 1945):533-575; "The Problem of Rationality in the Social World," *Economics* 10 (May 1943):130-149; "Concept and Theory Formation in the Social Sciences," *The Journal of Philosophy* 51 (April 1954):257-273. And also Aaron V. Cicourel and John I. Kitsuse, *The Educational Decision-makers,* Indianapolis: The Bobbs-Merrill Co., Inc., 1963; Aaron V. Cicourel, *The Social Organization of Juvenile Justice,* New York: John Wiley and Sons, Inc., 1968.

7. See Harold Garfinkel, "Common Sense Knowledge of Social Structures: The Documentary Method of Interpretations in Law and Professional Fact Finding," in Garfinkel, *Studies in Ethnomethodology,* Chapter 3; Alfred Schutz, "Common-Sense and Scientific Interpretation of Human Action," *Philosophy and Phenomenological Research* 14 (September 1953):1-37.

8. See Harold Garfinkel, "Studies of the Routine Grounds of Everyday Activities," in Garfinkel, *Studies in Ethnomethodology,* Chapter 2.

9. See Aaron V. Cicourel, *Method and Measurement in Sociology,* New York: The Free Press, 1964, p. 1.

10. George J. McCall and J.L. Simmons, *Issues in Participant Observation.* See the Introduction.

11. Ibid., p. 4.

12. Ibid., p. 5.

13. William J. Filstead, *Qualitative Methodology,* p. 4.

14. For methodological problems in this area, see W. Richard Scott, "Field Methods in the Study of Organizations," in James C. March (ed.), *Handbook of Organizations,* Chicago: Rand McNally and Co., 1965, p. 272.

15. Maurice G. Kendall, *Rank Correlation Methods,* London: Charles Griffin and Co., Ltd., 1962.

16. Howard S. Becker, Blanche Geer, Everett C. Hughes, and Anslem L. Strauss, *Boys in White: Student Culture in Medical School,* Chicago: University of Chicago Press, 1961, p. 22.

Index

Adult Authority (parole board), 44, 81
alcoholism, 101-102
Allen, Francis A., 8-9, 11
American Psychiatric Association, 20, 99
Atascadero State Hospital, 18, 42-44, 47-48,
    63, 67, 69, 74, 79-81, 83, 87, 98, 102,
    109, 121, 125, 131-132, 137

Barr-Walker Act, 146
Blumberg, Abraham S., 29
Borderland of Criminal Justice, 8
Bowman, Karl, 23
Bureau of Criminal Identification and In-
    formation, 61-62
Bureau of Criminal Statistics, 13, 121

calendar
    individual, 141-142
    master, 29, 49, 110, 130, 142
    pressures, 53-54
categorization of cases, 30-34, 50, 57, 113-
    116
child molest, 33, 47, 50, 73, 99, 105
    cases, 33-34
Cicourel, Aaron V., 155
civil commitment, 23, 63, 74, 79, 129, 140-
    152
    compared to criminal commitment, 1-4
    criminalization of, 129-152
    criticism of, 11
    definition, 1
    due process, 148-149
    form of social control, 1
    increased use of, 9-11
    relation to other sanctions, 43-48
    statistics, 4-7
    trends in, 151-152
classical school of criminology, 9
Contra Costa County, 13, 58, 75-76, 101-
    102, 111, 114, 122, 125-127, 165-166
    description of, 157-158
    probation department policy, 88-90, 93-
    94
criminal history
    of defendant, 34, 41-42, 61-62, 69-70,
    85-86
criminal justice system, 7-8, 141, 143

dangerous
    as element of law, 23
dangerousness, 77, 104
    problem of, 104-106
decisionmakers, 32, 35, 48, 62

attitudes toward sanctions, 43-49
decisionmaking, 11, 29
    in court, 12-13
    practical, 12
Department of Corrections, 44, 140
Department of Mental Hygiene, 18-19, 25,
    44
deportation
    of sex offender, 71
Dershowitz, Allen M., 9
Dession, George, 4
deterrence, 49
diagnosis
    typification of, 31
Diagnostic and Statistical Manual, 99
discretion
    of court, 12
diversion, 7, 10
divestment of the criminal law, 8
double jeopardy, 24
drunkenness, 5-6

Emerson, Robert, 31
ethnomethodology, 155
Etzioni, Amitai, 137
evidence, 117-118, 127, 132
exhibitionism, 34, 106

Fortas, Abe, 3

Garfinkel, Harold, 155
Gault, In re, 144-145
Glueck, Sheldon, 20-21

Hart, Henry, 3
heroin addiction, 6
hidden crime, 62, 86, 120-121
homosexual, 34
homosexuality
    cases, 114-116

Jackson v. Indiana, 149
Jacob, Herbert, 54
judge
    criminal master calendar, 49, 110, 130
justice, 96, 109
    individualization of, 84
    individualized, 127
    standardized, 84, 127-128

Kendall, Maurice G., 164
Kittrie, Nicolas, 4, 8, 9, 10

About the Author

Martin L. Forst received the bachelors degree in psychology (1966), the masters degree (1971) and D.Crim. (1974) in criminology from the University of California in Berkeley. In 1974 he was a research analyst for the Superior Court of San Francisco County in California, and later, through June of 1975, an assistant project director for the Judicial Pilot Program for Research for the Santa Clara County (California) Judiciary. After working on these projects, Dr. Forst received a post-doctoral fellowship at the Center for the Study of Law and Society (1975/76) at the University of California, Berkeley. He is a research criminologist at the Center for the Study of Law and Society, an instructor in the Criminal Justice Program at Golden Gate University in San Francisco, and a private criminal justice consultant. Dr. Forst is co-editor of the book *Crime and Justice in America* as well as the author of several journal articles.

F5